Black Religion/Womanist Thought/Social Justice

Series Editors
Dwight N. Hopkins
University of Chicago Divinity School
Chicago, IL, USA

Linda E. Thomas
Lutheran School of Theology Chicago
Chicago, IL, USA

The Black Religion/Womanist Thought/Social Justice Series produces works engaging any dimension of black religion or womanist thought as they pertain to social justice. Womanist thought is a new approach in the study of African American women's perspectives. The series includes a variety of African American religious expressions; traditions such as Protestant and Catholic Christianity, Islam, Judaism, Humanism, African diasporic practices, religion and gender, religion and black gays/lesbians, ecological justice issues, African American religiosity and its relation to African religions, new black religious movements or religious dimensions in African American "secular" experiences.

More information about this series at
http://www.palgrave.com/gp/series/14792

Danjuma G. Gibson

Frederick Douglass, a Psychobiography

Rethinking Subjectivity in the Western Experiment of Democracy

Danjuma G. Gibson
Calvin Theological Seminary
Grand Rapids, MI, USA

Black Religion/Womanist Thought/Social Justice
ISBN 978-3-030-09176-7   ISBN 978-3-319-75229-7   (eBook)
https://doi.org/10.1007/978-3-319-75229-7

Cover illustration: Glasshouse Images / Alamy Stock Photo

Printed on acid-free paper

This Palgrave Macmillan imprint is published by the registered company Springer International Publishing AG part of Springer Nature.
The registered company address is: Gewerbestrasse 11, 6330 Cham, Switzerland

ACKNOWLEDGMENTS

Roosevelt and Harriett, I am eternally grateful to you. It is because of you that I am what I am. Your endless love and dedication to my life has been the bedrock upon which I have built everything else. Thank you for believing in me. Thank you for loving me.

Secondly, I am indebted to all of my mentors and professors at Garrett-Evangelical Theological Seminary, especially those on my doctoral committee who were instrumental in my professional development as a scholar and theologian. A special thanks to Dr. Lallene Rector, Dr. Stephen G. Ray, Dr. Lee Butler, and Dr. Pamela Holliman for your encouragement and affirmation of my personhood, and guidance in my development as a scholar, theologian, and clinician. I am forever indebted to you.

Lastly, I am most appreciative of the support of Dr. Dwight Hopkins and Dr. Linda Thomas for believing in my project enough to include me in the Palgrave Macmillan series in Black Religion, Womanist Thought and Social Justice. Dr. Hopkins, your mentorship and wisdom has been particularly formational in my early years as a scholar. Thank you for your support throughout this process.

CONTENTS

CHAPTER 1

Introduction

*He would at times seem to take great pleasure in whipping a slave…the
louder she screamed, the harder he whipped, and where the blood ran
fastest, there he whipped longest…I remember the first time I ever
witnessed this horrible exhibition. I was quite a child, but I remember
it. I never shall forget it…it struck me with awful force. It was the
bloodstained gate, the entrance to the hell of slavery.*
(Douglass 1845, p. 6)
*The usual pretext for killing a slave is, that the slave has offered
resistance. Should a slave, when assaulted, but raise his hand in
self-defense, the white assaulting party is fully justified by southern, or
Maryland, public opinion, in shooting the slave down. Sometimes this is
done, simply because it is alleged that the slave has been saucy.*
(Douglass 1855, pp. 127–128)
*I was somewhat unmanageable at the first, but a few months of this
discipline tamed me. Mr. Covey succeeded in breaking me—in body,
soul, and spirit. My natural elasticity was crushed; my intellect
languished; the disposition to read departed, the cheerful spark that
lingered about my eye died out; the dark night of slavery closed in upon
me, and behold a man transformed into a brute.*
(Douglass 1881, pp. 119–120)
*From the hour that the loyal North began to fraternize with the disloyal
and slaveholding south; from the hour that they began to 'shake hand
over the bloody chasm;' from that hour the cause of justice to the black
man began to decline and lose its hold upon the public mind, and it has
lost ground ever since. The future historian will turn to the year 1883*

© The Author(s) 2018
D. G. Gibson, *Frederick Douglass, a Psychobiography*,
Black Religion/Womanist Thought/Social Justice,
https://doi.org/10.1007/978-3-319-75229-7_1

1

> *to find the most flagrant example of this national deterioration. Here he will find the Supreme Court of the nation reversing the action of the Government, defeating the manifest purpose of the Constitution, nullifying the Fourteenth Amendment, and placing itself on the side of prejudice, proscription, and persecution.*
> *(Douglass 1892, pp. 652–653)*

It is difficult to imagine the environment in which a person is forced to exist to write the things outlined above. What drives my investigation is this question: amid the extreme context of American slavocracy, how can we account for the robust subjectivity and agency of Frederick Douglass? In this context of extremity, a situation in which most contemporary psychological theory suggests the human spirit would be vanquished, how does Frederick Douglass emerge to become one of the most prolific and freest thinkers of the nineteenth century? In the context of extremity, how does a person experience himself as human? How can he still imagine and operate from a robust sense of self and the agency to self-determine?

To analyze the life of Frederick Douglass, it is necessary to begin at the end. For in his fourth and final autobiographical reflection, published just three years before his death, Douglass reflects on the Supreme Court's devastating decision to overturn the Civil Rights Act of 1875. His conclusion to his final anthology stands in stark contrast to the seeming conviction with which he concludes his third autobiography, written just six years after the landmark Civil Rights Bill of 1875 when Douglass was at the pinnacle of his life's achievements. The code by which Douglass lived seems to have yielded unimaginable dividends: "I have taught that the 'fault is not in our stars but in ourselves that we are underlings,' that 'who would be free, themselves must strike the blow'...forty years of my life have been given to the cause of my people, and if I had forty years more they should all be sacredly given to the great cause" (p. 488). Yet, as Martin Luther King Jr. toward the end of his life—in an interview with Sander Vanocur[1]—expressed how his dream of democracy had become more of a nightmare, so Frederick Douglass ended his final autobiography on a note of tempered resignation at the nadir of the nineteenth-century Reconstruction era and the dawn of an emerging twentieth-century Jim Crow reign of terror.

Ever since his epic battle with Covey the Negro-breaker, "striking the blow" to be free from the slave power had ordered Douglass' philosophical, political, and social framework of thinking, as well as his sense of identity and subjectivity. But that "blow" was not just for himself. His cause was his people. This is a mark of generativity: an emotional maturity that precipitates an internal desire for the well-being and prosperity of one's biological offspring—or others that may symbolize one's posterity and the continuation of one's lifework (Erikson 1980), in Douglass's case, his people as a race.

That same mature ego strength apparent in his interest in the wellbeing of his people is especially evident in his 1874 address to students at the Indian Industrial School. In that address, entitled *Self Made Men*, he indirectly likens himself to one who has been able to make the best of his personal gifts and talents and achieve much despite the "efforts of society and the tendency of circumstances to repress, retard, and keep them down" (p. 7), an obvious encouragement for his audience to do the same. In his first three autobiographies, Douglass' closing reflections had to do with exterior themes—ideas, values, and aspirations that were connected to the external world. He is thinking beyond his own personal survival, tapping into larger ideas that can bring freedom. For example, in the first edition of the *Life and Times of Frederick Douglass* (1881), he concludes his work with a more positive assessment of exterior social conditions for himself and his contemporaries, as well as his contributions to the Reconstruction era. In what he perceived to be (at that time) a final exhortation to his fellow black colleagues, Douglass wrote:

> I have aimed to assure them that knowledge can be obtained under difficulties; that poverty may give place to competency; that obscurity is not an absolute bar to distinction, and that a way is open to welfare and happiness to all who will resolutely and wisely pursue that way; that neither slavery, stripes, imprisonment, or proscription, need extinguish self-respect, crush manly ambition, or paralyze effort; that no power outside of himself can prevent a man from sustaining an honorable character and a useful relation to his day and generation…forty years of my life have been given to the cause of my people, and if I had forty years more they should all be sacredly given to the great cause.[2] (p. 488)

Nevertheless, circumstance has a way of disrupting fantasy of the American dream. Indeed, life has a brutal way of robbing us of the illusions of safety, security, orderliness and that human progress is somehow linear. The most formidable meaning-making task of his life challenged Douglass in his final anthology of 1892, for in 1883 the Supreme Court had ruled the Civil Rights Act of 1875 unconstitutional. All was lost! In the wake of the catastrophic collapse of Reconstruction, Douglass must have wondered what was the meaning of his life's work. With the promise of Reconstruction shattered—for Douglass and millions of others—how was hope of the future and the movement for freedom to be redefined? At first glance, it seems that Douglass concludes his life-story on a high note, determined to think positively about the context that precipitated the writing of this fourth edition:

> Contemplating my life as a whole, I have to say that, although it has at times been dark and stormy, and I have met with hardships from which other men have been exempted, yet my life has in many respects been remarkably full of sunshine and joy. Servitude, persecution, false friends, desertion and depreciation have not robbed my life of happiness or made it a burden… from first to last I have, in large measure, shared the respect and confidence of my fellow-men…I have had the happiness of possessing many precious and long-enduring friendships with good men and women.[3] (p. 752)

Are his final words an affirmation of American innocence and idealism and a trivialization of the horrors of the slavocracy? Do they ignore the dismantling of Reconstruction and the dawn of the Jim Crow era? Not at all. Rather, Frederick Douglass' words reflect an act of agency, the will to self-determine, an *interior show of force* to survive within a psychosocial matrix riddled with blowback and retaliation against the forward-moving progress of a now defunct Reconstruction era. In contrast to previous autobiographies, Douglass' closing words in his final biopic read as a *resistance against interior despair*. Despite the sociocultural context that suggested that his life and life's work did not matter, Douglass responded with a counter-hegemonic ending narrative that asserted that he and his life's work were still meaningful. Under the overwhelming weight of structural evil, hegemony, and hopelessness precipitated by the removal of federal troops from southern states and the decision of the Supreme Court to rescind the Civil Rights Bill of 1875, Douglass composed a life-giving closing narrative—a life-story with sufficient integrity to withstand the load of hopelessness and the fog of despair.

If the reader is unconvinced by this interpretation of Douglass's concluding words in his final autobiography, a portion of his speech of January 9, 1894 at the Metropolitan AME Church in Washington, DC, just over a year before his death leaves no question as to the despair that Douglass was attempting to resist. Decisively countering the erroneous and growing public sentiment that mob lynching in the Jim Crow south was justified due to the alleged (but unfounded) rape of white women by black men, as well as the growing momentum to disenfranchise black citizens, Douglass (1894) lamented the degenerative state of the Union:

> I have sometimes thought that the American people are too great to be small, too just and magnanimous to oppress the weak, too brave to yield up the right to the strong...He is a wiser man than I am, who can tell how low the moral sentiment of this republic may yet fall. When the moral sense of a nation begins to decline and the wheel of progress to roll backward, there is no telling how low the one will fall or where the other may stop...The Supreme Court has surrendered, State sovereignty is resorted. It has destroyed the civil rights Bill, and converted the Republican party into a party of money rather than a party of morals...The cause lost in the war, is the cause regained in peace, and the cause gained in war, is the cause lost in peace. (pp. 23–24)

In so many ways then, where Douglass found himself in 1894 is where so many of us found ourselves in 2017 after eight years of a black presidency. There is something hauntingly consistent and repetitious about the life-cycle stages of a nation experimenting with democracy.

This book is a psychobiography of one of the most prolific African American writers and thinkers of the nineteenth century: Frederick Douglass (1818–1895). It is primarily a psychoanalytical examination of Frederick Douglass's four autobiographies: *Narrative of the Life of Frederick Douglass* (1845), *My Bondage and My Freedom* (1855), *Life and Times of Frederick Douglass* (1881), and the revised edition of *Life and Times of Frederick Douglass* (1892), hereafter referred to as books 1, 2, 3, and 4, respectively. To understand and interpret Douglass' life better, I examine not only the cultural, political, and religious environment that influenced the personhood or subjectivity of Douglass—and the counter-effect he exuded on his environment—but also his own thoughts and experiences as articulated in his four autobiographies and other primary source documents such as his speeches and articles.

To return to the question with which I opened the book, what drives my investigation is the question of what accounts for Douglass' robust subjectivity and agency, his free thinking despite his context of such extremity? To address this question, this project engages in a psychoanalytic examination of all four of Frederick Douglass' autobiographies: two written antebellum and two written postbellum. As with a client in the therapeutic space, rather than prioritize objective historical facts, I am more concerned with examining when, how, and why Douglass tells his story in the manner he does, how his story shifts *(or takes shape)* with each successive autobiography, and the psychodynamic, social, cultural, religious, and practical theological implications of that shaping.

I begin with the assumption that Frederick Douglass was one of the most significant and prolific thinkers and writers of the nineteenth century, having a profound influence on his contemporaries—especially Abraham Lincoln—as well as the political and cultural landscape of his time. Douglass' subjectivity and agency, as evidenced in his ideological and philosophical investments into the sociopolitical conversations of the time, contributed significantly to the North's involvement in the Civil War and Lincoln's executive decision to pen the Emancipation Proclamation. Given these major achievements and contributions, I wonder: how can we account for the robust strength of Douglass' *interior world* amid American slavocracy? More broadly, I wonder: in the context of extremity, how does a person experience herself as human? How can she still imagine and operate from a robust sense of self and the agency to self-determine?

Based on the writings of Douglass, I suggest that in such extreme conditions the most fundamental emotional, psychical, and spiritual task of the human enterprise is to experience oneself within the interpersonal milieu or matrix in which one is embedded, its individual and collective subjectivity, agency, narratives, histories, cultures, heritages, and religiosity.

For such *interior force of being* can resist the pervasive threat of nonself. When a person is forced to live beyond the edges of meaning, or in a context of extremity that undermines the human spirit, the *experience of self* becomes her core psychological, emotional, and spiritual task. When radical evil and the traumatic are normalized, as they were in American slavocracy and as, arguably, they still are for many persons today, the genius to survive and to live and the experience of selfhood can be the sole resources left to an oppressed person. What I have learned and want to show you from Frederick Douglass's writings is that this genius to survive, this force of being, is something that he developed and cultivated. He cultivated it (1) by engaging liminal spaces of play, imagination, and interior reflection; (2) by practicing agency over his body; and (3) by bearing witness over his entire life span to his life experiences and personhood, something he did by creating and accumulating life-stories and counter-narratives that built up the experience of his self. By extension, I want to suggest that this is a survival strategy available to those forced to exist at the margin.

Such an examination of Douglass' survival strategies makes sense only with a good grasp of the psychosocial, cultural, and religious environments that influenced Douglass, as well as his counter-influence on those same environments. As part of that examination, I give special attention to the development of Douglass' religious identity, for his multiple enactments of black religious expression acted as a counter-hegemonic force against both the terror of American slavocracy and the concomitant theo-political imagination that underwrote and justified its existence.

How we think about individual trauma and the evolving concept of social and cultural trauma is important in this project. For the way in which history is told and memory unfolds forms individual and group subjectivity, for better or worse. Douglass' personal narrative already alerts us to this psychological phenomenon, for during Reconstruction he was greatly concerned about how antebellum and postbellum narratives of the nation would be constructed for contemporary and future generations. Would they be stories of grandeur, innocence, and triumphalism? Or stories of the horrors of slavocracy and of the war that was necessary (directly or indirectly) to end the atrocities against black people? We shall see that Douglass had an acute understanding of the importance of story and memory.

Who, Then, Was This Person, Frederick Douglass? How Does He Tell His Story?
In 1818 (as far as he can tell) Douglass was born to Harriet Bailey in the district of Tuckahoe, Talbot County, Maryland. The name given to him by his mother is Frederick Augustus Washington Bailey. Early on in his life—in part out a necessity for concealment, but also for the sake of identity formation—Douglass changed his name several times. According to him, even before fleeing Maryland, Douglass dispensed with his two middle names (Augustus Washington). He eventually replaced Bailey with Johnson in order to hide from fugitive slave hunters. Shortly thereafter he married Anna Murray and followed the suggestion of Nathan Johnson, an abolitionist that provided for Douglass and Anna, that he change his last name from Johnson to Douglass, as there were already too many Johnsons in the New Bedford area. Agency to determine his name was clearly of

great importance to Douglass, as the way he narrates this episode in the first three autobiographies varies, possibly suggesting multiple psychological and emotional needs at the time of the writings. In the first autobiography, arguably written when he was in a post-traumatic state, Frederick Douglass tells the story of how his last name ultimately became Douglass by emphasizing his personal insistence that he retain his first name, Frederick, in order to maintain a personal sense of identity. In his first rendition of this episode, Douglass stressed that because there were so many other persons in New Bedford with the last name of Johnson, he found it necessary to change his name in order to distinguish himself and that he gave the "privilege" of choosing a last name to Nathan Johnson. As he narrates this episode in the second and third autobiographies, he demonstrates a tendency to idealize another figure, an ego ideal that he finds in Nathan Johnson. Here, Frederick Douglass emphasizes that Nathan Johnson, who was allegedly indisposed to having another person in New Bedford with the last name of Johnson, chose the last name of Douglass, an idea he came up with after Johnson read *Lady of the Lake*. In books 2 and 3, Douglass reveals that because of the reverence and regard he held for Nathan Johnson, he was personally honored to be named by him—especially with a name that represented nobility in Scotland. It is not until book 2 that we learn that Nathan Johnson was black. Because Frederick Douglass writes about Nathan Johnson with such regard and endearment in books 2 and 3, one is left wondering if Johnson was a kind of surrogate father for Douglass, especially as Douglass was emerging (or birthing) into a new identity for himself, having just fled the trauma of the plantation system. Indeed, it was Nathan Johnson who first gave living quarters to Douglass and his new wife Anna as they escaped the slaveholding grip of the south. Compared to Douglass's response to his repressed awareness that his former plantation master was probably his biological father, it is easy to understand the much more benevolent impact of Nathan Johnson on Douglass' identity formation and therefore his acceptance of the name Johnson proposed for him as a father figure.

    Back to our story. By 1824 at roughly the age of six, Frederick Douglass left the direct care of his grandparents to live among the wider population of bond servants on the plantation of Col. Edward Lloyd. Douglass' direct master (who resided on Lloyd's plantation) was Aaron Anthony. A few years later, after Aaron Anthony died, his son-in-law Thomas Auld became Douglass' new master. For about the next 12 years, Douglass lived between Tuckahoe and Baltimore. When in Baltimore, he was under the oversight of Thomas Auld's brother Hugh and his wife. How Douglass narrates this period of his life is important because of the impact that it has on his subjectivity and identity formation. It was from Sophia Auld that Douglass learned to read, one of the most pivotal moments in his life. Literacy exposed him to anti-slavery, abolitionist, and other such literature that not only deepened his thirst for freedom but enhanced his personal sense of identity. Then, in 1838, after one earlier failed attempt, Douglass escaped to New York and married Anna Murray, his first wife. From this marriage, he had five children, two girls and three boys. Seven years later in 1845, he published his seminal work, *Narrative of the Life of Frederick Douglass*. It was also around this time that he toured Great Britain—another formative experience in Douglass' identity formation and subjectivity. In Great Britain, for the first time in his life, Douglass was able to experience himself more fully as a human—within an intersubjective matrix whereby he was not enslaved. No doubt, such experiences were accretive to his post-traumatic recovery—both psychologically and spiritually—after he escaped the stronghold of the American slavocracy in the south.

In 1855, just ten years after the *Narrative*'s publication, Douglass wrote his second autobiography, *My Bondage and My Freedom*. Even though written some 17 years after his initial escape, we can still feel the trauma and fear in Douglass' narrative. This second work is sandwiched between two fateful decisions enacted by the US government: the Fugitive Slave Act of 1850 and the Supreme Court's Dred Scott decision of 1857. The Fugitive Slave Act of 1850 required that any official (particularly in the northern free states), regardless of their position on slavery, return all escaped human beings to their enslavers in the south. The Dred Scott decision of 1857 held that because he was a descendent of enslaved Africans, Scott was not a US citizen and therefore had no legal standing to sue for his freedom, even though he resided in a free state with his enslavers. Both death-dealing acts of the federal government would be influential on the identity formation of the entire country as well as the intersubjective matrix in which Douglass crafted his second work. Douglass wrote this second autobiography under great risk and danger. Antebellum political and social tensions were at an all-time high between the slave powers of the south, northern free states, and various abolitionist organizations. Understood in this light, we can see that his narrative was a show of force—a *force of being* to show agency—and an act of outright defiance to the intersubjective milieu of a nation and the slave power structure.

In 1881 Douglass published his third autobiography, *The Life and Times of Frederick Douglass*, which many know as his final autobiography. It was published 11 years after the adoption of the 15th amendment to the constitution (making it illegal to deny citizens the right to vote because of their race) and six years after the Congress passes the Civil Rights Act of 1875, arguably the peak of the Reconstruction era. During this year, Douglass' first wife died. Three years later in 1884, he married Helen Pitts, a white woman, an action that precipitated a kind of social backlash, both in the white and black communities to which Douglass responded in an August 27 letter to his friend Amy Post, "what business has the world with the color of my wife?"

In 1892 Douglass published a revised edition of this third autobiography. For our purposes in this book, I regard this revised edition as a fourth anthology, as Douglass added a relatively extensive addendum (to the third autobiography), partly in reaction to the Supreme Court's 1883 ruling that declared the 1875 Civil Rights Act unconstitutional. On the morning of February 20, 1895, Frederick Douglass, a member of the National Woman's Suffrage Association, attended its triennial conference in Washington DC. During the evening hours at their home in the Anacostia neighborhood of Washington DC, as he excitedly shared with his wife the events of the day, he slowly sunk to the ground and passed away, apparently of a heart attack. While by all accounts—both from his wife and others—he appeared to be in very good health, one witness recalled seeing Douglass earlier that day repeatedly rubbing his left hand with his right, as if it were somehow agitated (*The New York Times* 1895). While at the end of his life he may have witness a reversal in the forward-moving progress of liberation for black people, Frederick Douglass nonetheless died engaged in his life's work: advocating and working tirelessly for those at the margin, the downtrodden.

MAIN ARGUMENT

Force of being is the drive, desire, capacity, and agency to imagine and experience one's subjectivity and body—interdependently—within the intersubjective matrix in which one is embedded, along with the requisite agency and autonomy to effect or transgress (i.e. to make oneself known or felt) the psychosocial components (or interplay) that sustains that intersubjective matrix. The psychosocial components or interactions that make up the intersubjective milieu can consist of religious, political, social, class, gender, or racial elements. For any individual or group, this *force of being* is developed and cultivated by: (1) engaging sacred spaces of play and reflection, (2) practicing and exercising personal agency over one's body, and (3) creating personal life-stories and counter-narratives that are accretive to the experience of self.

I suggest that what most fundamentally drove Frederick Douglass was not to satisfy the psychosocial objectives generally put forth by traditional psychoanalytic theory, objectives such as oedipal resolution, conflict-free spaces, object seeking, relational seeking, and so on, but that he was *fundamentally life-seeking*. In the extreme environment of the slavocracy where survival could not be taken for granted, and life itself was all he had to fall back upon, Douglass was psychologically and spiritually sustained by his interior *force of being*—an offense for life (and defense against death) that propelled him through one of the darkest periods in modern history. While other psychodynamic frameworks may be useful to interpret Douglass' life, such frameworks are secondary or tertiary at best, as *they fail to account for life in the context of extremity. Force of being* attempts to account for contextual and sociocultural extremity.

In this project, I construct and then develop the notion of an *interior force of being* from the firsthand accounts of Douglass in his autobiographies. Chapter 2 describes in some detail the psychosocial environment of the slavocracy, for to address adequately the psychodynamic question of the etiology of selfhood within Frederick Douglass, we must be able to feel and imagine the horrors that Douglass experienced in his environment. Chapter 3 examines the narratives and theoretical detail that underwrites my proposed concept of the *force of being*. Through several key examples taken from all four autobiographies, I demonstrate that it is *at the limits of an individual or group's material and existential existence that exerting one's interior force of being is the most fundamental psychic and spiritual task*. Chapter 4 then addresses the key rhetorical question of why Douglass writes not one but four autobiographies of over one thousand pages in total. Beyond some brief reflections on the concept of cultural trauma and resiliency, Chap. 4 suggests that this repeated practice of writing his life-story was a potent counter-hegemonic strategy against structural and sociocultural oppression, evil, an attempt to make invisible and to "other" certain people and to promote their self-hate. By repeatedly writing his story, Douglass in a deliberate and ongoing way developed his interior *force of being*, in the face of a society that refused to recognize his humanity—both antebellum and postbellum.

But Douglass' story has implications not only for him and his survival and well-being. I see his internal force of being as the foundation for a theology of deliverance, a theology that incorporates many of the same liberation objectives as black liberation theology. That is the topic of the fifth chapter. The sixth and final chapter follows on from this by outlining a public theology for the internal *force of being*, arguing for a Eucharistic ritual that communally laments and remembers the often unspoken tragedy and unmourned history and legacy of slavery within the intersubjective space. I suggest that such a praxis would lay the groundwork for indigenous communal therapies that are conducive for healing and reconciliation. For in this project, the term slavocracy is not limited to the institution of slavery itself but reflects the confluence of a great variety of ideological, philosophical, political, social, religious, and material apparatus that colluded and continue to collude in a way that normalized and normalizes the brutalization of black and brown bodies and depreciated and still now depreciates black subjectivity. More importantly, this understanding of term "slavocracy" begs the question of how its legacy remains present in the religious, economic, and sociopolitical environment and the lingering effect on black and white subjectivity within the western democracy experiment.

This project addresses a fundamental question related to black subjectivity: given the pervasive terror inflicted upon black bodies and black subjectivity in the slavocracy, how do we account for Frederick Douglass? From where does he derive his incredible force of being? How did he survive psychologically? For though Douglass was one of the most prolific thinkers of the nineteenth century, we see in his autobiographies that Douglass had access to very few—if any—of the interpersonal or psychosocial resources that traditional or contemporary psychoanalytic theory suggests would have been vital for the emergence of the robust selfhood observed in Douglass. Likewise, contemporary trauma theory mostly suggests that a personality like Frederick Douglass could not emerge in slavocracy, that it was impossible for a person to thrive and develop a healthy ego or sound psychic organization without a nurturing environment. How then do we account for the subjectivity and agency we find in Frederick Douglass? How did he develop into a person regarded as one of the most esteemed social, political, philosophical, and religious voices of the nineteenth century?

The preponderance of traditional psychodynamic theory (and theology for that matter) has been imagined through the lens of modernity's

European male subject. This observation is not intended to invalidate psychological theory derived as such but instead to decenter European typology in the investigation of human subjectivity and interrogate the neocolonial propensity to universalize the human project through the singular lens of modernity's prized subject. The effect of modernity's anthropological interpretation on the humanities and soft sciences has been significant and deleterious for ethnic minorities, women, and peoples forced to the margin of our society—especially as a monolithic Eurocentric male hermeneutic of human experience has caused these same groups to be objectified, harmed, or to incur secondary trauma, as marginalized persons seek out care in psychotherapy, counseling, pastoral psychotherapy, Christian counseling, or any other form of interpersonal care.

This psychobiography of Frederick Douglass is thus also a much-needed remedial exercise in anthropological value creation, giving voice to the expression of black subjectivity beyond a singular (but still crucial) modality of resistance to oppression. It is a movement toward reimagining black subjectivity through a methodology that prioritizes black lived experience, heritage, culture, and religious expression and that postulates how black subjectivity illumines what it means to be human and self-aware. Furthermore, it augments how we understand psychological and spiritual growth and development, pathology and brokenness, healing and human flourishing, and a theory of change. Like resilience studies of other human atrocities, the reality of black experience in the slavocracy calls for a psychoanalytic examination of firsthand testimony and personal narrative that chronicles antebellum and postbellum black life and religious experience.

This approach is constitutive to understanding and reimagining black diasporic subjectivity, as first-person accounts from the American slavocracy chronicle human existence in extremity—a necessary precursor to understanding the contemporary intersection between anthropology, psychology, and religion. Examining first-person narratives found in the writings of Frederick Douglass (and his contemporaries) can illuminate how in the most heinous of environmental circumstances people nonetheless sustained their human subjectivity for generations. The historicizing of African American subjectivity is crucial to any serious conversation about black subjective life and identity formation and, for that matter, white subjectivity as well. That conversation is derived from the embodied experiences and context of African American life and religious expressions, with Douglass' slave narrative in four separate autobiographies serving as the point of departure for a psychological examination of his life.

The body of work composed by Frederick Douglass in many ways reflects not only his own particular life but is representative of antebellum and postbellum black life in general. From a sociopolitical perspective, narratives created by blacks who were formerly in bondage are a counter-hegemonic challenge to the arguments that propped up the evil system of slavery (Bruce, Jr. 2007). The narrative literary category destabilized illusions of southern grandeur and hospitality, debunked (white) attempts to romanticize plantation life, problematized illusions of slavery working in concert with democratization, and drew attention to ideas of freedom. Bruce suggests that "the slave narratives as a body of writing are rich in their literary and historical characteristics and implications" and warns that "one should be careful never to reduce them to any single dimension" (p. 42).

A HERMENEUTIC OF AFFECTIVE ATTUNEMENT

In responding to the central question of this project of where the subjectivity of Frederick Douglass came from given the human atrocities of the slavocracy, it is important to imagine and experience—as much as possible—the world as Frederick Douglass experienced it. This project does not so much seek to rehash an historical account of slavery as it strives to engage the reader and help the reader to attune their affect or to empathize with what Douglass relates. Empathy, understood as an epistemological category, is a critical skill and function in any discipline, but all the more so in psychology, practical theology, and for the public theologian. For any psychotherapist, observer, or reader, the use of self is critical when seeking to understand and interpret the context and worldview of another individual.

So I invite the reader to attune him- or herself affectively in engaging this psychobiography, for awareness of one's own emotion is just as informative and diagnostic as cognition. I will have failed in my goal if the reader does not get an emotional sense of what Douglass felt and experienced as he encountered the terror of slavery for nearly half of his life, the excitement and hope of the future when he escaped the bonds of the slave power, his pervasive fear of being recaptured and sent back into bondage, the excitement around Lincoln's executive order of emancipation and the ensuing period of Reconstruction, and the collapse of hopes and dreams when the Civil Rights Act of 1875 was struck down by the Supreme Court. This personal engagement in reading firsthand slave narratives and this awareness of one's internal affect (such as shame, guilt, anger, and revulsion about what the traumatic circumstances of Douglass' life) will necessarily impact how the reader interprets the data and how we understand each other.

Consequently, entering into an intersubjective space with Frederick Douglass as a hermeneutical approach is methodologically imperative to engage the question of how the agency and subjectivity of Douglass could emerge amidst the terror of a slave nation. Far more than cognition, the reader must be self-aware and willing to immerse herself through imagination and empathy to experience the terror and horrors that Douglass experienced in order to appreciate fully the psychological tasks that he faced.

Theoretically, I rely here on Gadamer's (1988) work on the principle of effective history and the fusion of past and present horizons. For Gadamer, an understanding of any historical figure requires an empathic fusion with the past "in terms of its own being, not in terms of our contemporary criteria and prejudices, but within its own historical horizon ... so that what we are seeking to understand can be seen in its true dimensions" (p. 270). Central to this project is grasping the experience of terror that Douglass and his black contemporaries experienced daily. Gadamer warns that "if we fail to place ourselves in this way within the historical horizon out of which tradition speaks, we shall misunderstand the significance of what it has to say to us" (p. 270). The goal is not to be subsumed in the context of the past but to place the historical horizon in dialogue with the present horizon of the reader. For Gadamer, our presuppositions and prejudices govern the hermeneutical situation, and these same unconscious prejudices constitute the present horizon of the reader. Yet the present horizon is never static or stable but is constantly being tested and constructed. Part of the testing of the present horizon of the reader is the:

> encounter with the past and the understanding of the tradition from which we come. Hence the horizon of the present cannot be formed without the past. There is no more an isolated horizon of the present than there are historical horizons. Understanding, rather, is always the *fusion of these horizons* which we imagine to exist by themselves ... this process of fusion is continually going on, for there old and new continually grow together to make something of living value.[4] (p. 272)

To this end, Gadamer's conception of the hermeneutical situation and the proposed hermeneutic of affective attunement are helpful to this project and offer a much-needed corrective to the ideological tendency in the academy, scholarship, the church, and society at large to exclude, erase, or claim as irrelevant the histories and traditions of those who have existed on the underside of history, especially the history of people and groups who are of African descent. The present and the future cannot be properly understood without awareness of how tradition and the past affect how we interpret any phenomenon or event. The goal of racial reconciliation in certain parts of the church seems to impose limits to any conversation about race in the present; as if the past of extreme violence, slavery, genocide, and radical evil (both interpersonally and structurally) are not material realities upon which the United States was built. It has become politically correct and a facade of goodwill for churches and denominations to boast about ministries or initiatives related to racial reconciliation. Yet these same organizations may lack the spiritual courage and requisite ego-strength to acknowledge the truth of our history and tradition, fail in the most basic understanding of the trauma and suffering imposed on generations of black people, refuse to grieve and lament the related human atrocities perpetrated and condoned by the church and state, and lack individual or communal contrition—all of which are prerequisites to any form of redemptive and sustained reconciliation.

Gadamer's explanation of the hermeneutical situation and the fusion of horizons is a helpful framework in response to the naïve observation (or question) of how the United States could still be wrestling with issues of nationalism, bigotry, racism, or white supremacy in 2017 (as if the passage of time could replace truth, healing, repentance, or justice). Like the situation in which Frederick Douglass found himself in 1892—scrambling to make meaning of what appeared to be a catastrophic reversal of the forward-moving momentum and progress of Reconstruction—so many find themselves in 2017 after eight years of the first black family occupying the White House. Like the backlash Douglass and his contemporaries experienced in 1883 when the Supreme Court struck down the Civil Rights Act of 1875, we are witnessing similar sociopolitical and psychosocial blowback in 2017: the brazen celebration of neo-Nazism and white supremacy, ignoring or even normalizing xenophobia, misogyny and rape culture, sexism, bigotry and racism, or the state-sanctioned brutality and murder of black bodies at the hands of law enforcement and the seeming inability of juries to convict (even with video footage as prime evidence).

In the history of the American democracy experiment, there seems to be an indelible pattern of repetition: a massive resistance against injustice, structural oppression, and radical evil—a period of social and political progress for those at the margin—followed by a violent counterreaction and movement toward a status quo of Eurocentric normativity and domination across all domains of western existence. My examination of Douglass' writings calls into question how we define and understand "progress" in the United States. When efforts at reconciliation are proffered at the expense of erasing history and truth, what we end up with is facades of progress—illusions of a Christian nation propped up by bankrupt hermeneutics that mistake the simple passage of time and the neoliberalist economic advancement for moral progress and democratic idealism.

This psychobiography of Frederick Douglass is not a confirmation of western idealism. During his life, he refused to cooperate passively with the evil slavocracy. So now as we reflect on Douglass' body of works after his death, we experience in him a human subjectivity that refuses to cooperate with *our need* to grasp and pigeonhole the subjectivity of another human being, our need to demystify the alterity of our neighbor. Frederick Douglass offers us a subjectivity that is complex, ambiguous, and liminal—difficult to narrow down to a consumerist and parochial western ego ideal that is easy to grasp. And it is in this kind of subjectivity, a subjectivity that refuses to cooperate with radical evil—a *subjectivity governed by a force of being*—that we may see the fullest embodiment and expression of the American democratic experiment. Perhaps more than any of the personalities that we traditionally associate with the formation of western democracy (George Washington, Thomas Jefferson, John Adams, Benjamin Franklin, etc.), the life of Frederick Douglass represents a more excellent display of the essence of democracy. In his examples of self-made men (1874), it is interesting to note that Douglass mentions none of the founding fathers or any of his American white contemporaries (except for Elihu Burritt and Abraham Lincoln, who he says emerged from the "backwoods.")

This would then be consistent with Douglass' description of self-made men "who are not brought up but who are obliged to come up, not only without the voluntary assistance or friendly co-operation of society, but often in open and derisive defiance of all the efforts of society and the tendency of circumstances to repress, retard and keep them down" (p. 7). The founding fathers, along with many of their contemporaries, benefited from privilege, oppression, and violence upon black and brown bodies in their enactment of the democratic experiment, an outright paradox and irony of the very principles they espoused. But Frederick Douglass benefited from no such structures or privileges in his pursuit of freedom and selfhood. In a life that reflected tragedy and triumph, trauma and attempts to recover, joys and sorrows, progress and setbacks, and hopes and fears, the life of Frederick Douglass compels us to reimagine how we might expand our understanding of human subjectivity in the fragile and often violent experiment called American democracy.

NOTES

1. Martin Luther King Jr.'s interview with Sander Vanocur in May of 1967 (just under a year before his assassination), aired on NBC on June 11, 1967.
2. The argument here is that context, as well as a sense of generativity, informs Frederick Douglass' experience of self as he concludes his third autobiography. In Erik Erikson's seventh life-cycle stage, the crisis to be managed is generativity over and against stagnation, with generativity representing a desire to share gifts, talents, legacy, heritage, and so on, with posterity or successive generations. The virtue that represents the offspring of a successful negotiation of this critical life-cycle stage is a capacity to share—and Frederick Douglass' words seem to fit squarely with Erikson's observations on generativity.
3. In the final words of his last autobiography, Frederick Douglass seems to again follow Erik Erikson's final life-cycle stage of integrity vs. despair. In this interpretation, Douglass seeks to fortify his sense of personhood and subjectivity by creating a life-story with sufficient integrity (or strength) to sustain the weight of disappointment related to shattered dreams and expectations which, in this context, reflects in part, the violent end of Reconstruction in the latter years of the nineteenth century. According to Erikson, the goal is to construct such a story that will combat the despair that stems from the tragedies of life. If not negotiated successfully, an individual runs the risk of internalizing melancholy. At worst, groups may run the risk of unmitigated nihilism (Erikson E. H. 1980).
4. My emphasis.

BIBLIOGRAPHY

Bruce, D. D., Jr. (2007). Politics and political philosophy in the slave narrative. In A. A. Fisch (Ed.), *The cambridge companion to the African American slave narrative* (pp. 28–43). Cambridge: Cambridge University Press.

Douglass, F. (1845). *Narrative of the life of frederick douglass, an American slave: Written by himself.* Boston: Published at the Anti-Slavery Office.

Douglass, F. (1855). *My bondage and my freedom.* New York: Miller, Orton & Mulligan.

Douglass, F. (1874). *Self-made men*. Carlisle: Indian Print, Indian Industrial School.

Douglass, F. (1881). *Life and times of Frederick Douglass: His early life as a slave, his escape from bondage, and his complete history to the present time*. Hartford: Park Publishing Company.

Douglass, F. (1892). *Life and times of Frederick Douglass written by himself: His early life as a slave, his escape from bondage, his complete history to the present time*. Boston: De Wolfe, Fiske & Company.

Douglass, F. (1894, January 9). *Address: The lessons of the hour*. Washington, DC: Press of Thomas and Evans.

Erikson, E. H. (1980). *Identity and the life cycle*. New York: W. W. Norton & Company.

Gadamer, H. G. (1988). The history of understanding. In K. M. Vollmer (Ed.), *The hermeneutics reader: Texts of the German tradition from the enlightenment to the present* (pp. 256–291). New York: Continuum.

The New York Times. (1895, February 21). Obituary: Death of Frederick Douglass. *The New York Times*, pp. 1, 3.

CHAPTER 2

The Intersubjective Matrix of the Slavocracy: Experiencing the World of Frederick Douglass

*I have been frequently asked how I felt when I found myself in a free
State…I was yet liable to be taken back, and subjected to all the tortures
of slavery… But the loneliness overcame me… I was afraid to speak to
any one for fear of speaking to the wrong one, and thereby falling into
the hands of money-loving kidnappers, whose business it was to lie in
wait for the panting fugitive, as the ferocious beasts of the forest lie in
wait for their prey…The motto which I adopted when I started from
slavery was this—"Trust no man!" I saw in every white man an enemy,
and in almost every colored man cause for distrust. It was a most
painful situation; and, to understand it, one must needs experience it,
or imagine himself in similar circumstances.*
*Frederick Douglass (1845, pp. 107–108); My emphasis for Douglass'
call for a hermeneutic of affective-attunement*

The above passage captures well the environment in which Douglass
existed. Even when physically free from the material confines of his enslavement, his selfhood and agency were still enthralled in the intersubjective
matrix of a slave nation. In Chap. 1, I defined the intersubjective milieu as
the interpsychic space that a group of individuals or community in a specific context (be it geographic, sociopolitical, class, religion, ethnicity,
race, etc.) co-create and inhabit based on individual and collective subjectivity, agency, narratives, histories, cultures, or heritages. When this
collectively constructed interpersonal psychic space pushes the limits of

© The Author(s) 2018   21
D. G. Gibson, *Frederick Douglass, a Psychobiography*,
Black Religion/Womanist Thought/Social Justice,
https://doi.org/10.1007/978-3-319-75229-7_2

human survival—such as slavery—I suggest the most basic psychosocial task is to experience selfhood within that intersubjective space. In order to better understand the subjectivity of Frederick Douglass, this chapter captures the terrifying intersubjective milieu of the slavocracy and the stranglehold it had on the persons and psychic space within its grip.

In contemporary psychoanalytic literature, the point of departure for human subjectivity tends to be on how an individual uses the immediate parental or caregiver environment to form an object relation, create self-objects, establish relatedness, or form interpersonal affective connections. For the most part, this literature gives scant attention to the social, political, historical, and economic contexts in which the individual is embedded and how such complex environments and culture inform subjectivity and identity formation. This is not to suggest that culture was never considered at all in the annals of classical theory or object relational literature. In the early stages of psychoanalytic formulation, Freud's *Totem and Taboo* (1913/1990) used an evolutionary lens to make a connection (albeit limited) between the individual subject and the evolution of civilization. Interpersonalists such as Harry Stack Sullivan (1964) went well beyond what classical theory was willing to recognize in culture, rebuffing the notion of an isolated individual who stood apart from culture. Sullivan protests that "no great progress in this field of study can be made until it is realized that the field of observation is what people do with each other... no such thing as the durable, unique, individual personality is ever clearly justified" (p. 221). Erikson's (1994) work on the life-cycle stages is of note as well, as he enumerates the requisite psychological tasks within each stage is using a psychosocial lens. Notwithstanding such efforts, the momentum and trajectory of psychodynamic discourse seems to have aligned itself with modernity's quest for universality, individualism, and independence.

Seldom is the question asked about how overarching narratives or the constructed history of a group, culture, or nation is formative for the psychic structure of the individual. Psychoanalytic theory does little to address how social and political narratives prop up or undermine ego strength. For much of contemporary psychoanalytic discourse, the environment of the theorist is rarely taken into consideration when reflecting upon the respective theory. The absence of such deliberation mistakenly assumes that time and space are irrelevant to the formulation of a theory of mind and that any given theoretical formulation recognizes the humanity of all persons equally. This is not the case for people of African American descent.

In all of his autobiographies, Frederick Douglass gives witness to the extreme forms of torture and violence that were routinely inflicted upon persons of African descent during slavery and postbellum. His firsthand accounts of this emotionally, psychologically, and traumatizing environment are crucial to this project. Yet the caregiving social environment that depth psychology presupposes is available (immediately or eventually) to nurture the pre-oedipal subject reflects a critical theoretical assumption that people of African descent could not take for granted in the slavocracy. For Frederick Douglass and his contemporaries, to internalize basic trust was not a realistic psychical option. Elliott (2002) critiques Erikson's linear psychosocial developmental theory for a similar assumption when he observes that such a presupposition postulates that "contemporary social conditions provide an all-inclusive framework for affirmative identity, an ideological vision which is at one with much contemporary multinational advertising, such as the projected world unity of 'The United Colours of Benetton.' Here Erikson's positive gloss on society...becomes a way of underwriting the cultural values of late capitalism" (p. 71).

The environment into which Frederick Douglass (and other victims of the slavocracy) was born was sadistic and violent toward black bodies and black subjectivity. Immanuel Kant's (1793/2009) coining of the term radical evil, while useful in pointing toward evil that transcends even the most extreme self-serving, malignant, or unconscionable human passions, only scratches the surface in describing the physical, religious, and psychosocial environment in which black subjectivity was embedded during the slavocracy. Martin Matustik (2008) characterizes Kant's description of this brand of innovative evil as "gratuitous destruction and invidious violence... shaming radical evil's logical self-contradiction...does us existentially no good...Radical moral evil lies in humans willing destruction even at the cost of their own downfall" (p. 8).

In examining the narratives of Frederick Douglass, it is reasonable to conclude that the radical evil (and its purveyors) entrenched in the slavocracy was immune to theological or political critique. Douglass (1845) challenges this hypocrisy in the appendix of his first autobiography: "we have men sold to build churches, women sold to support the gospel, and babes sold to purchase Bibles for the poor heathen...all for the glory of God and the good of souls" (p. 119). Over time, such tolerance of the genuine evil inherent in the slavocracy ossified the soul of a nation and subverted the democratic principles upon which it was founded. For both the architects of the deadly system as well as the onlookers and bystanders, the toleration of radical evil anesthetizes and eventually denigrates the internal moral compass that leads humanity to communal love and justice.

In the wake of World Wars I and II, the Shoah, and other twentieth-century atrocities, scholars have extended significant intellectual capital to examine and understand the irrational, incomprehensible nature of radical evil. It seems that twentieth-century human atrocities are the point of departure for much of this needed work. In Bernstein's (2002) philosophical examination of the nature of radical evil, he ponders the work of several scholars including Nietzsche, Freud, Levinas, Jonas, and Arendt. For Bernstein, in the wake of inconceivable and unimaginable atrocities against humanity that have occurred in the twentieth century alone, we must rethink our conceptions of evil:

> Traditional concepts are no longer adequate in helping us to understand what appears so incomprehensible. Each of these thinkers warns us that there is no reason to think that in the future we will not face new forms of evil and new questions. The truth is that we do not have to wait for the future. For we are constantly being confronted with unanticipated forms of brutal ethnic cleansing, militant religious fanaticism, terrorist attacks, and murderous varieties of nationalism. (p. 226)

Bernstein is sound on this point. The contours of innovative social evil remain prevalent in the American democracy experiment. The events of Charlottesville, VA, in August 2017 where a white woman was killed and several others injured while peacefully counter-protesting a neo-Nazi, white supremacy, and alt-right demonstration convincingly turns a common conventional wisdom on its head: the erroneous belief that the passage of time automatically (or magically) precipitates racial progress. The old adage that *time heals all wounds* has permitted the latent and malignant evil that resides in the western psyche to go unchallenged as if it doesn't exist, while such evil continues to yield deadly material results.

Commendable scholarship continues to be generated in examining the nature and causes of human atrocities. In a collection of essays on group violence and trauma edited by Robben and Suarez-Orozco (2000), scholars reflect on how nation-states can be consumed with the proliferation of innovative destruction (mass rapes, ethnic cleansing, torture camps, etc.). The editors suggest that an interdisciplinary approach that engages soft sciences such as sociology, psychology, or anthropology can shed light on questions of extraordinary evil. Again, the point of departure reflects data taken from twentieth century atrocities as the authors assert "in the last decades of the twentieth century we have witnessed the resurgence of systematized torture, forced disappearances, group rapes, and ethnic massacres and 'cleansings' as organized practices for dealing with historical and cultural chagrins, political dissent, ideological orthodoxy, and ethnic and gender difference" (p. 6).

While such scholarship is laudable, what is conspicuously missing from these philosophical and psychological reflections on radical evil is the over 400-year-long holocaust of slavery in the western hemisphere. Of course, there are a few scholars who note this. For example, as it relates to trauma literature, Gump (2000) laments that "slavery is peculiarly absent from the trauma literature...[A] lthough attention is given to the Holocaust, Three Mile Island, the Buffalo Creek Disaster, floods, earthquakes, sexual abuse, rape, even the Depression, except for a brief mention here and there slavery is missing from the canon" (p. 625).

To understand the psychodynamic framework of his life as understood within his autobiographies, we cannot skip the psychosocial environment of the slave nation into which Frederick Douglass was born. For the psychosocial environment of slavery reflected the sociopathic, concupiscent, and sadistic craving of constituents beholden to the white power structure to mutilate, rape, torture, and destroy black bodies and black subjectivity. All such actions were carried out arbitrarily and with impunity. Contemporary historiography interpretations that delimit the slavocracy to an economic rationale are inadequate, misguided, and represent the pervasive propensity to diminish feelings of cultural guilt, anxiety, or shame-related historical culpability. They deliberately ignore the overwhelming evidence of the sociopathic brutality and genocide foundational to the slavocracy. The documented record of depraved brutality that Frederick Douglass and his contemporaries were subjected simply impeaches the economic hermeneutic—as the sole rationale—for the creation of a slave nation.

THE SLAVOCRACY

I use the terms slavocracy and slave power to describe the ubiquitous stranglehold of white slaveholding power over every aspect of society. The ideologies that willingly and often energetically sustained the slavocracy included philosophy, religion, culture, politics, social contracts, and interpersonal relationships. The historical institution of slavery was absolutely not limited to the workings of a few people or a small group of individuals in the American South. Nor was the institution of slavery incidental to the building of America. No, it was absolutely foundational to the emergence of the American democratic project.

The existence of American slavery is in no way unique to western expansionism. Despite it being among the most brutal systems of genocide and oppression in modernity, slavery has long existed throughout human history. Rehearsing this history is well beyond the scope of this project. Generally speaking, scholars of history of slavery tend to differentiate between cultures or social orders that had slaves within them and social orders whereby slavery was constitutive of its very cultural identity (Berlin 2003). According to Berlin, in the former, slave labor represented but one production resource among others. Nevertheless, brutality was still a part of the slave system. Conversely, in societies in which slavery was integral to the cultural identity, "slavery stood at the center of economic production, and the master-slave relationship provided the model for all social relations: husband and wife, parent and child, employer and employee" (p. 9). So central was the enslavement of black people to western expansion, American identity formation, and its alleged manifest destiny, that Baptist (2014) makes a rather compelling argument that America's capitalism and economic prowess owes its success—and has it foundation—in the brutal labor market of the slavocracy. While particular strands of historical accounts attribute the success of modern-day American capitalism to nineteenth- and twentieth-century financial moguls, venture capitalists, or clever inventors, according to Baptist, "the expansion of slavery in both geography and intensity was what made American capitalism[;]...the more that enslaved people were tortured, the more efficiently they produced" (p. 421). Indeed, Douglass' own account of the slavocracy would seem to suggest that America was indeed what Berlin refers to as a *slave nation*. Understanding that the psychosocial context in which Douglass and his contemporaries existed was that of a *slave nation* is crucial to a psychoanalytic examination of his subjectivity and identity formation—as well as other psychological categories such as trauma, self-objects, and agency.

In explicating the evils of the slave power, Douglass not only exposes the evil of individuals who were advocates of slavery, but, through the prose of personification, he illuminates the ubiquitous grip that the slave power imposed on the collective unconscious and imagination of the nation. In book 2, he describes slavery as if it were a nation itself or society within a nation. In other places, Douglass (1855) spoke of slavery as if it were a person. Depicting the slavocracy as a living personality that desired to hide itself from others, Douglass described the evil institution in the state of Maryland as living in "secluded and out-of-the way places...where slavery, wrapt[ed] in its own congenial, midnight darkness, can, and does, develop all its malign and shocking characteristics: where it can be indecent without shame, cruel without shuddering, and murderous without apprehension or fear of exposure" (p. 62).

Douglass notes a social caste system within the slave power, a hierarchy made of up slaveholders, overseers, and those in bondage. Douglass further notes that the slavocracy values isolation, in that broader public opinion serves as a kind of buffer against the "cruelty and barbarity of masters, overseers, and slave-drivers, whenever and wherever it can reach them" (p. 61). Unfortunately, there were many such places of seclusion and isolation throughout the south (and even in the border states) that were ripe for the cultivation of and perpetuation of cruelty and thus slavery. Such was the place in Maryland where Douglass grew up in slavery, as he describes here:

> *That plantation is a little nation of its own, having its own language, its own rules, regulations and customs.* The laws and institutions of the state, apparently touch it nowhere. The troubles arising here, are not settled by the civil power of the state. The overseer is generally accuser, judge, jury, advocate and executioner. The criminal is always dumb. The overseer attends to all sides of a case. There are no conflicting rights of property, for all the people are owned by one man... religion and politics are alike excluded. One class of the population is too high to be reached by the preacher, and the other class is too low to be cared for by the preacher... the politician keeps away, because the people have no votes, and the preacher keeps away, because the people have no money...In its isolation, seclusion, and self-reliant independence, Col. Lloyd's plantation resembles what the baronial domains were, during the middle ages... there it stands, full three hundred years behind the age, in all that relates to humanity and morals.[1] (p. 64)

Numerous sources describe this heinous environment in which Frederick Douglass existed, including firsthand accounts by *human beings* formerly in bondage as well as the testimonies of slaveholders. Among them is that of Weld (1839), a nineteenth-century abolitionist, who compiled the testimonies of dozens of witnesses who attested to the arbitrary and brutal nature of the daily life of slaves. The accounts are alike in their testimonies of rapes, murders, beatings, mutilation of flesh, and tor-ture. Further, on many occasions, it seems as if the slave power inflicted its brutality with a sense of enjoyment or internal fulfillment or a psychotic sense of self-righteous, all evidence of a sociopathic nature. Weld's obser-vation is worth quoting at length:

> Many masters whip until they are tired—until the back is a gore of blood— then rest upon it: after a short cessation, get up and go at it again; and after having satiated their revenge in the blood of their victims, they sometimes *leave them tied, for hours together, bleeding at every wound.*—Sometimes, after being whipped, they are bathed with a brine of salt and water. Now and then a master, but more frequently a mistress who has no husband, will send them to jail a few days giving orders to have them whipped, so many lashes, once or twice a day. Sometimes, after being whipped, some have been shut up in a dark place and deprived of food, in order to increase their torments: and I have heard of some who have, in such circumstances, died of their wounds and starvation. Such scenes of horror as above described are so common in Georgia that they attract no attention. (p. 20)

Black existence was so unbearable in the slavocracy, Kreiger (2008) identifies a common theme of preferring the "horror" of death over life in slavery. For many persons in bondage like Frederick Douglass and Harriet Jacobs, "death wishes are expressed so often that they become the mantra of the enslaved, their echo enhancing the narrative's already morose tone" (p. 610). The nineteenth-century literary genre of the gothic illustrates the brutality and terror experienced by black women embedded in the patriarchal structure of plantation life. Kreiger describes a scene from the biography of Harriet Jacobs where a person was punished by being encased in a cotton gin for four days. After succumbing to such horrific torture, the person was found partially eaten by rodents and vermin.

Foster (2011) highlights that not only black women but also black men were subject to the horror of rape throughout the plantation system. Rape was so common and intertwined in slavocracy that Foster argues it served as a "metaphor for enslavement" (p. 445). The sexual exploitation that slave masters and mistresses imposed upon black men ranged from sod-omy, forced breeding, castration, and genital mutilation. Ultimately, Foster believes that the sexual abuse of black men by masters and mis-tresses is seldom recognized due to the "current and historical tendency to define rape along gendered lines, making both victims and perpetrators reluctant to discuss male rape … The sexual assault of men dangerously points out cracks in the marble base of patriarchy that asserts men as penetrators in opposition to the penetrable, whether homosexuals, children, or adult women" (p. 448).

But there is more. That whites abused the bodies of those in bondage for medical experimentation is seldom recognized. Yet in her work to expose medical experimentation on the victimized, Washington (2006) details multiple accounts of black females being subjected to various gynecological surgeries without anesthetics by the man who is venerated as the father of gynecology, Dr. James Marion Sims. Washington wrote an account of a black woman in bondage named Betsy, who is depicted in an oil painting along with Dr. Sims as fully clothed, calm, and compliant, while Sims and other physicians observe her. Washington contrasts this painting with the reality of black female victims engaged in a violent struggle, having to be restrained on a bed by other physicians, while "Sims determinedly sliced, then sutured her genitalia ... The other doctors, who could, fled when they could bear the horrific scenes no longer ... It then fell to the women to restrain one another" during the enforced surgery (p. 2). Washington poses the rhetorical (but sarcastic) question of whether Sims was a savior or a sadist.

Bruce (2007) highlights the prevalence of such sadism, unconstrained passion, and arbitrariness in the violence imposed on slaves and black bodies. He notes that the violence frequently inflicted by slave owners "slipped over into sadism: ingenious, gratuitous, even inflicted for pleasure ... sadism was both possible and prevalent in the slave regime" (p. 39). He offers an account of a slave named Patsey who was stripped, staked to the ground, and beaten until she became unconscious, all while her mistress observed the event with "an air of heartless satisfaction" (p. 39). Similarly, in book 1, Douglass (1845) testifies to the arbitrariness of the violence imposed by slave masters in everyday situations:

A mere look, word, or motion,—a mistake, accident, or want of power,—are all matters for which a slave may be whipped at any time. Does a slave look dissatisfied? It is said, he has the devil in him, and it must be whipped out. Does he speak loudly when spoken to by his master? Then he is getting high-minded, and should be taken down a button-hole lower. Does he forget to pull off his hat at the approach of a white person? Then he is wanting in reverence, and should be whipped for it. Does he ever venture to vindicate his conduct, when censured for it? Then he is guilty of impudence,—one of the greatest crimes of which a slave can be guilty. Does he ever venture to suggest a different mode of doing things from that pointed out by his master? He is indeed presumptuous, and getting above himself; and nothing less than a flogging will do for him. Does he, while ploughing, break a plough,—or, while hoeing, break a hoe? It is owing to his carelessness, and for it a slave must always be whipped. (p. 79)

This pathological brutality of the slaveholding imaginary consumed the entire country, implicitly and explicitly, directly and indirectly. The brutality on black bodies manifested itself in other ways as well, even with how the slavocracy conducted itself on the national seen with its political counterparts. Epps (2004) describes as such the context that precipitated the crafting of the 14th amendment, arguing that the slave power was an intimidating threat that extended beyond blacks in the south to the Northern political power structure. For Epps, "the southern…civilization was from the beginning inclined toward obtaining its way in national affairs by bullying and threatening Northern politicians into bartering sectional rights for Southern votes … Northern victory ensured…a new nation purged of the constitutional influence of slavocracy" (p. 185). Epps characterizes the growing power and influence of the bullying slave power in the decade preceding the civil war. Provoking fears in the northern Republican party, Epps argues that this slave power "or the 'slavocracy,' was bent on using the federal machinery to take over the free states and impose a slave system on them" (p. 199).

Similarly, the slave power imposed an infinite and existential terror on black people everywhere in the Union. Its terror was not limited to enslaved victims in the south. This terror also extended to the few who were either born free or had escaped north to a free state but were in constant danger of being kidnapped or recaptured. Indeed, even after he fled captivity into the northern free states, Douglass (1881) laments that the joy of having escaped from his slaveholder's grasp was temporary because "I was not out of the reach and power of the slaveholders … a sense of loneliness and insecurity again oppressed me most sadly" (p. 203). The mesmerizing influence of slavocracy in the north held out the real possibility that Douglass could be captured and returned to the south, where he would be sure to experience unfettered punishment and torture. Douglass describes an encounter with a fugitive slave that he knew from the south, depicting the precariousness of his situation in the following:

He told me that New York was then full of southerners returning from the watering places north; that the colored people of New York were not to be trusted; that there were hired men of my own color who would betray me for a few dollars; that there were hired men ever on the lookout for fugitives; that I must trust no man with my secret; that I must not think of going either upon the wharves, or into any colored boarding-house, for all such places were closely watched; that he was himself unable to help me; and, in fact, he seemed while speaking to me to fear lest I myself might be a spy, and a betrayer. (pp. 203–204)

When you can't trust or be trusted even by people of your own color, when you fear for your life even when you are free, then the intrapsychic terror and horror imposed by the slavocracy is indeed complete.

THE INTRAPSYCHIC HORROR OF THE SLAVOCRACY

In several places, Douglass offers firsthand accounts of the extreme cruelty to which those in bondage were subjected. Just several pages into his first autobiography, Douglass (1845) describes one of the first scenes of violence (and experience of terror) he ever witnessed, at the age of five or so, of his Aunt Hester being beaten by their master, Aaron Anthony, for dating Edward, a slave on another plantation (a prior experience being his forced removal from his grandmother's care to enter the plantation system):

I remember the first time I ever witnessed this horrible exhibition. I was quite a child, but I well remember it. I never shall forget it whilst I remember any thing. It was the first of a long series of such outrages, of which I was doomed to be a witness and a participant. It struck me with awful force. It was the blood-stained gate, the entrance to the hell of slavery, through which I was about to pass. It was a most terrible spectacle. I wish I could commit to paper the feelings with which I beheld it ... Before he commenced whipping Aunt Hester, he took her into the kitchen, and stripped her from neck to waist, leaving her neck, shoulders, and back, entirely naked. He then told her to cross her hands, calling her at the same time a d–d b–h. After crossing her hands, he tied them with a strong rope, and led her to a stool under a large hook in the joist, put in for ... I was so terrified and horror-stricken at the sight, that I hid myself in a closet, and dared not venture out till long after the bloody transaction was over. (pp. 6–8)

Douglass' inability to "commit to paper the feelings" he experienced some 23 years removed from the traumatic incident when he writes his first autobiography in 1845 reflects a post-traumatic stress reaction consistent with trauma literature. Judith Herman's (1997) work in trauma seems to support this position, as elevated levels of alertness can haunt victims of trauma well beyond the actual traumatic event. As time progressed, and subsequent autobiographies became materially longer than the first, Douglass was able to articulate his feelings around this event in much greater detail.

It was not simply a matter of chance that Douglass' subsequent writings were much longer than the first. A significant portion of each autobiography contained the same information as the previous book. However, at the time of the first writing in 1945, Douglass had not been long out of the direct trauma of slavery (approximately seven years removed) and, as such, was arguably living in a relative state of hyper-arousal and shock. He had not yet internalized a relative sense of safety and, consequently, did not have the emotional faculties to adequately remember and mourn the traumatic losses in his life—hence his statement "I wish I could commit to paper the feelings with which I beheld" the beating of his Aunt Hester. At that moment, words were inadequate and could not fully capture the event in question. Such responses mesh with Herman's articulation of trauma recovery in three main stages: the establishment of safety, remembrance and mourning, and reconnection with ordinary life.[2]

By the time he writes book 2, having experienced a greater sense of safety (which included being removed from his traumatic environment by his travels in Europe), Douglass (1855) offers far more description and interpretation of the horrific scene he witnessed, saying of his Aunt Hester, "this was a young woman who possessed that which is ever a curse to the slave-girl; namely, personal beauty" and that "slavery provides no means for the honorable continuance of the race" (pp. 85–86). By the time of book 3, when he is even further removed from the direct traumas of childhood and has had more time of safety and for remembering, Douglass (1881) seems to remember additional details of the event with Aunt Hester, noting that "the scene here described was often repeated, for Edward and Esther continued to meet, notwithstanding all efforts to prevent their meeting" (p. 38).

From a very early age then, Douglass knew nothing of the facilitating or holding environment commended by traditional psychoanalytic theory as necessary for a child's health development, and indeed such theory does not take into account those forced to live in traumata, those who exist at the edges of meaning. For Douglass, an environment of wholesome relationships and the availability of amicable self-objects were effectively nonexistent. Instead, the psychosocial environment to which Douglass was subjected is best summed up in book 3 when he laments as follows:

> One of the commonest sayings to which my ears early became accustomed, was that it was "worth but a half a cent to kill a nigger, and half a cent to bury one." While I heard of numerous murders committed by slaveholders on the eastern shore of Maryland, I never knew a solitary instance where a slaveholder was either hung or imprisoned for having murdered a slave. The usual pretext for such crimes was that the slave had offered resistance. Should a slave, when assaulted, but raise his hand in self-defense, the white assaulting party was fully justified by southern law, and southern public opinion in shooting the slave down, and for this there was no redress. (p. 53)

Given this psychosocial space of the slavocracy, we can logically conclude that there was no place that Frederick Douglass (or any other bondperson) could avoid being subjected to terror and violence. The violence of slavocracy was inherently and pervasively traumatic, systemic, structural, and chronic. If the reader finds the description of the slavocracy unbelievable, revulsive, depressive, or horrifying, at least such reactions reflect the potential for a hermeneutic of affective attunement. This would be consistent with Gadamer's conception of a fusion of the historical and present horizons of the historical subject and the reader of Douglass' narratives. The feelings of frustration, repulsion, shame, or even unbelief that one experiences as one reads scenes of pervasive terror in Douglass' or others' firsthand accounts are necessary in order to understand the environment to which this slaveholding society subjected black selfhood. This project's central question is how Douglass' remarkably agential selfhood was constructed in such a hostile environment.

Context then is an inextricable consideration when considering a clinical picture of any life or human being. Moreover, a violent context that forces people to the edges of meaning is necessarily informative to psychic structure. The life of Frederick Douglass, as told through his own words, problematizes how various schools of thought in depth psychology (ego psychology, object relations, self-psychology, relational, etc.) conceptualize the human project. The common point of departure for psychoanalytic theory—a relatively safe environment that can facilitate emotional and psychological growth—reflects the uninterrogated presupposition of colonial privilege afforded to white existence and subjectivity. This nefarious prerogative locates the etiology of psychic health on the privileged assumption that an individual subject will have access to parents or caregivers, a *typical expectable environment*,[3] viable object relations, a facilitating environment, self-objects, relational dyads, or intersubjective dyads that facilitate the accrual of a healthy psychic structure. Within this paradigmatic framework, the etiology of neurosis or pathology tends to be situated in compromises to this privileged psychic space.

Yet, in the psychosocial environment of a slavocracy, these universal assumptions are turned on their head. In the life of Douglass, while individual instances of self-objects, object relations, or caregivers can be identified, on balance he endured trauma his entire life. Psychoanalytic literature does not take into account that an individual could be born into a universe of terror. We have already read above discrete and pervasive descriptions of this terror. In every segment of the slavocracy, black bodies and black subjectivity were objectified and rendered abject. Black bodies were subordinated to every *other body* in society and as such were experienced as objects to be used at the pleasure of the stakeholders and observers within the slavocracy: that is to say, there were no innocent bystanders that could not benefit from the exploitation of black bodies.

While it is conceivable to use psychoanalytic theory as a hermeneutical tool in certain instances to understand slave narratives, it cannot be done uncritically or universally. For to do so would erroneously suggest that elements of slavery may have been psychologically and spiritually redemptive to black selfhood. Said differently, if it is argued that within the slavocracy, *over the long run*, Frederick Douglass or his contemporaries could find structure-building objects to internalize, or that facilitating environments or viable self-objects, then this suggests that the suffering imposed by the slavocracy was in some way psychologically, emotionally, or spiritually redemptive. Western guilt, fragility, and anxiety that props up the illusion of American innocence and exceptionalism stands ready and willing to adopt such nefarious hermeneutics.

A converse way to argue this position is to note how psychoanalytic literature significantly underestimates the extent to which political, social, economic, and historical narratives prop up and sustain individual and group psychic structure. Traditional psychoanalytic theory alone seems inadequate to account for black subjectivity amid the psychosocial terror of the slavocracy and the concomitant unconscious deep structures of oppression. As currently constructed, depth theory makes little to no mention of the slavocracy, its primacy in the American democratic project, its impact on the psychic structure of the architects and benefactors of the slavocracy and souls that were in bondage, or its anthropological and psychosocial legacy in contemporary American life. The uninterrogated assumption that all persons (to varying degrees) will be accepted and embraced in a social milieu that recognizes them as subjects (and not denigrated as objects to be acted upon) reflects an unconscious colonial logic. In such a schema, the grand narratives of western expansion, socioeconomic progress, and manifest destiny cover over and trump the counter-realities of Native American genocide, the Middle Passage, and the slave industrial complex.

Furthermore, psychoanalytic theory does not mention the extent to which historical and contemporary western narratives of grandeur, power, and manifest prop up the ego structure building processes of western subjectivity. Spillers (2003) critiques the psychoanalytic field's silence on race. She observes that "its initial subjects were, to a degree, quite comfortably installed in the environment and were even 'at home' in it ... It seems that Freud wrote as if his man/woman were Everybody's, were constitutive of the social order, and that coeval particularities carried little or no weight" (p. 384). Indeed, while object relations, self-psychology, and relational theorists sought to distinguish and distance themselves from Freud's contention of drive and libidinal motivations, they remained well within his tradition by failing to account for how the psychosocial environment impacts the availability of early life-cycle psychic resources or how the social environment necessarily influences any conception of a developmental trajectory. Spillers is correct to warn that "because its theories seduce us to want to concede, to 'give in' to its seeming naturalness, to its apparent rightness to the way we live, we must be on guard all the more against assimilating other cultural regimes to its modes of analyses too quickly and without question, if at all" (p. 385).

In recent years, a growing number of psychoanalytic theorists, specifically ethnic minorities and people of color, have begun to recognize and publish on the impact of culture and society on the individual psyche and subjectivity. Relatively speaking, however, such recognition still remains greatly underemphasized in western depth psychological discourse, especially as it relates to black experience in America. Joy DeGruy Leary's project *Post Traumatic Slave Syndrome* (2005) highlights the enduring traumatic effects that the legacy of slavery has inflicted upon African

American psychological and emotional health across generations. Kimberlyn Leary (2000) talks about "racial enactments" within the therapeutic encounter; she notes that no matter how its effects are denied, the underpinnings of race inevitably influence both therapist and client, suggesting "when racial enactments emerge in treatment, they offer—perhaps even more acutely that other enactments—the potential to open up an important piece of clinical understanding or to derail the exchange if they are not effectively metabolized" (p. 642). Janice Gump (2010) focuses on the nuances of the identity formation and how cultural and sociopolitical factors influence subjectivity. She argues conclusively that "African American subjectivity is marked by trauma...infusing and determining both intrafamilial and societal traumatic acts is the historical fact of slavery" (p. 48). Dorothy Holmes (1999) argues that when ignored and repressed, racial enactments or phenomena can undermine the success of the therapeutic process, especially in the countertransference of the therapist, as race is an inescapable social construction that is foundational to western society. Instead, she suggests the therapist must be intentional in addressing issues on race in their own therapy, as "therapists who achieve conscious, voluntary management of racially conflicted affects and drive derivatives are optimally suited to help patients who express their conflicts in racial terms" (p. 327).

In my own experience and observation, it is quite shocking to observe the number of seasoned analysts and therapists that oversee and direct psychoanalytic training programs and are responsible for the future of countless students but remain oblivious (and in denial) to personal, interpersonal, and institutional racism. Many will go so far as to argue that race has no place in the therapeutic encounter nor should be brought up—despite the growing literature that suggests otherwise. Ethnic minorities in training programs continue to face significant challenges, often arguing to no avail that the instantiation of race—if ignored—presents a clear and present danger for change and healing in the therapeutic space, as well as the training institution. While Holmes made this argument in 1999, her point remains compelling and relevant today.

Altman (2010) suggests the broader culture influences the individual meaning-making system, arguing that "any attempt to understand how the interpersonal world looks to a patient or how meaning is created within a dyad must account of the cultural meaning-making systems brought to the interaction by each participant" (pp. 167–168). For him, based on context or circumstance, cultural considerations may be in the background, and in other situations, in the forefront. While Altman acknowledges the role of culture and the interpersonal world, he does not take the argument far enough. In examining the narratives of Frederick Douglass, I suggest that culture is not simply juxtaposed against the individual psyche but that it encapsulates the individual psyche, thereby being either accretive or derogative to psychic structure and subjectivity.

Suchet (2007) highlights the conspicuous absence of race in the majority of depth literature and employs psychoanalytic tools to deconstruct the ideology of whiteness. Naming the backdrop of white invisibility that has pervaded psychoanalytic discourse for most of the twentieth century, she rightly observes that "the burden of writing about race has until very recently fallen on those with darker skins who have been trying to tell us for decades that a racialized subjectivity is crucial" (p. 868). She goes further than Altman and closer to the contention of this project that contemporary and historical grand narratives are additive to psychic structure building (or destructing) when she posits that "psychoanalysis has been especially neglectful of the importance of power in the structuring of psychic processes. Foucault showed that ... psychoanalysis cannot be separated from the power structures in which the knowledge was created" (p. 869).

Seeley (2000) contours a detailed critique of the supposed universality of psychoanalytic theory and its inability to recognize its own cultural embeddedness, as well as the political and social structures that formulate and sustain the theories. Challenging what Pine has called the four psychologies (i.e. classical psychoanalysis, ego psychology, object relations, and self-psychology) and even the individualism-corrective that relational theory purports to solve, she calls into question depth psychology's holy-grail concepts of transference, drives, self-objects, the unconscious, and so on. For Seeley, "both clinical theory and clinical practice embed taken-for-granted" presuppositions and narratives "which are particular to limited segments of Western societies at the turn of the twenty-first century" (p. 31). Seeley espouses a postmodern construction of theory which postulates that any theory is culturally and historically conditioned. She calls into question theory that divorces human subjectivity from the social structures in which it is contained, concluding that "despite its claims that it is scientifically objective and value-free, psychotherapeutic practice works to produce a relatively narrow set of treatment outcomes, all of which embody contemporary Western ideals of selfhood and behavior" all the while eschewing "forms of behavior, consciousness, and relationship that are highly valued by other populations, but that do not resonate positively in the West" (p. 31).

Sheppard (2011) offers up a much-needed corrective, even going beyond the critique of other black psychoanalysts. For Sheppard, there is an irreducible link between gender and race. While it remains a crucial (and conspicuously missing) element in the vast majority of psychoanalytic discourse, race alone is inadequate for deconstructing psychoanalytic theory in a way that recognizes those existing on the underside of modernity. Otherwise, for black people and other ethnic minorities who exist outside of a heteronormative framework, "we find that it is close to being nonexistent" in the psychoanalytic project (p. 101). Although Sheppard has been trained in self-psychology and is a psychoanalyst by trade, she recognizes that "black women's experiences problematize many assumptions in self psychology because placing black women at the center of self psychology reveals that the conceptualizations of self-objects' functions have presumed a privileged position for the developing child in the family and the broader culture … we must reckon with the impact of a mirroring that projects not only opportunities for healthy acceptance but also a distorted reflection" (p. 120). She argues that negative mirroring by cultural objects requires active intervention from the child's caregiver. As we will see in the next chapter, a sound argument can be made that such intra-communal interventions by older black people within the plantation system shaped Frederick Douglass' formation of subjectivity.

Pastoral theologians and pastoral psychologists have long lamented the obvious omission of broader social constructs in psychoanalytic theory and universal conceptualizations of the human project. Archie Smith (1982) is concerned about the black church's identity and call as a liberation vehicle against personal and systematic evil and oppression against African Americans. While his immediate concern is the black church, Smith believes that the black church and the community it serves reflects a microcosm of American society and is symbolic of any victim of oppression. For Smith, the emergence of the middle and bourgeois classes within the black community has compromised the liberating mission and potency of the black church. Smith believes that social sciences, such as ethics, sociology, and psychotherapy, can be used as deconstructive tools that "engage in radical criticism of the existing structures of domination" (p. 25). Yet, Smith also recognizes that the same social science resources he seeks to use as deconstructive tools have "served to adjust the individual within the established norms and structures of society, thereby strengthening the status quo ... [R] ather than serve as a source of radical criticism of society, the practice of psychoanalysis has often helped to legitimate established social practices ... it has often served to dull even more the potentially critical and emancipatory, reconciling and healing task called for in the suffering of victims" (p. 26).

Based on this critique, Smith recognizes that western psychoanalysis, because of the oppressive system in which it was crafted, can be self-deluding for its theorists and practitioners and harmful to its clientele. Consequently, such social science tools cannot be engaged uncritically. As a pastoral theologian and counselor himself, Smith argues that "psychoanalysis premised on a different, but historically self-critical and liberating paradigm, will require the support of a different human subject and social order to be effective" (p. 25).

The work of Drs. Lee Butler and Carol Watkins-Ali seems to have received relatively little attention within the academy but remains critical in their call for a life-giving psychologic for black experience. Watkins-Ali's (1999) work was groundbreaking in that she employed womanist theology in her approach to crafting a pastoral theology for African American experience. She takes to task the traditional presupposed pastoral functions of healing, sustaining, and guiding as posited by Hiltner (1958) and proposes instead a pastoral approach whose "point of departure for theological reflection [is] the experience of those who inhabit the cultural context" and that "the pastoral caregiver's experience be regarded as secondary to the experience of the cultural context" (p. 123). Her call for a change in praxis methodology has gone largely unheeded in the field of pastoral theology. With cultural context as her point of departure, and informed by womanist theology and an African American context, Watkins-Ali adds nurturing, empowering, liberating, and an expanded understanding of reconciling to the traditional pastoral functions. But more specific to this project, Watkins-Ali rejects any form of western psychology (even if modified or contextualized by a theorist of color) as being useful for understanding the African American experience. Borrowing from the work of Kobi Kambon, Watkins-Ali posits that only a psychology informed by an Afrocentric worldview can be considered viable for African American pastoral care.

Butler (2006) has long held that psychoanalytical discourse fails to recognize the presence of oppressive structures and presumes a universality of its theories, with theorists that are oblivious to the context and culture in which their theories were crafted. Butler concludes that "using the psychodynamic personality theories to evaluate the African American community without making any theoretical modifications will result in inappropriate assessments and inaccurate conclusions" (p. 81). In *Liberating Our Dignity, Saving our Souls*, Butler critiques the psychodynamic theories of Freud, Jung, and Erikson, questioning their effectiveness in assessing African American experience. Rightfully being recognized as foundational to the field of psychoanalysis, all three theorists have had a profound influence on the field of pastoral theology and psychology in the latter half of the twentieth century, informing notions of anthropology, pathology, the human capacity for change, and human development.

Butler interrogates these theorists in his work. After problematizing the universality of psychodynamic development, Butler goes on to conceptualize an alternative schema of identity formation he calls the Theory of African American Communal Identity Formation (TAACIF). For Butler:

> the TAACIF suggests that the African American psyche, which moves according to its roots in African spirituality, makes accommodations according to the circumstances of a given moment ... the African American psyche does not respond according to the expectations of the context ... it cannot be predicted by the stage descriptions ... the African American psyche moves according to the psyche's understanding of the issues and self-conception". (p. 159)

The point made here is not to question the veracity of any arguments or conclusions Butler makes but to highlight his methodological approach in using psychological theory to explicate black experience.

Similarly, Ed Wimberly (2006) observes the sociopolitical impact on black subjectivity when he reconceptualizes pastoral counseling as inherently a political process in the black church. Consistent with the major premise of this chapter, Wimberly believes that political power is about the capacity to shape the discourse and conversations that impact how people experience themselves and form selfhood. The intent of this observation is not to smear the distinction between psychotherapy and pastoral counseling. But as a clinician in his own right, Wimberly does well to point out the inseparable connection between social and individual contexts. To this end, he concludes that "the role of pastoral counseling is to enable individuals, married couples, families, and mediating structures that bridge between the individual and the wider society to edit or re-author the negative internalized stories and identities that African Americans have embraced. The editing needs to facilitate and enable us to participate fully in society" (p. 22).

In this project, I seek to expand on the work already done by various black psychoanalytic theorist, psychotherapists, pastoral theologians, and other scholars, by situating the point of departure for studying black subjectivity in one of the most extreme and heinous periods in modern history: the American slavocracy that was fundamental to the western democratic experiment. If progressively minded scholars, theorists, and practitioners take seriously the culture of African Americans, then methodologically the task of a culturally relevant African American psychoanalytic inquiry must necessarily include history and heritage, beginning its observation in antebellum slavery, postbellum reconstruction, Jim Crow, and subsequent sociocultural periods. The proposed methodology reveals how in the most heinous environmental circumstances generations of people nonetheless preserved their human agency and subjectivity. The historicizing of African American subjectivity then is a critical—but relatively absent—component to how we understand the human enterprise.

THE SLAVOCRACY, THE PATRIARCHAL FAMILY, AND CARICATURES OF HUMANITY

The preponderance of psychoanalytic literature privileges the nuclear family as the basis of the emergent self. Classical theory's conception of *the self* is predicated on how successfully the parents or caregivers assist the child in managing drive frustration and negotiating oedipal conflict. In Freud's ([1927] 1961) conception of subjectivity, the structural model recognizes the influence of the parents in the superego. He goes so far to assert that "genetically the super-ego is the heir to the parental agency ... it often keeps the ego in strict dependence and still really treats it as the parents, or the father, once treated the child, in its early years" (p. 164). In the tradition of classical discourse, the conception of selfhood in object relations locates the etiology of selfhood in the parental dyad as well and presupposes the availability of caregiving objects that are able to be internalized. Winnicott's (1960) formulation of selfhood presupposes that nurturing caregiving objects is available for the child to depend upon and that a facilitating environment is accessible. He even goes so far to assert that "there is no such thing as an infant, meaning, of course, that whenever one finds an infant one finds maternal care, and without maternal care there would be no infant" (p. 587). Obviously Douglass and generations of other African Americans who were snatched away from their maternal caregivers by the evil dictates of slavery greatly challenge this position.

On balance, psychoanalytic theory has remained lodged in this parental dyad construct, with a view that the human project, in one way or another, is fundamentally in pursuit of other humans (whether in the form of objects, self-objects, or relational experiences). Summers (1994) succinctly characterizes object relations theory as "the view that the fundamental human motivation is for object contact" and that "all object relations theories view the formation of object relations as the primary human motivation" (p. 345). Kohutian thought conceives of parental figures as self-objects that can be idealized or provide mirroring (i.e. self-affirming functions) to the individual subject in an effort to bolster psychic structure and self-esteem. Kohut (1984) casts the human project in the form of a tension arc where the self seeks to "establish an uninterrupted tension arc from basic ambitions, via basic talents and skills, toward basic ideas. This tension arc is the dynamic essence of the complete, nondefective self; it is a conceptualization of the structure whose establishment makes possible a creative-productive, fulfilling life" (pp. 4–5).

Yet the psychical use and privilege of a nuclear family or the availability of amicable objects was foreign to Frederick Douglass and others who were the victims of a slavocracy. The reality of the slavocracy and its destruction on the black family is undisputed. Thus the reality of Frederick Douglass seriously calls into question the tradition of psychoanalytic theory's etiology of selfhood within a parental dyad or nuclear family.

In all four books, Douglass speaks with utter contempt for how slavery destroys the experience of family among the slaves. In book 1, he speaks of his mother in more of a detached manner than he does in subsequent books. In books 2 and 3, Douglass extols his mother with a kind of compassion that reflects a deep regret for never having the opportunity to establish a familial or emotional connection with her. However, in all of his autobiographical writings, Douglass makes it clear (notwithstanding the first five years of his life that were spent with his grandmother and grandfather, Betsey and Isaac Bailey) that the slavocracy allowed for no emotional connection or relationship with a family. In the first couple of pages of book 1, Douglass (1845) introduces the precarious nature of the family victimized by slavery:

> My mother was named Harriet Bailey. She was the daughter of Isaac and Betsey Bailey, both colored, and quite dark. My mother was of a darker complexion than either my grandmother or grandfather. My father was a white

man. He was admitted to be such by all I ever heard speak of my parentage. The opinion was also whispered that my master was my father; but of the correctness of this opinion, I know nothing; the means of knowing was withheld from me. My mother and I were separated when I was but an infant—before I knew her as my mother. It is a common custom, in the part of Maryland from which I ran away, to part children from their mothers at a very early age. Frequently, before the child has reached its twelfth month, its mother is taken from it, and hired out on some farm a considerable distance off, and the child is placed under the care of an old woman, too old for field labor. For what this separation is done, I do not know, unless it be to hinder the development of the child's affection toward its mother, and to blunt and destroy the natural affection of the mother for the child. This is the inevitable result. I never saw my mother, to know her as such, more than four or five times in my life; and each of these times was very short in duration, and at night.

Douglass' observation that the child's affection toward the mother and that the natural affection of the mother for the child are both blunted seriously puts into question whether or not individuals are *fundamentally* object or relational seeking. Any notion of fatherhood was essentially non-existent. Information about his father reflected fleeting rumors at best. Douglass could only assume that based on the dark complexion of his mother, and his lighter skin tone, that his father was indeed white as postulated by rumor. Douglass concludes the discussion of his mother in book 1 in a matter-of-fact way, suggesting that for him, even upon receiving the news of her death, he felt no more connection and therefore sadness than if she had been any other stranger that he encountered:

Never having enjoyed, to any considerable extent, her soothing presence, her tender and watchful care, I received the tidings of her death with much the same emotions I should have probably felt at the death of a stranger. Called thus suddenly away, she left me without the slightest intimation of who my father was. The whisper that my master was my father, may or may not be true; and, true or false, it is of but little consequence to my purpose whilst the fact remains, in all its glaring odiousness, that slaveholders have ordained, and by law established, that the children of slave women shall in all cases follow the condition of their mothers; and this is done too obviously to administer to their own lusts, and make a gratification of their wicked desires profitable as well as pleasurable; for by this cunning arrangement, the slaveholder, in cases not a few, sustains to his slaves the double relation of master and father. (pp. 3–4)

In book 2, Douglass (1855) further develops his argument on how the slavocracy destroys the black family and dehumanizes the individual, observing that

> the practice of separating children from their mothers, and hiring the latter out at distances too great to admit of their meeting, except at long intervals, is a marked feature of the cruelty and barbarity of the slave system ... But it is in harmony with the grand aim of slavery, which, always and everywhere, **is to reduce man to a level with the brute** ... It is a successful method of obliterating from the mind and heart of the slave, all just ideas of the sacredness of the family, as an institution. (pp. 37–38)

In positing that the slave can be "reduced to the level with the brute," Douglass debunks the myth that slaves are somehow a subclass of human being that are unaffected by the destruction of one's family or are somehow endowed with special strength to endure hardships. In recognizing that the slave can be reduced to "a level with the brute," Douglass is indirectly asserting the full humanity of himself and his contemporaries that are engulfed in the terror of the slavocracy. In another place where Douglass reflects upon the horror he experienced when being separated from his grandmother so that he could be integrated into the plantation system, he laments, "children have their sorrows as well as men and women; and it would be well to remember this in our dealings with them. SLAVE-children are children, and prove no exceptions to the general rule" (p. 39).

In the world of the slavocracy, classical theory's developmental achievement of the oedipal resolution or even Kohut's conception of an idealizing self-object are compromised, as both systems assume the availability of a father figure. But Douglass explicates how the system of slavery ravages the fraternal capacity within the black family system. Douglass asserts that his lack of knowledge with regard to his father is not only normative in a slavocracy but an intentional effort to ensure the viability of a hegemonic systemic social structure:

> I say nothing of father, for he is shrouded in a mystery I have never been able to penetrate. Slavery does away with fathers, as it does away with families. Slavery has no use for either fathers or families, and its laws do not recognize their existence in the social arrangements of the plantation. When they do exist, they are not the outgrowths of slavery, but are antagonistic to that system. The order of civilization is reversed here. The name of the child

is not expected to be that of its father, and his condition does not necessarily affect that of the child...my father was a white man, or nearly white. It was sometimes whispered that my master was my father. (pp. 51–52)

In reflecting on the tradition of psychoanalytic discourse, Mitchell (1999) extols human relatedness as universal. He challenges a key argument in this project: that theory is culture specific. For Mitchell, such an argument is self-defeating, as the notion of cultural specificity makes the similar universal claim that it is arguing against. I quote Mitchell at length because he gives voice to many who view relational theory as a universal lens useful for dissecting the human project:

Why is everything culturally relative? It can only be because human beings are fundamentally, thoroughly cultural creatures. But why would culture be so important? It can only be because human beings become human beings through attachments to and internalizations of their caregivers and the particular culture they embody. Thus, the postmodern critique of relationality as universal and fundamental depends on the presumption of relationality as universal and fundamental. We are so much embedded in our relations with others that those very relations are difficult to discern clearly. We are so in the thick of relationality that it is almost impossible to fully appreciate its contours and inner workings—a bit like the eye trying to see itself. (p. 89)

Mitchell's argument is compelling. Indeed, relational discourse is a welcome departure from the notion of the isolated mind that dominated classical theory as well as modernity's anthropological conception of what constitutes humanness. Nevertheless, what seems to be taken for granted is the very context in which Mitchell and others are embedded: the context allows for the development of a *free self* or a *structurally unoppressed self* whereby human relatedness represents the fundamental drive of a healthy clinical picture. Mitchell's position fails to consider the subaltern subject and the abject body that cannot experience either *life, well-being, or survival* as a foregone conclusion. My argument is not to suggest that relationality—or any other object need—is irrelevant to the nature of selfhood but just that it is not *universally fundamental* to human subjectivity as many contemporary psychoanalytic thinkers contend. A prime example of this is the countless number of bonds-persons who escaped to the north, while leaving family behind. Albeit a difficult choice to make, Frederick Douglass (and countless others) made difficult decisions (and oftentimes fateful choices) to abandon familial systems for the sake of freedom.

Even in northern free states, a relational framework seems problematic in understanding Douglass' subjectivity, as he contended that the threat of being betrayed or recaptured prohibited his basic trust of anyone, white or black, enslave or free.

I cannot overstate this point. For when a particular clinical orientation is posited as fundamental, it necessarily determines how we understand and interpret pathology, wholeness, development, and ultimately, the human project. That those forced to exist at the edges of meaning in the slavocracy challenge how twentieth-century psychoanalytic theory understands familial systems, object relations, classical theory, interpersonal theory, or even self-psychology is a challenge to which we simply must attend, a challenge we must honor. They know something that many of us do not. They have experienced something many of us have not. Another way of stating this argument is that many contemporary psychoanalytic theorists and practitioners fail to appreciate the social matrix and narratives (both historical and contemporary) that prop up their own self-structures and influence even the way they theorize. At the margins, survival is not a foregone conclusion. At the margins, life and relationships are different than at the center. When such is the case, the clinical equation must account for this critical variable if it is not to be considered shamefully and willfully uninformed about life beyond a western Eurocentric worldview.

Any effort to envision subjectivity or selfhood is precarious work. So we proceed with caution, a sense of humility, and acknowledgment of the psychosocial context in which we, as observers, are embedded. The attempted canonization of any anthropological or psychosocial project is a slippery slope that opens the door to oppression and colonization of the other.

Fanon (1952) recognized the dangers of universalizing subjectivity and selfhood within the domain of psychoanalysis. He notes that

> ontology does not allow us to understand the being of the black man, since it ignores the lived experience. For not only must the black man be black; he must be black in relation to the white man...the black man has no ontological resistance in the eyes of the white man. From one day to the next, the Blacks have had to deal with two systems of reference ... Their metaphysics, or less pretentiously their customs and the agencies to which they refer, were abolished because they were in contradiction with a new civilization that imposed its own. (p. 90)

When social context (like the slavocracy) threatens the very survivability of *the self*, or construes the *black self* as abject, theories that conspicuously ignore such harsh conditions cannot be universally imposed as the fundamental essence of human experience. For example, in the following passage, Douglass' own (1855) account of his strained emotional connections to family and siblings seem to turn on its head *human relatedness as the fundamental emotional task* of the human project on its head:

> I had never seen my brother nor my sisters before; and, though I had sometimes heard of them, and felt a curious interest in them, I really did not understand what they were to me, or I to them. We were brothers and sisters, but what of that? Why should they be attached to me, or I to them? Brothers and sisters were by blood; but slavery had made us strangers. I heard the words brother and sisters, and knew they must mean something; but slavery had robbed these terms of their true meaning. The experience through which I was passing, they had passed through before. They had already been initiated into the mysteries of old master's domicile, and they seemed to look upon me with a certain degree of compassion; but my heart clave to my grandmother. Think it not strange, dear reader, that so little sympathy of feeling existed between us. The conditions of brotherly and sisterly feeling were wanting—we had never nestled and played together. My poor mother, like many other slave-women, had many children, but NO FAMILY! The domestic hearth, with its holy lessons and precious endearments, is abolished in the case of a slave-mother and her children. "Little children, love one another," are words seldom heard in a slave cabin. (p. 48)

Despite his protestations, we do witness the fundamental nature of relatedness in Douglass' connection with his grandmother for the first five years of his life. The love and care Douglass' grandparents provided during the first years of his life had a profound influence on his emotional and character formation. The internal object constancy that was realized by Douglass' unique situation (in the slavocracy) that allowed him to exist in a relatively non-traumatic environment with his grandparents proved to be a major psychical asset once he was exposed to the horror of plantation life. In his work on object constancy and psychopathology in adult years, Akhtar (1994) observes,

> The attainment of object constancy assures the mother's lasting presence in the child's mental structure. The attainment of self constancy establishes a

coherent, single self-representation with minimal fluctuations under drive pressures. Together, these achievements result in (and in a dialectical fashion, are themselves contributed to by) the disposal of aggression towards self and object by repression, rather than by splitting. Capacity for tolerating ambivalence now emerges on the psychic horizon. (p. 443)

Consistent with an object relational lens, Akhtar goes on to suggest the growing capacity for an individual to develop sophisticated object relations and tolerate ambivalence—all because of the object constancy of a caregiving object internalized in adolescent years, even in the absence of the originating object. Frederick Douglass' reference to the importance of his grandmother in several of his autobiographies evidences her influence over his life and grants credence to an object relational lens. However, even this relationship was not unaffected by the slavocracy and cannot be compared to an environment that is conducive to fostering the kind of viable subjectivity that is envisioned by object relations or any other contemporary psychoanalytic discourse. Even with his grandmother, Douglass experienced a continuous and pervasive threat, although he was too young to fully comprehend it. Douglass (1855) relates that

> children have their sorrows as well as men and women...the liability to be separated from my grandmother ...haunted me...I dreaded the thought of going to live with that mysterious 'old master,' whose name I never heard mentioned with affection, but always fear ... I look back at this as among the heaviest of my childhood's sorrows". (pp. 39–40)

Although he could not fully appreciate the danger, Douglass was haunted by a cloud of dread that somehow this experience of life with his grandparents was only temporary. And even while he was with his grandmother, to imagine that the early relationship with his grandmother—under the traumatizing influence of the slavocracy—can fully account for the robust subjectivity we witness in Frederick Douglass is a tenuous proposition at best.

Of course, there is the temptation to imagine that even within the slavocracy, while less than optimal, Douglass and other bond-persons may have been able to form object relations or encounter mirroring self-objects through their interactions with other enslaved persons or the free white persons within the patriarchal family structure in the south. Perhaps. Yet, to envision nourishing object relations or relational dyads in the context of extremity necessarily means minimizing, denying, or even romanticizing the reality of the everyday terrors the slave power perpetrated. It blurs and trivializes the distinction between victim and perpetrator, compromises sustained theological reflection on modernity's project of western expansion, and problematizes pastoral ethics and a theological praxis that *should* compel a nation and society to mourn an unspeakable heritage of genocide and enslavement.

To conceive of life-giving psychic structures that could be cultivated within the slavocracy begets a treacherous agenda that endeavors to identify redemptive elements within slavery. Moreover, such thinking is contrary to the firsthand account of what Douglass (1855) puts forth, as he challenges the idea that anything redemptive can come from people victimized in the southern patriarchal plantation. Even when the slave owner is the father of an enslaved child, the victim's relationship within that family is precarious at best. It is hard to conceive of healthy object relations, self-objects, relational attachments, or any other life-giving psychogenic asset being formed and cultivated. I quote Douglass at length here in order to reinforce the evil in psychologies or theologies that find the good in everything:

One might imagine, that the children of such connections, would fare better, in the hands of their masters, than other slaves. The rule is quite the other way; and a very little reflection will satisfy the reader that such is the case. A man who will enslave his own blood, may not be safely relied on for magnanimity. Men do not love those who remind them of their sins—unless they have a mind to repent—and the mulatto child's face is a standing accusation against him who is master and father to the child. What is still worse, perhaps, such a child is a constant offense to the wife. She hates its very presence, and when a slaveholding woman hates, she wants not means to give that hate telling effect. Women—white women, I mean—are IDOLS at the south, not WIVES, for the slave women are preferred in many instances; and if these idols but nod, or lift a finger, woe to the poor victim: kicks, cuffs and stripes are sure to follow. Masters are frequently compelled to sell this class of their slaves, out of deference to the feelings of their white wives; and shocking and scandalous as it may seem for a man to sell his own blood to the traffickers in human flesh, it is often an act of humanity toward the slave-child to be thus removed from his merciless tormentors. (p. 59)

The task of this project centers on understanding how a selfhood like that of Douglass could emerge in the terror of the slavocracy. Exercises in reductionism that explain away the everyday horrors experienced on the plantation short-circuit the possibility of developing a more robust under-standing of human subjectivity in the American democratic experiment.

CARICATURES OF RELIGION, FAMILY, AND BLACK SUBJECTIVITY

Consistent with Douglass' testimony about the fallacy of alleged benefits in the patriarchal plantation family system, Andrews (1986) highlights the ongoing tensions between abolitionists and slave proponents regarding the would-be familial advantages of the plantation system. Not unlike present day examples where Christian symbols and rituals are employed to justify white supremacy, structural evil, and systemic oppression, in a show of brazen irony and passion, proponents of slavery put forth allegedly "biblically based" arguments for the institution of family and Abrahamic patriarchy as support for maintaining the hegemonic slave system. The collective psychic space that supported slavocracy was replete with ideological red herrings that propped up the *normalcy* of slavery and the alleged religious, social, and familial benefits that it brought to black exis-tence. Conversely, many abolitionists sought to dispel the redemptive myths of slavery by using firsthand accounts of escaped slaves to expose the diabolical nature of the plantation. Andrews asserts that

> Each side of the slavery issue claimed the institution of the family as its guid-ing ideal and the protection of the domestic well-being of black slaves as one of its chief reasons for existence...southern apologists labored to domesti-cate the so-called domestic institution of slavery by likening it to the ideal-ized Victorian family, wherein one found "cheerful obedience and gratitude on the part of children (read slaves), and paternalistic wisdom, protection, and discipline on the part of the father (read master)." Masters compared themselves favorably to...patriarchal authority and claimed that they pre-sided necessarily and benevolently over...the blood family, the slave families, and the larger family of the entire plantation community. (pp. 242–243)

In speaking of abolitionists such as William Lloyd Garrison and others, Andrews says that these individuals "stigmatized the 'patriarchal institu-tion' as a haven, indeed, a harem, of interracial libidinousness, in which the 'absolute power' of the unholy patriarch combined with the male's supposedly innate 'lust of dominion' to produce the lurid image of the 'Erotic South'" (p. 243). Indeed, one would be hard-pressed to find nourishing objects to internalize or mirroring self-objects in such an environment. But even the abolitionist's characterizations of the horrors of the plantation patriarchal family reflected the objectification of black bodies, as most descriptions reflected moral themes of lust or eroticism. Such descriptions of what occurred in the plantation caricature of family may have been directionally correct but were still misguided. Terms like erotic, lust, and libidinal indicate an interaction between two mutually recognized subjects, which was not the case in the slavocracy. The plantation family was a place of rape and sadism imposed upon objectified black bodies by plantation masters and mistresses. The autobiographies of Douglass affirm this representation.

The work of Hartman (1997) sheds further light on the essence of this chapter. For Hartman, the terror of the slavocracy and its impact on black selfhood is not only found in explicit acts of terror and dehumanization (such as beatings, torture, and mutilation) but in the parodies of subjectivity and enjoyment imposed by the slave power upon the black subject. Such examples include enactments of the blackface mask in the minstrel, scenes of "black happiness" at the auction blocks, or even circumscribed events of lasciviousness (such as rape being recast as black lust or seduction) or festivities that were contrived by the slave power. In such instances, slaves were compelled to mimic joy and contentment with their situation and their slave masters. Hartman contends that "the barbarism of slavery did not express itself singularly in the constitution of the slave as object but also in the forms of subjectivity and circumscribed humanity imputed to the enslaved" (p. 6). Consistent with the inner workings of the slavocracy, Hartman's project rests upon the overlooked fact that "in civil society—the submission of the slave to all whites" (p. 24) was the normalized way of life.

This is the danger of uncritically applying psychoanalytic discourse as an interpretive lens to the life of Frederick Douglass or any other slave narrative: it does further violence to the narrative and identity of a people already burdened with cultural trauma. It risks romanticizing the horror and trauma of the slavocracy just to fit neatly with a psychodynamic framework (or religious framework, for that matter). To apply insight theory uncritically risks misconstruing contrived images of subjectivity (that have been imputed by the slave power) as authentic black selfhood. Because by law, social contract, and ideology black subjugation was virtually total, Hartman rightly surmises that, "the laws of slavery subjected the enslaved to the absolute control and authority of any and every member of the dominant race. At the very least, the relations of chattel slavery enhanced whiteness by racializing rights and entitlements, designating inferior and superior races, and granting whites domination over blacks" (p. 24). But the totality of domination runs deeper into the recesses of personhood to how the victimized on the plantation engaged in leisure activities, as such activities were used as an indirect method of emotional control. Hartman observes "the contours of antebellum enjoyment reveal less about 'the nature of the Negro' than the terms of interracial interaction that engendered the understanding and imputation of black excess" (p. 24).

Nowhere is this seen more clearly than in Douglass' (1855) testimony and interpretation of why plantation owners permitted bond-persons to celebrate Christmas. According to Douglass, the only time enslaved persons on the plantation were allowed off during the year was the days between Christmas and New Year's Day. The celebration that was demanded by the masters was imposed upon the slaves and carried an "expectation" of appreciation and ingratiation. Understood through a Freudian lens, it is almost as if the celebrations served as a kind of perverse fetish for the slave power: the celebrations were a symbol and practice that served to absolve guilt, making the plantation owners think that they were something (i.e. good-willed, noble, altruistic, etc.) they were not. Speaking of the victimized participating in such celebrations, Douglass observes,

> The majority spent the holidays in sports, ball playing, wrestling, boxing, running foot races, dancing, and drinking whisky; and this latter mode of spending the time was generally most agreeable to their masters. A slave who would work during the holidays, was thought, by his master, underserving of holidays. Such an one had rejected the favor of his master. There was, in this simple act of continued work, an accusation against slaves; and a slave could not help thinking, that if he made three dollars during the holidays, he might make three hundred during the year. Not to be drunk during the holidays, was disgraceful; and he was esteemed a lazy and improvident man, who could not afford to drink whisky during Christmas. (p. 252)

Indeed, the requirement of bond-persons to satisfy the colonial imagination and of the slave power was complete.

As Douglass saw it, the slave masters used such celebrations strategically to get bond-persons to take their minds of the true state of their infirmity. The holiday celebrations were meant to *change the subject*, such that the enslaved might not think of insurrection and escape, and to make them more cooperative and content with the idea of bondage. Similar to illusions of a benevolent patriarchal family, slave masters *preferred* for bondpersons to be drunk or preoccupied with "celebration" during this short week of the year. Taken uncritically, one could become affectively enthralled in scenes of mimicry that caricature images of black selfhood shrouded in celebration that is supposedly attributable to slave-power benevolence. It would be mistaken to believe that in such environments sustainable and suitable relations or self-objects were available for psychic structure building. We would be left with the belief (often portrayed in Hollywood projects) that plantation life couldn't have been too awful. Douglass warns of the ulterior motives that underwrite such illusions of humanity. Again, I quote Douglass at length here because he offers profound insight into the sadistic psychic space of the slavocracy in which he and his contemporaries were forced to exist:

The holidays are part and parcel of the gross fraud, wrong, and inhumanity of slavery. They are professedly a custom established by the benevolence of the slaveholders; but I undertake to say, it is the result of selfishness, and one of the grossest frauds committed upon the down-trodden slave. They do not give the slaves this time because they would not like to have their work during its continuance, but because they know it would be unsafe to deprive them of it. This will be seen by the fact, that the slaveholders like to have their slaves spend those days just in such a manner as to make them as glad of their ending as of their beginning. Their object seems to be, to disgust their slaves with freedom, by plunging them into the lowest depths of dissipation. For instance, the slaveholders not only like to see the slave drink of his own accord, but will adopt various plans to make him drunk. One plan is, to make bets on their slaves, as to who can drink the most whisky without getting drunk; and in this way they succeed in getting whole multitudes to drink to excess. Thus, when the slave asks for virtuous freedom, the cunning slaveholder, knowing his ignorance, cheats him with a dose of vicious dissipation, artfully labelled with the name of liberty. The most of us used to drink it down, and the result was just what might be supposed: many of us were led to think that there was little to choose between liberty and slavery. We felt, and very properly too, that we had almost as well be slaves to man as to rum. So, when the holidays ended, we staggered up from the filth of our wallowing, took a long breath, and marched to the field,—feeling, upon the whole, rather glad to go, from what our master had deceived us into a belief was freedom, back to the arms of slavery. I have said that this mode of treatment is a part of the whole system of fraud and inhumanity of slavery.

It is so. The mode here adopted to disgust the slave with freedom, by allowing him to see only the abuse of it, is carried out in other things. (pp. 75–76)

This description of the motivations of the slave power calls into question that the universalization of any contemporary psychodynamic theory can exclusively account for what we observe in the agency and subjectivity of Frederick Douglass. The sadism inherent in the slavocracy compels us to search deeper in a robust account of a clinical picture of one of the most prolific thinkers of the nineteenth century. Hartman (1997) is thus correct in noting that "the barbarism of slavery did not express itself singularly in the constitution of the slave as object but also in the form of subjectivity and circumscribed humanity imputed to the enslaved" (p. 6).

Even today, concocted illusions of the antebellum southern plantation system in history books, Hollywood, and the media tend to trivialize at best, or romanticize at worst, the psychosocial space of the slavocracy, all in an effort to alleviate American guilt and shame about the systemic and unspeakable atrocities of slavery that effectively underwrote and enabled the country's democratic experiment. There seems to be no institution or western discourse (including church and theology) that in one way or another does not minimize the extent to which the legacy of slavery has (and continues to) overrun the American psyche. For example, in 2012, while significant attention and conversation was given to the film *Django* (a spaghetti western which depicted a slave attempting to rescue his wife from a southern plantation owner), far less attention and conversation was given to the film *Abraham Lincoln: Vampire Slayer*, a story about Abraham Lincoln partnering with enslaved persons and others to kill vampires that had taken over the south. Viewing the film from an affective perspective, one could almost come away feeling that the southern plantation system *wasn't that bad* and that the horror of slavery was a black problem that is historically compartmentalized to African American culture, as opposed to it being intertwined with (and in many respects, the essence of) American history. Contemporary scholarly and literary discourse continues to undermine the historicity of American complicity in slavery and genocide, and to run roughshod through black phenomenology and subjectivity over the last four centuries.

Noted scholar and historian James Oliver Horton (1999) observes the difficulty of articulating and integrating the reality of slavery in American history. He asserts that most northern public schools teach very little on the subject matter, and that southern public schools are even worse. Many

Americans choose to understand slavery as a southern problem that surfaced just prior to the Civil War. Horton laments about how many people have accepted the pro-slavery argument of a "benevolent system, well suited to the limitations of black people." He quotes a nineteenth-century historian as rationalizing slavery on the basis that "blacks were 'indolent, playful, sensual, imitative, subservient, good-natured, versatile, unsteady in the purpose, devoted, and affectionate'" (p. 22). And indeed, from a psychosocial perspective, these are character stereotypes that are still at work today. Hartman (1997) is right to conclude that the "fixation on the slave's 'good times' conceals the affiliations of white enjoyment and black subjection and the affective dimensions of mastery and servitude....the seemingly casual observations about black fun and frolic obscure this wanton usage and the incorporation of the captive body in realizing the extensive and sentient capacities of the master subject" (p. 25). In book 3, Douglass (1881) echoes this when he laments,

> The remark in the olden time was not unfrequently made, that slaves were the most contented and happy laborers in the world, and their dancing and singing were referred to in proof of this alleged fact; but it was a great mistake to suppose them happy because they sometimes made those joyful noises. The songs of the slaves represented their sorrows, rather than their joys. Like tears, they were a relief to aching hearts. It is not inconsistent with the constitution of the human mind, that avails itself of one and the same method for expressing opposite emotions. Sorrow and desolation have their songs, as well as joy, and peace. It was the boast of slaveholders that their slaves enjoyed more of the physical comforts of life than the peasantry of any country in the world. My experience contradicts this. (pp. 44–45)

The matrix of the slavocracy was thorough in overwhelming and captivating the hearts and the imagination of its citizenry; both black and white, slave and free, victim, perpetrator, or bystander. Politically, legally, socially, and ideologically, black bodies and subjectivities were rendered subhuman, objects to be used at the pleasure not only of slave masters but of any white persons. Efforts to compartmentalize slavery to some small facet of western history or to confine its motivations to economic rationales reflect efforts to repress group and collective guilt and shame and to reorchestrate grand narratives that prop up the psychic space of the majority.

Patterson's (1982) seminal work on the dynamics of slave societies describes well the slavocracy in which Douglass and his contemporaries

were embedded: a web of human power relations at all levels that emphasize domination and powerlessness. Patterson understands three essential
elements that govern the power relations that underwrite the slavocracy:
(1) physical violence to assert control over the subordinate subject, (2)
psychological persuasion that convinces victim slavery is in their best interest, and (3) a cultural ethos that transforms the hideousness of slavery into
narratives of obedience and obligation. It was in this horrific matrix that
black selfhood was objectified and subjectivity was defined.

This is the environment in which this project examines the subjectivity
of Frederick Douglass. It cannot be smoothed over for the sake of universalizing and uncritically imposing twentieth-century depth psychology on
human subjectivity across space, culture, and time. In the American democratic experiment, canonizing the formation of agency and human subjectivity presupposes that survival is a foregone conclusion. For Douglass and
his contemporaries, any psychic space that allowed them to endure the day
was an achievement in and of itself. Conceptions of the fundamental motivation of selfhood are necessarily dependent on the cultural and sociopolitical environment in which the individual is embedded. And this was
Douglass' environment.

SLAVERY AND THE CORRUPTION OF THE BYSTANDER

Studies of genocide, or cultural and group trauma such as slavery in the
United States, rightfully focus on the deleterious effects these human
atrocities had on their victims, future generations of the victims, and the
prospective legacy of structural and systemic oppression that is the offspring of gross crimes against humanity. Post-Holocaust scholarship—
especially within the psychoanalytic community—has produced exceptional
work in this regard. Fewer studies, however, focus on the effects that
human atrocities have on the surrounding onlooking community—the
bystander(s). Again, I argue that for the most part this gap in scholarship
regarding the effects that human atrocities have had on the surrounding
community is ok. Otherwise, we run the risk of facilitating an erroneous
equivalency (which some actors try to create in order to absolve group
guilt). To state it succinctly: there is unequivocally no comparison to speak
of in terms of suffering and adversity in how the legacy of human atrocities—whether speaking of slavery or any other heinous crime—negatively
impacts the posterity of those who have been brutalized and victimized.

That being said, there are other considerations in terms of the more latent psychosocial and spiritual effects that the slavocracy had on the larger community—the bystanders. Such considerations include group-level maladaptive behavioral and personality disorders that position the broader society to function as enablers who collude in some way to underwrite present and future human atrocities. In the slavocracy, there was no such place as a demilitarized zone. One was either a victim, a perpetrator, an intentionally *disquieted* beneficiary (i.e. abolitionist or other anti-slavery advocate), or a *bystander*, defined in this project as an intentionally or unintentionally *quieted* individual or community who through (conscious or unconscious) privilege can exercise their sociopolitical right and psychosocial capacity to ignore radical evil and oppression—and exist amidst evil and oppression—as if evil and oppression does not materially exist.

Bearing witness to the ubiquitous and arbitrary nature of the extreme violence inflicted upon slaves, Douglass tells of events that demonstrate that the slaveholding community was not unaffected by the violence that occurred. In addition to the actual owners of bond-persons and the direct perpetrators of atrocities against black bodies, there were enablers and bystanders in the slavocracy, both in the church and in the greater community, that helped to maintain the slave culture. In examining Douglass' firsthand testimony, it seems that the slavocracy, similar to how a psychologist described the surrounding German community in the Shoah, displayed a collective split or dissociated psyche, where part of the person (or group) yielded to a position of inflicting terror on black bodies, while another part of the same person (or group) recognized the wrong that was being done. In book 1, Douglass (1845) describes how in Baltimore two girls in bondage, Henrietta and Mary, were regularly beaten so severely by their mistress, Mrs. Hamilton, that "the head, neck, and shoulders of Mary were literally cut to pieces" (p. 35). Douglass describes Mary's head as being covered with sores because of the punishment inflicted by Mrs. Hamilton, while the mistress spewed out epithets such as "take that, you black gip" or "move faster, you black gip" (p. 35). In book 2, Douglass' (1855) description of public opinion on Mrs. Hamilton and her treatment of her slaves reflects a kind of collective vertical split, where on the one hand the community disapproves of the abuse and torture, but on the other hand, the community believes it is more important not to interfere with the actions of the slaveholder and her slaves.

It is some relief to this picture of slavery in Baltimore, to say—what is but the simple truth—that Mrs. Hamilton's treatment of her slaves was generally condemned, as disgraceful and shocking; but while I say this, it must also be remembered, that the very parties who censured the cruelty of Mrs. Hamilton, would have condemned and promptly punished any attempt to interfere with Mrs. Hamilton's right to cut and slash her slaves to pieces. There must be no force between the slave and the slaveholder, to restrain the power of the one, and protect the weakness of the other; and the cruelty of Mrs. Hamilton is as justly chargeable to the upholders of the slave system, as drunkenness is chargeable on those who, by precept and example, or by indifference, uphold the drinking system. (p. 150)

Douglass' account of how the community viewed Mrs. Hamilton's actions is indicative of a collective unconscious splitting of the ego, where two diametrically opposed ideas that are held within the group psyche are not denied but are split apart and disavowed, prevented from being fused together or put in dialogue with each other. To put such competing ideas in conversation with each other (full awareness of torturing a human being vs. maintaining the system of slavocracy) would be intolerable to the individual or collective psychic space of the community—a community in and through which the idea of American freedom and democracy propped up individual and collective experiences of identity. To be sure, knowledge of the heinous acts of the individual slaveholder and the community is fully available to them, but as Douglass describes it, such awareness is disavowed for the sake of self and communal preservation.

Kohut's (1971) conception of a vertical split is useful here to demonstrate how incompatible perspectives or psychological positions can coexist within the same psychic structure. For Kohut, "the ideational and emotional manifestations of a vertical split in the psyche—in contrast to such *horizontal splits* as those brought about on a deeper level by repression and on a higher level by negation—are correlated to the side-by-side, conscious existence of otherwise incompatible psychological attitudes *in depth*" (p. 177). To be sure, the slaveholding power knew the heinous nature of what it enacted, but at the same time, it didn't want to know.

In book 3, Douglass (1881) provides another account of an enslaved girl who was killed by her mistress. The vicious murder was precipitated by the mistress's own crying baby: she felt the enslaved girl did not respond quickly enough to the child during the night. Douglass indicated that the girl was beaten to death by her mistress with a piece of fire wood. The scene he describes reinforces the arbitrariness of the terror that was imposed on black bodies:

> This wicked woman, in the paroxysm of her wrath, not content at killing her victim, literally mangled her face, and broke her breast-bone. Wild and infuriated as she was, she took the precaution to cause the burial of the girl; but, the facts of the case getting abroad, *the remains were disinterred*, and a coroner's jury assembled, who, after due deliberation, decided that "the girl had come to her death from severe beating." The offense for which this girl was thus hurried out of the world was this, she had been set that night, and several preceding nights, to mind Mrs. Hicks' baby, and having fallen into a sound sleep the crying of the baby did not wake her, as it did its mother. The tardiness of the girl excited Mrs. Hicks, who, after calling her several times, seized a piece of fire-wood from the fire-place, and pounded in her skull and breast-bone till death ensued. *I will not say that this murder most foul produced no sensation. It did produce a sensation. A warrant was issued for the arrest of Mrs. Hicks, but incredible to tell, for some reason or other, that warrant was never served, and she not only escaped… punishment, but the pain and mortification as well of being arraigned before a court of justice.*[4]

The bold portions of the above passage again show evidence of this collective split; on the one hand, there was enough awareness to have the body of the slave girl exhumed for examination as well as to have an arrest warrant issued for the mistress, but on the other hand, the warrant is never executed. Whether it was the torture of Mary and Henrietta by Mrs. Hamilton, or the murder of a little girl by Mrs. Hicks, both acts represent the acts of sociopaths and the most extreme forms of archaic grandiosity and exhibitionism (the destruction of another human life). Kohut (1972) alludes to the destructive behaviors and actions that can be enacted by the individual with a vertical split, suggesting that "defensive and archaic forms of exhibitionism and grandiosity are split off from the 'reality ego' and as such are no longer subject to modification by "later external influences" or by a "corrective emotional experience" (p. 372). I suggest that this collective unconscious split was necessary to preserve the individual and collective identity of the slave power.

The group and psychosocial behavior of bystanders as described by Douglass is consistent with observed behavior of citizens of Nazi Germany during the Holocaust. In his examination of the rise of genocide in the twentieth century, Kressel (1996) employs the concept of cognitive dissonance to explain how German citizens became enablers and bystanders to the atrocities carried out in concentration and death camps. For Kressel, cognitive dissonance reflects that anxiety or tension that arises in an individual or group when one's internal belief system conflicts with one's external behaviors. The goal for the individual or group then is to reduce the tension. Kressel argues that, unfortunately, it is easier for individuals or groups to adjust or change their attitudes or belief systems than it is to change behaviors that have gained traction and momentum. When cognitive dissonance is present, reducing the tension becomes the unequivocal goal of the neurotic group. Kressel concludes that,

> to reduce this dissonance, they developed consistent Nazi attitudes…by performing Nazi behaviors publicly, they became committed to the behaviors… watching others model the behaviors contributed to the pressure to conform…if people whom you respected were behaving like Nazis, then perhaps such behaviors were not immoral after all. (p. 153)

Kressel's conclusion aligns well with Douglass' firsthand account of the surrounding community within the slavocracy.

Identifying the role of the bystander in the slavocracy is crucial in order to rebuff the tendency to assign the culpability of slavery to the actual owners of slaves. The slavocracy was mature, ubiquitous, and entrenched in every aspect of society. Slavery was a community effort; it was maintained by the community. In Douglass' account, those who didn't own slaves but were bystanders and turned a blind eye to the violence perpetrated against black bodies were nonetheless partakers in a depraved society. Douglass' observations of the community at large in the American south and its propensity to ignore brazen violence toward a particular group of human beings is strikingly similar to Barnett's (1999) examination of the psychosocial behavior of bystanders during the Holocaust. She examines the role of religion, institutions, groups, the social role of totalitarianism, and attitudes of indifference, among other factors, that contributed to the advancement of Nazi objectives. Similar to Douglass' position, Barnett contends that "the genocide of the European Jews would have been impossible without the active participation of bystanders to carry it out and the failure of numerous parties to intervene to stop it…The Holocaust did not occur in a vacuum…There was a general failure" (p. 11).

Reflecting on the terror of the environment in which Frederick Douglass and his contemporaries were forced to exist is a condition precedent to understanding his genius to survive, live, and create, such that he was arguably one of the most prolific thinkers of the nineteenth century. Moreover, it further emphasizes the crucial role that the proposed interior force of being plays in the lives of the subaltern at the margin.

NOTES

1. My emphasis.
2. Judith Herman's last stage, reconnecting with ordinary life, is problematic in the context of understanding the selfhood of Douglass or for that matter, any other enslaved person. For Douglass, the definition of trauma must extend beyond a violation from normal life, as African Americans were born into a life of extremity. They lived and died in a world of violence. This violence perpetrated by the slavocracy was not the exception, but the rule. It begs the question then of how to expand our understanding of trauma beyond a baseline of normativity.
3. Term used by Heinz Hartmann (1939). *Psycho-Analysis and the Concept of Health. The International Journal of Psychoanalysis*, 20: 308–321.
4. My emphasis.

BIBLIOGRAPHY

Akhtar, S. (1994). Object constancy and adult psychopathology. *The International Journal of Psychoanalysis, 75*, 441–455.

Altman, N. (2010). *The analyst in the inner city: Race, class, and culture through a psychoanalytic lens* (2nd ed.). New York: Routledge.

Andrews, W. L. (1986). *To tell a free story: The first century of Afro-American autobiography, 1760–1865*. Urbana/Chicago: University of Illinois Press.

Baptist, E. E. (2014). *The half has never been told: Slavery and the making of American capitalism*. New York: Basic Books.

Barnett, V. J. (1999). *Bystanders: Conscience and complicity during the holocaust*. Westport: Praeger Publishers.

Berlin, I. (2003). *Generations of captivity: A history of African-American slaves*. Cambridge: The Belknap Press of Harvard University Press.

Bernstein, R. J. (2002). *Radical evil: A philosophical interrogation*. Malden: Blackwell Publishing Inc.

Bruce, D. D., Jr. (2007). Politics and political philosophy in the slave narrative. In A. A. Fisch (Ed.), *The cambridge companion to the African American slave narrative* (pp. 28–43). Cambridge: Cambridge University Press.

Butler, L. H. (2006). *Liberating our dignity, saving our souls: A new theory of african american identity formation*. St. Louis: Chalice Press.

Douglass, F. (1845). *Narrative of the life of frederick douglass, an American slave: Written by himself.* Boston: Published at the Anti-Slavery Office.

Douglass, F. (1855). *My bondage and my freedom.* New York: Miller, Orton & Mulligan.

Douglass, F. (1881). *Life and times of frederick douglass: His early life as a slave, his escape from bondage, and his complete history to the present time.* Hartford: Park Publishing Company.

Elliott, A. (2002). *Psychoanalytic theory: An introduction.* Durham: Duke University Press.

Epps, G. (2004). The antebellum political background of the fourteenth amendment. *Law and Contemporary Problems, 67*(3), *Conservative and Progressive Legal Orders,* 175–211.

Erikson, E. H. (1994). *Identity and the life cycle.* New York: W.W. Norton & Company, Inc.

Fanon, F. (1952). *Black skin, white masks.* Paris: Editions du Seuil.

Foster, T. A. (2011). The sexual abuse of black men under american slavery. *Journal of the History of Sexuality, 20,* 445–464.

Foster, C. R., Smith, F., & Shockley, G. S. (2004). *Black religious experience.* Nashville: Abingdon Press.

Freud, S. (1913/1990). *Totem and taboo: Some points of agreement between the mental lives of savages and neurotics.* New York: W. W. Norton & Company.

Freud, S. ([1927] 1961). Humour. In J. Strachey (Ed.), *The standard edition of the complete psychological works of sigmund freud, volume XXI (1927–1931): The future of an illusion, civilization and its discontents, and other works* (pp. 159–166). London: The Hogarth Press.

Gump, J. P. (2000). A white therapist, an African American patient—Shame in the therapeutic dyad: Commentary on paper by Neil Altman. *Psychoanalytic Dialogues, 10,* 619–632.

Gump, J. P. (2010). Reality matters: The shadow of trauma on African American subjectivity. *Psychoanalytic Psychology, 27,* 42–54.

Hartman, S. V. (1997). *Scenes of subjection: Terror, slavery, and self-making in nineteenth-century america.* New York: Oxford University Press.

Herman, J. L. (1997). *Trauma and recovery: The aftermath of violence—from domestic abuse to political terror.* New York: Basic Books.

Hiltner, S. (1958). *Preface to pastoral theology: The ministry and theory of shepherding.* Nashville: Abingdon Press.

Holmes, D. E. (1999). Race and countertransference: Two "blind spots" in psychoanalytic perception. *Journal of Applied Psychoanalytic Studies, 1,* 319–332.

Horton, J. O. (1999). Presenting slavery: The perils of telling America's racial story. *The Public Historian, 21*(4), 19–38.

Kant, I. (1793/2009). *Religion within the bounds of bare reason* (W. S. Pluhar, Trans.). Indianapolis: Hackett Publishing Company, Inc.

Kohut, H. (1971). *The analysis of the self: A systematic approach to the psychoanalytic treatment of narcissistic personality disorders*. Chicago: The University of Chicago Press.

Kohut, H. (1972). Thoughts on narcissism and narcissistic rage. *The Psychoanaltyic Study of the Child, 27*, 360–400.

Kohut, H. (1984). *How does analysis cure?* Chicago: The University of Chicago Press.

Kreiger, G. (2008). Playing dead: Harriet Jacobs's survival strategy in "incidents in the life of a slave girl". *African American Review, 42*(3/4), 607–621.

Kressel, N. J. (1996). *Mass hate: The global rise of genocide and terror*. New York: Plenum Press.

Leary, K. (2000). Racial enactments in dynamic treatment. *Psychoanalytic Dialogues, 10*, 639–653.

Leary, J. D. (2005). *Post traumatic slave syndrome: America's legacy of enduring injury and healing*. Portland: Joy DeGruy Publications Inc.

Matustik, M. B. (2008). *Radical evil and the scarcity of hope: Postsecular meditations*. Bloomington: Indiana University Press.

Mitchell, S. A. (1999). Attachment theory and the psychoanalytic tradition: Reflections on human relationality. *Psychoanalytic Dialogues, 9*, 85–107.

Orlando, P. (1982). *Slavery and social death: A comparative study*. Cambridge: Harvard University Press.

Seeley, K. M. (2000). *Cultural psychotherapy: Working with culture in the clinical encounter*. Lanham: Rowman & Littlefield Publishers, Inc.

Sheppard, P. I. (2011). *Self, culture, and others in womanist practical theology*. New York: Palgrave Macmillan.

Smith, A., Jr. (1982). *The relational self: Ethics and therapy from a black church perspective*. Nashville: Abingdon.

Spillers, H. J. (2003). *Black, white, and in color: Essays on american literature and culture*. Chicago: The University of Chicago Press.

Suarez-Orozco, M. M., & Robben, A. C. (2000). Interdisciplinary perspectives on violence and trauma. In M. M. Suarez-Orozco & A. C. Robben (Eds.), *Cultures under siege: Collective violence and trauma* (pp. 1–41). New York: Cambridge University Press.

Suchet, M. (2007). Unraveling whiteness. *Psychoanalytic Dialogues, 17*, 867–886.

Sullivan, H. S. (1964). *The fusion of psychiatry and social science*. New York: W.W. Norton & Company, Inc.

Summers, F. (1994). *Object relations theories and psychopathology: A comprehensive text*. New York: Psychology Press.

Washington, H. A. (2006). *Medical apartheid: The dark history of medical experimentation on black Americans from colonial times to the present*. New York: Doubleday.

Watkins Ali, C. A. (1999). *Survival and liberation: Pastoral theology in african american context.* St. Louis: Chalice Press.

Weld, T. D. (1839). *American slavery as it is: Testimony of a thousand witnesses.* New York: American Anti-Slavery Society, Office. No. 143.

Wimberly, E. (2006). *African American pastoral care and counseling: Politics of oppression and empowerment.* Cleveland: The Pilgrim Press.

Winnicott, D. W. (1960). The theory of the parent-infant relationship. *The International Journal of Psychoanalysis, 41,* 585–595.

Yelling, J. F. (2004). *Harriet Jacobs: A life.* New York: Basic Civitas Books.

CHAPTER 3

Reimagining Black Subjectivity: A Psychoanalysis of Frederick Douglass

*A man's troubles are always half disposed of when he finds endurance
the only alternative. I found myself here; there was no getting away;
and naught remained for me but to make the best of it.*
—*Frederick Douglass (1881, p. 27)*
*A man, without force, is without the essential dignity of humanity.
Human nature is so constituted, that it cannot honor a helpless man,
although it can pity him; and even this it cannot do long, if the signs of
power do not arise.*
—*Frederick Douglass (1855, p. 247)*

In the previous chapter, I established that the broader psychosocial environment and the cultural and social narratives impact how we understand
human subjectivity, as well as how we experience our subjectivity.
Throughout this project, I employ the phrase anthropological subjectivity
to name what it means to be human and how we human beings experience
ourselves in our interior space, interpersonally, and with the Divine. The
intersection of these two schools of thought (anthropology and human
subjectivity) cannot be overemphasized in this psychobiography, as all of
the players in American slavocracy colluded actively or passively to prop up
the system. Understanding human subjectivities, their interpersonal relatedness, and the expressions of what it meant to be human within in the
spaces that constructed the western democratic experiment is crucial to

© The Author(s) 2018
D. G. Gibson, *Frederick Douglass, a Psychobiography*,
Black Religion/Womanist Thought/Social Justice,
https://doi.org/10.1007/978-3-319-75229-7_3

this project. It provides insight into of how the architects, benefactors, bystanders, and victims of the American slavocracy understood and experienced themselves in relation to self, other, and the Divine.

The self-experiences of the architects of the slavocracy—self-experiences in relation to the Divine, culture, and black bodies—together anesthetized their subjectivities against any form of guilt, shame, or conviction about the destruction of black bodies. Uncovering and interpreting self-experience helps us to understand human motivation and behavior. The interplay and dance of contemporary human subjectivities that perpetuate white supremacy, racism, or any other form of oppression and bigotry can often be traced to the historical subjectivities that created and maintained the slavocracy.

As we see in the autobiographies of Douglass, examples of such self-experience by the designers of the slavocracy in relation to the darker bodies of the victimized included superiority, sadism, paternalism, fear, and domination. That Douglass could resist these shows his robust subjectivity and his ability to self-determine in the extreme context of the slavocracy. Reflections upon anthropology and the psychodynamics of human subjectivity are critical to examining Frederick Douglass, how he navigated the traumatizing contours of the slavocracy and oppression in the nineteenth century and how the legacy of that environment continues to influence us today.

An increasing number of scholars and practitioners in the world of psychology are beginning to recognize the interdisciplinary value of anthropology and psychodynamic discourse. Women and scholars of color have long challenged the propensity of psychodynamic theory to locate the etiology and essence of human subjectivity within the individual (or even two individuals), as if outside factors have no impact on them. Realizing the value of the intersection of anthropology and psychodynamic discourse, Seeley (2000) suggests "anthropologists …offer psychotherapists various new ways of thinking about culture[;…] by focusing on individuals, on their psychological processes and characteristics, and on their social worlds, these new conceptions of culture directly address clinical interests" (p. 74). The intersectionality of anthropological subjectivity becomes important for practical theology to the extent that such soft sciences are engaged in combination with the requisite God-talk to examine the practices of the church.

Psychodynamic discourse in many ways still tends to essentialize the foundation of human subjectivity within the confines of the individual or in some form of a human dyad (whether that be with parents, significant caregivers, past and contemporary relationships, etc.). Yet, a psychoanalytic examination of the autobiographies of Frederick Douglass suggests we should not universalize these theories. For when conceptions of human subjectivity limit the accomplishment of psychical, emotional, or spiritual tasks to the individual or a human dyad, such theorizing presupposes that human survival is a foregone conclusion because they assume that exterior cultural forces are conducive to the formation of the human subjectivities in question. Yet those who have traditionally existed on the underside of history (such as slaves in a slavocracy) do not have the luxury of taking for granted the continuity of existence in a hostile environment. Groups of people who are objectified in the social contract of any given society cannot internalize the most basic trust of survivability that is necessary for the flourishing of human subjectivity. This observation seems to be conspicuously absent from mainstream psychoanalytic theory.

INTRODUCTION OF THE FORCE OF BEING

I suggest that even more elementary to the basic psychosocial tasks of forming human subjectivity is seeking life. Frederick Douglass was not motivated to resolve oedipal conflict, nor was he primarily object,[1] relational, or self-object seeking. He sought life, plain and simple, what I call the *interior force of being*. I derive this term from Douglass' (1855) own words. In his second autobiography, after reflecting on a prolific fight with the so-called slave-breaker Covey, Douglass asserts that "a man, without force, is without the essential dignity of humanity...human nature is so constituted, that it cannot honor a helpless man, although it can pity him; and even this it cannot do long, if the signs of power do not arise" (p. 247). I understand this "essential dignity of humanity" to be the lifelong quest for human subjectivity.[2]

Examples of this thought can be seen in other human atrocities such as the Holocaust. When one is forced to exist under extreme circumstances, the human develops what Des Pres (1976) observed a Shoah survivor from the Treblinka Nazi extermination camp coin as the "talent for life" (p. 192). Des Pres set out to understand how the survivors of the camps were able to live in the face of unspeakable horror. "[Their testimony," he reported, "reveals a world ruled by death, but also a world of actual living conditions, of ways of life which are the basis and achievement of life in extremity" (p. v). For Des Pres, the survivors manifested psychic structures and traits that are not unique to them but are found in those subjected to extreme conditions. To be sure, existence in the slavocracy was an existence in extremity. Des Pres observes that "survivors act as they do because they have to; and what their predicament reveals is that in extremity life and humanness depend on the same set of activities…**when external props collapse, survivors fall back on life itself**"[3] (p. 191). Likewise, for Frederick Douglass, all external props were compromised such that the pursuit of life, of being itself, was Douglass' most fundamental psychic task.

Interestingly, Des Pres notes that the phrase "talent for life" did not signify special gifts and talents that only certain people have and others lack. I believe he makes a very important observation. Theologically and psychologically, to suggest that survivors of such duress possessed special power or endurance runs the risk of creating a subcategory of humanity that only reinforces the evil imposed upon them. It also suggests that those who didn't survive somehow lacked character. This is an area that resilience literature tends to overlook. Instead, the survivor in Des Pres' work was describing how he personally "experienced" the death camp. Des Pres reflects on the testimony of one of the survivors:

> The survivor just quoted is describing how it felt to him as *experienced*; and for the phrase "talent for life" we might substitute "magic will" or "imperishable power" or "life itself" or any of the other phrases survivors use. The reference is always to something other and greater than the personal ego, a reservoir of strength and resource which in extremity becomes active and is felt as the deeper foundation of selfhood. This is as much as survivors can say of their experience, but in coming to this limit we touch upon a further implication—a view reached precisely at the limit of personal experience. Survivors act as if they were *prepared* for extremity; as if anterior to learning and acculturation there were a deeper knowledge, and elder wisdom, a substratum of vital information biologically instilled and biologically effective. (p. 192)

Des Pres' observation that survivors seemed to be "prepared for extremity" and that they appeared to possess a "deeper knowledge" or "elder wisdom" that enabled them to withstand extremity suggests a baser psychogenic endeavor with which the individual subject is tasked, *a task that traditional psychoanalytic discourse tends to overlook or take for granted.* How might a psychoanalytic picture account for those born into extremity? Based on time, space, context, and location, one could argue that the task to experience being—*the task for human dignity* or the *force of being*—

represents the fundamental psychosocial task. This task is largely out of the realm of awareness and taken for granted if the larger culture and context is structured to psychically affirm the human subject. To put it succinctly, if the environment is not designed to affirm or recognize a person or group, the bedrock *intra-subjective task for human dignity* is no longer latent; it is the fundamental psychological and spiritual undertaking.

This project defines *force of being* as the interior life force that resists the threat of non-self. When a person is forced to live beyond the edges of meaning, in a context of extremity that undermines the human spirit, the *experience of self* becomes the intrinsic psychical and spiritual aspiration. When radical evil and the traumatic are normalized, as in the American slavocracy, or when a person is born into such an environment, then life and the *experience of self* become all that to which its victims can retreat. I propose further that a person develops and cultivates this force of being psychologically and spiritually by: (1) engaging sacred spaces of play and interior reflection, (2) practicing agency over the body, and (3) bearing witness to one's life experiences and personhood through personal testimony and creating life stories and counter-narratives.

By the first, sacred spaces of play and contemplation, I refer to the intermediary liminal space between Douglass' inner imaginal composition and the external horror of the slavocracy. This was the space in which Douglass was able to imagine and experience himself as something other than an object of the slavocracy. Bodily redemption or practicing agency over the body is the *effort* to reclaim one's body, in any way and to any extent, from the objectified roles that the slavocracy assigned to it. The upshot of this central argument is that the victimized (i.e. those in bondage) who were not fortunate enough to have access to sacred spaces of play or contemplation, to witness or practice bodily redemption, or to exert counter-narratives into the surrounding intersubjective matrix (through personal testimony, autobiographies, etc.), *effectively experienced the depletion of their interior force of being.*

Frederick Douglass' most basic psychological and spiritual task was to develop and use his internal force of being in the surrounding intersubjective matrix. In the extreme environment of the slavocracy where survival could not be taken for granted and life itself was all he had to fall back upon, Douglass' internal force of being sustained him. Spiritually, emotionally, and psychologically, it propelled him through one of the darkest moments in modern history. It enabled him to survive a permanent state of acute duress, in which survival is not a foregone conclusion. Important to understanding how the proposed interior force of being governed Frederick Douglass is to understand how this internal psychical and spiritual resource functioned in relation to other human subjectivities and the psychosocial environment. The broader environment, and how it is psychosocially constructed, is relevant to this project. The interior force of being does not operate in isolation.

THE INTERSUBJECTIVE MATRIX/MILIEU

More recent scholarship in psychoanalytic literature takes into account the psychic space between subjectivities critical to the definition of *force of being*. In particular, Stolorow and Atwood (1996) articulated the distinctiveness of their theory of intersubjectivity from other psychoanalytic theories by dispelling what they perceived to be the myth of the isolated mind. For Stolorow and Atwood, the self is not to be found in preexisting, organic psychological content with universalized developmental needs such as self-objects, separation-individuation tasks, or the dissolution of illusions of omnipotence. Rather, they found the self in the ongoing reciprocal interaction of the child-caregiver dyad, a self that is formed by the constant interaction between two subjectivities, and beyond that, in "the larger relational system or field in which psychological phenomena crystallize and in which experience is continually and mutually shaped." They envisage not an isolated mind or a preexisting self, but the person as "one of interacting subjectivities, reciprocal mutual influence, colliding organizing principles, conjunctions and disjunctions" and "attunements and malattunements" (p. 181). Anticipating others' critique, they refute the notion that they have simply constructed a gullible variation of environmentalism. For to them, such critique "ignores the contribution of that individual to each intersubjective transaction that occurs...intersubjective fields, are by definition, codetermined and thus cocreated" (p. 189).

In another place, Stolorow (1995) suggests that self-psychology most closely aligns with his theory of intersubjectivity in that a psychology of the self conceptualizes the experience of selfhood "through the felt responsiveness of others" (p. 394). While Stolorow believes that Kohut was on track to craft a theory of intersubjectivity, he believes self-psychology fell short of this task, as its ultimate goal of an independent center of initiative suggests an isolated self and is even contradictory to Kohut's own assertion that the self is experienced dyadically through the empathic responsiveness of a caregiver or another person.

I touch upon this conversation on intersubjectivity, as I believe *force of being* necessarily includes the mutual impact of the intersubjective matrix in which one is embedded. When viewed through the lens of Douglass' life, I suggest three areas of constructive inquiry are in order regarding Stolorow's understanding of intersubjectivity.

First, while a shift from the "myth of the isolated mind" is a welcome departure from the western theoretical infatuation with individualism, I believe Stolorow's position goes too far in locating the self exclusively in the intersubjective dyad. Such a position simply cannot account for the subjectivity and agency of Douglass in the extreme environment of a slavocracy. As I emphasized in Chap. 2, the influence of the slavocracy was ubiquitous and consumed the imagination of both private and public life. The social contract demanded the objectification of black subjectivity. If Stolorow's position is uncritically applied to Douglass, then we run the risk of either minimizing the horror of slavery (a very common approach) or of suggesting that there were redemptive elements in slavery, both of which are unacceptable. If this is the case, then what was the source of Douglass' imagination? How did he manage to imagine that which was unimaginable (i.e. black subjectivity)? I suggest it was thanks to his "self" or a *force of being* in the intersubjective milieu. Douglass demonstrates that the fundamental psychological task is the effectuation of an interior *force of being*. Human subjectivity always seeks to operationalize its potency of life within any intersubjective milieu in which it is embedded. For individuals and groups that have not been forced to exist on the underside of history, this tends to be a dormant psychological and spiritual task or ability. For Douglass and many others like him, it was the only life-giving choice.

Gehrie (1994) takes up this problem of the independent mind as well, questioning the subject that is located solely in the intersubjective dyad and warns "it is one thing, I think, to describe a person's mind as independent and quite another to derive from that a position of 'alienation' or essential separateness from others" (p. 251). Acknowledging Stolorow and Atwood's position, Gehrie agrees that "there is a danger of reification in talking about the mind or the self as if it were a thing" that was completely isolated, but he laments that "one could argue, however, that perhaps we shouldn't throw out the baby with the bathwater, that only by knowing one's own mind is true access to that of others possible" and "that having a 'mind' need not condemn us to isolation" (p. 252). Gehrie's position is consistent with what I observe of Douglass: he did indeed bring his self to the intersubjective encounter.[4]

Such a preexisting self and the intersubjective space are not necessarily mutually exclusive phenomena. In her sabbatical lecture, Holliman (2013) raises the relational importance of engaging the space between two subjectivities, noting that the "other" can be located in one of three places: (1) over there, (2) in between, or (3) inside of you. She argues that when the "other" is located inside of another subject (as opposed to the space between two or more subjects), it results in conflict with no room for negotiation. The point that is implicit in her relational/intersubjective schema is that a "self" does indeed exist *a priori* in the psychic space between two subjects.

The second area of constructive inquiry I propose regarding Stolorow's understanding of intersubjectivity viewed through the lens of Douglass' life is this: that we can no longer speak of an intersubjective dyad solely between two individuals or the child-caregiver system, but must speak in terms of a robust intersubjective matrix that encapsulates multiple subjectivities. The intersubjective milieu in the definition of the *force of being* is more robust than the space between two individuals. It is an intersubjective ecology that has been determined by individuals, cultural groups, religion, politics, economics, deep structures of a society, social contracts, historical and contemporary narratives, and unconscious interpretations of nation-state history. The convergence of these discourses can create an intersubjective milieu that props up the psychic structure of the majority (individually and collectively) and undermines the psychic space of a minority. The interaction between this intersubjective matrix and the individual is circular and reciprocal, as both are benefactors or casualties of the same process. It is within this multidimensional intersubjective space that Douglass sought to effectuate his *force of being*. In this definition of the intersubjective milieu, I use the term "effectuate" to suggest that the *individual seeks to experience themselves in a self-determining way*, regardless of whether they are positively affirmed by other elements in the matrix. Hence, the quest for his subjectivity was not just between Douglass and the constituents in his immediate surrounding, but between Douglass and the slavocracy and between Douglass and the American democratic experiment.

In considering how culture and history impact the individual psyche, the work of Frie (2012) is particularly helpful. He calls attention to how social dimensions impact the conscious and are relevant to psychoanalysis. He critiques the common assumption that "culture and history are …'out there,' as though in some way existing in a separate register from personal experience" (p. 331). Frie employs the concept of narrative unconscious to explicate the unconscious system of meaning making into which all individuals are born. This meaning-making construct does not necessarily represent the agency of the individual, but a social hermeneutic that represents the confluence of multiple discourses that ultimately shapes the personal experience and identity of the individual subject and creates a framework for determining "us" versus the "other." Narrative unconscious is then useful for understanding the notion of an intersubjective matrix and its capacity to prop up the individual psyche. Frie concludes as follows:

> The hermeneutic tradition suggests that there is no psychological experience that is not constituted by the sociocultural and interpretive contexts in which we find ourselves. Our experience is always contingent on contexts that constitute our personhood by way of interpretations and practices. It is not the case that the person is merely "influenced" by sociocultural factors and contexts. It is not enough to view selfhood and culture as interacting variables. Rather, the experience of selfhood is fundamentally embedded and forged within communal contexts. We exist in the world by way of shared cultural understandings. (pp. 335–336)

Third, in any reflection of intersubjective discourse, an assumption of co-creativity is not a foregone conclusion. The idea of co-creativity presupposes individual agency and dyadic mutuality. But human subjectivities that exist on the underside of history often cannot take self-determination and co-creativity for granted. Douglass was not an equal co-creator of the intersubjective space in which he was embedded. Yet he was compelled by an internal force of being either to resist the meanings (and roles) imposed on him by certain intersubjective matrixes, to join whatever spaces that were suitable for the operationalization of his force of being, or to carve out a psychic space within the broader intersubjective milieu.

Conversely, within the paradigm of the interior force of being, emotional and spiritual neurosis (or pathology) suggests that to some extent the individual subjectivity unconsciously accedes to the predetermined roles assigned by the intersubjective milieu in a way that is harmful to the experience of selfhood. Neurosis as an extreme response to this reflects the inability to reimagine "self" as something other than what has been hegemonically crafted in the intersubjective space. In her work on a psychoanalytic social theory of oppression, Oliver (2004) refers to the presumed mutuality of subjectivities that is found in much of psychoanalytic theory as a perverse privileging. For Oliver, alienation that results from psychic anxiety related to separation-individuation tasks is a far cry from "the debilitating alienation of being thrown there as one incapable of meaning making... debilitating alienation is the result of being thrown into a world of preexisting meanings as one incapable of meaning making" (p. 15). While Oliver connects this debilitating alienation to being thrown into the world, I argue that it is being thrown into intersubjective spaces where one's agency for mutual and interactive meaning making is compromised. She concludes that "the greatest pain of this alienation comes from the fact that even the meaning of one's own body has been already defined" (p. 15).

Consequently, in the definition of force of being (the interior life force that resists the threat of non-self), the notion of interdependence is vital. In advocating for interdependence, both psychic dependence and independence can lead to an unhealthy self. As regards the life of Frederick Douglass, if subjectivity is solely to be found in the intersubjective space, it would seem that Douglass and his contemporaries could not have resisted the psychic onslaught of the slavocracy and its constituent stakeholders given its pervasiveness and dominance. In an intersubjective paradigm that assumes there is no element of a preexisting subject, in short without the psychic and emotional resources to resist or counter-imagine, Frederick Douglass should have submitted spiritually, psychologically, and emotionally to the desires of the environment—and indeed, many of those in bondage submitted. When viewed through the lens of traditional psychoanalytic theories, an argument can be made that Frederick Douglass *should have* considered his enslavement as normative, and consistent with social design and God's divine plan. And some of those who were enslaved—as well as the bystanders and onlookers—did indeed internalize the ideology of slavery, the result of neurosis or of a traumatized state. Yet Douglass did not internalize this ideology. This suggests to me that an element of selfhood does indeed exist before the intersubjective dyad or milieu. That is to say, the self is not totally *dependent* on the intersubjective dyad.

Yet neither is the self-constructed *independent* of the intersubjective milieu. A psychology of the self is useful in this regard. Kohut conceptualized the continuous psychic need for twinship association, reflective self-object (i.e. a person) affirmation, and the idealization of self-objects (i.e. person) over the entire lifespan. From this perspective, the self, to some degree, necessarily depends on another person. In Kohut's construct, there exists a self-aware subject from birth. In this conception, the overall goal of one's psychological project is to become an independent center of initiative comprised of basic goals, ambitions, and ideas which are achieved through the deployment of skills and talents. When viewed through the life of Douglass however, I believe Kohut's formulation still presents problems, as psychological health is delimited to the "self" being empathically mirrored by another or by the "self" being soothed through the idealization of another. Such self-affirming self-objects (i.e. people) or self-soothing idealized self-objects would have been scarce for Douglass or any other slave in the slavocracy.

While instances of mirroring and idealization can be found in Douglass' autobiographical recollections, there is no example that demonstrates a sustained developmental trajectory, as most in-depth literature suggests, is necessary for the individual to become psychologically mature. At best, we only see brief instances of such psychic reciprocation between Douglass and certain others. Additionally, if a self-psychological hermeneutic is applied uncritically, Douglass' selfhood is delimited to being affirmed by the subjects within a slavocracy. Such subjects lack the capacity to recognize Douglass as a human being, let alone to affirm him. Can it truly be argued that over an extended period of time Douglass could idealize his enslavers and the benefactors and architects of the plantation system? Such an expectation reflects a racist ideology that is incapable of experiencing or imagining African Americans as complex beings that encounter a full array of human experiences including suffering, pain, grief, or even hate and resentment for their enslavers and oppressors.

Moreover, it is methodologically flawed to interpret a theory of anthropology, human development, pathology, or change exclusively through a lens that does not adequately account for life in extremity. It runs the risk of diagnosing as regressive (or pathological) certain actions that individuals employ in order to resist or survive. Lastly, Kohut's formation still calls for the goal of psychological maturity to reflect an independent center of initiative. While his scheme does recognize the importance of an empathic influence by a caregiver (or another person) on another person's psyche, his construct doesn't fully consider the reciprocal self-forming influence of each subject within a given dyad, let alone a complex intersubjective matrix.

While traditional psychodynamic themes for human development may have been beneficial and occasionally present in a slavocracy, they were not absolutely necessary for the construction of Douglass' psychic structure. Empathic attunement from the other within the intersubjective matrix, while typical and beneficial, did not appear absolutely necessary to the formation of a subjectivity existing in extremity. Instead, for Douglass it seems that the drive for self-experience (or the drive to be or exist) within the intersubjective field was structure building in and of itself.

LIVING IN THE INTERSUBJECTIVE MATRIX

A *force of being* is constructed in the framework of *interdependence* within an intersubjective milieu. Interdependence recognizes that selfhood is both dependent on the intersubjective space in which one is embedded and yet sufficiently independent or autonomous either to influence the intersubjective milieu with one's own self-meaning or to transgress an objectified role or assignment that the space has created for an individual. In challenging Stolorow's view that the self is to be found only in the intersubjective dyad, I will borrow from Summers' (1996) argument that "autonomy has never meant freedom from environmental influence, but a degree of control over it...isolation is not the psychoanalytic meaning of autonomy" (p. 167). Whether or not one agrees with Summers' argument (that in psychoanalytic discourse isolation is not synonymous with autonomy), his conception of autonomy is useful for the argument of interdependence being put forth. If the selfhood of Douglass was totally dependent on the empathic affirmation of power brokers in the slavocracy, self-development would have been severely arrested.

But we see from the example of Douglass that resistance to the threat of non-self or conversely the desire and agency to transgress (or defy) the norms and social contracts of the slavocracy's intersubjective milieu were conducive to building one's psychic structure and selfhood. Simply put, resistance of any kind built the personhood of Frederick Douglass. The upshot of this position is that the selfhood of Douglass or any of his contemporaries was not necessarily contingent upon a material freedom (which many were not able to secure) but on awareness that one *should be free*. Such awareness transgressed the intersubjective milieu of the slavocracy.

Thus, the interdependency of *force of being* divorces selfhood from the Hegelian (1977) binary that suggests subjectivity is to be found only in being recognized by the other. If this is the case, then the selfhood of oppressed people is arguably limited to the eradication of racist ideologies in any given environment. Attributing oppressed people's progress to the moral progress of the oppressor is a sign of this fallacious argument.

However, recognition by the other is not absolutely necessary for developing a force of being. We see in Douglass that one's ability to transgress the intersubjective matrix (whether or not the other chooses to recognize or affirm the subject) is sufficient grounds for self-experience and subjectivity and is never futile. Because of the very act of fighting his overseer, Douglass (1855) was able to claim that "this spirit made me a freeman in fact, while I remained a slave in form" (p. 247). The autobiographies of Frederick Douglass suggest that under oppressive conditions, the interior force of being reflects the most fundamental spiritual and psychological task that props up human subjectivity.

I was caught off guard by finding an interior force of being that functioned interdependently. I had approached this project expecting to find a Frederick Douglass whose identity was more subsumed in idealistic notions of subjectivity through community—an epistemological perspective that is held by many scholars and theologians of color. But after examining and coding four autobiographies of Frederick Douglass, I had to concede that while at times his subjectivity was formed in the intersubjective community of other blacks in the plantation community, at other times it seemed that his selfhood emanated from another source outside of the community. This both/and dialectic is captured well in the notion of interdependence central to this project.

Nowhere is the concept of interdependence better exemplified than in a speech/publication of Douglass entitled *Self-Made Men*. Douglass made this speech in 1874 to a group of students at the Indian Industrial School in Carlisle, PA. In it, he clearly states that he doesn't believe any person can truly be independent. For Douglass, there is no state of existence that "can lift a man into absolute independence of his fellowmen, and no generation of men can be independent of the preceding generation. The brotherhood and inter-dependence of mankind are guarded and defended at all points." He goes on: "I believe in individuality, but individuals are, to the mass, like waves to the ocean. The highest order of genius is as dependent as its lowest" (pp. 5–6). But after establishing that he does not necessarily believe in absolute independence, Douglass defines:

[s]elf-made men [as...] the men who, under peculiar difficulties and *without the ordinary helps of favoring circumstances*, have attained knowledge, usefulness, power and position and have learned from themselves the best uses to which life can be put in this world, and in the exercises of these uses to build up worthy character. They are the men who *owe little or nothing to*

birth, relationship, friendly surroundings; to wealth inherited or to early approved means of education; who are what they are, without the aid of any of the favoring conditions by which other men usually rise in the world and achieve great results. In fact they are the men who are not brought up but who are *obliged to come up,* not only without the voluntary assistance or friendly co-operation of society, but often *in open and derisive defiance of all the efforts of society and the tendency of circumstances to repress, retard and keep them down.* They are the men who, in a world of schools, academies, colleges and other institutions of learning, are often compelled by unfriendly circumstances to acquire their education elsewhere and, amidst unfavorable conditions, to hew out for themselves a way to success, and thus to become the architects of their own good fortunes. They are in a peculiar sense, indebted to themselves for themselves.[5] (pp. 6–7)

Clearly, Douglass is speaking of himself here. By the time of this speech, Douglass had garnered popularity and wealth on the lecture circuit. He exercised an agency that seemed to enable him to be both connected and disconnected in the intersubjective spaces he inhabited, whether it was with other slaves or blacks or even in the plantation system. In certain instances, Douglass' selfhood seemed to erect emotional and psychic boundaries that prevented his subjectivity from being overwhelmed by the dictates and imagination of the slavocracy. As we shall see in this chapter, if the intersubjective milieu was not conducive to his personhood, Douglass' interior force of being seemed to exhibit a kind of autonomy that defied—or transgressed—the oppressive interpsychic field. Conversely, if the intersubjective space was conducive to Douglass' force of being, his selfhood seemed to be found more interdependently. An example of this can be seen in Douglass' gradual transition from believing that freedom for blacks could only be realized by a total and complete extraction from the American context to a position that such freedom may be achievable within the American socioeconomic and political framework.

These observations present a complex understanding of community, selfhood, and intersubjective spaces that seems to be absent from the psychodynamic literature. Moreover, the essence of Douglass' definition of self-made men is not that there are such self-made individuals in any ontological sense of the word, but that such individuals didn't benefit from the favorable psychological conditions and requisites that psychoanalytic theory assumes are available to everyone. In this speech, Douglass effectively crystalizes what Oliver (2004) refers to as a perverse privileging that is presupposed in western conceptions of selfhood. This observation is consistent with the proposed conception of the *interior force of being*. Saidiya Hartman (1997) argues against an ontological construction of community and challenges reducing the concept of community to race. Hartman distinguishes between a "community" in fact versus a "community" in form. In the slavocracy, Hartman argues that community for African Americans was not built on common identity but on a common goal of liberation. For Hartman, to reduce community to race ignores the complexities, nuances, and diversity of black culture and subjectivity. For Hartman then, community among the slaves was less about any common identity and more about a common goal to eradicate slavery. She argues that

> contrary to identity providing the ground of community, identity is figured as the desired negation of the very set of constraints that create commonality—that is, the yearning to be liberated from the condition of enslavement facilitates the networks of affiliation and identification...yet it is important to recognize that the relations among slaves were characterized as much by antagonisms, distrust, contending interest, values, and beliefs as by mutual cooperation and solidarity. (p. 59)

We see an example of the complex community that Hartmann describes and what I consider to be an example of interdependence within the intersubjective matrix in Douglass' recollection of an incident that occurred while he was a fugitive in New Bedford, CT, shortly after escaping from the plantation in Maryland. In all of his autobiographies, Douglass (1845) recalls an incident in which "a colored man and a fugitive slave were on unfriendly terms," with the former threatening the latter that he would report his whereabouts to his master. According to Douglass' report, New Bedford was an abolitionist stronghold and a safe haven for fugitive slaves. Douglass recounts that once the news spread in New Bedford that this colored man had threatened to expose this fugitive slave to his master:

> [s]traightway a meeting was called among the colored people, under the stereotyped notice, "Business of importance!" *The betrayer was invited to attend.* The people came at the appointed hour, and organized the meeting by appointing a very religious old gentleman as president, who, I believe, made a prayer, after which he addressed the meeting as follows: "*Friends, we have got him here, and I would recommend that you young men just take him outside the door, and kill him!*" With this, a number of them bolted at him;

but they were intercepted by some more timid than themselves, and the betrayer escaped their vengeance, and has not been seen in New Bedford since. I believe there have been no more such threats, and should there be hereafter, I doubt not that death would be the consequence.[6] (p. 115)

This incident is a provocative example of the complex community to which Hartman speaks. There was a betrayer who was willing to compromise another fugitive. Some in the community attempted to kill the betrayer for the sake of the broader community, while others interceded to protect the betrayer. All of this occurred within the same intersubjective milieu that represented an extreme context for all parties involved. But more specifically, it emphasizes an interdependent concept of selfhood or an interdependent center of initiative. An interdependent scheme necessarily incorporates the formational and reciprocal influences of any intersubjective dyad (that includes people) or milieu (that includes culture, narratives, social contract, etc.) and concomitantly incorporates the uniqueness of selfhood that is organic and precedes the intersubjective dyad. In what follows, I propose that such a conception is a more suitable psychological and anthropological hermeneutic by which to interpret the complex life of Frederick Douglass and his contemporaries.

More recent conversations in psychoanalytic literature address individualistic notions of selfhood (i.e. "I think therefore I am") with the conception of one- and two-person psychologies. The more traditional models that focus solely on the intrapersonal construction of selfhood are interpreted as a one-person model, juxtaposed against two-person models that attempt to account for the construction of the self with others. Relational proponents such as Aron (1996) argue that the most important component of relationality is that it conceives of the relation between "the individual and the social, internal objects and external interpersonal relations, self-regulation and mutual regulation" (p. 63). Aron asserts that the relational movement's focus on the two-person paradigm is due to the fact that "in the history of psychoanalysis and in Western culture more generally, our bias has been so strongly in favor of an individual view and our values are so highly individualistic that a correction has been needed" (p. 63). Yet while the relational paradigm locates selfhood in the reciprocity of the dyad, it does not include the social and cultural as much as I think necessary. Altman (2010) augments the "correction" of which Aron speaks by calling for a three-person model which incorporates larger societal elements. For Altman, the construction of a three-person model emphasizes "the analytic significance of the racial, cultural, and social class status of patient and analyst, as well as the institutional context of their work" (p. 61).

While both Aron and Altman make great strides toward incorporating social and historical influence in the conception of the human subject, they fall short in my estimation. In the two or three-person configuration, the social element seems to be construed as *an option* that is available for consideration. In this project, I argue that contemporary and historical narratives and the larger political, legal, economic, and social contracts of any society are *necessarily formational* in how we conceive the human project and experience *the other*. Many psychoanalytic theorists, practitioners, and even theologians and religious scholars fail to grasp the extent to which the western intersubjective complex underwrites their psychic structure in a way that they can conceive of theories that take human survivability and continuity for granted.

EXAMINING FREDERICK DOUGLASS' GOD-IMAGE AND RELIGIOUS DISPOSITION

We see Douglass' force of being in his capacity to imagine the unimaginable or to imagine that which his intersubjective milieu postulated was nonexistent. Throughout his autobiographies, Douglass was constantly imagining his selfhood in a culture and context that did not recognize him or other victims of the slavocracy as having subjectivity. So the central question persists: how could Douglass, from a very early age, imagine freedom and what he refers to as "manhood" for himself, when he was embedded in an environment that condoned and justified slavery on a political, legal, social, familial, theological, and religious basis?

In book 1, Douglass makes little mention of having thoughts of freedom and selfhood at an early age. It is conceivable that at the time of this first writing in 1845, Douglass wrote in a state of hyper-arousal,[7] catatonic shock, or post-traumatic stress disorder, as he remained in real danger of being recaptured. Deep reflections upon selfhood were clearly not at the forefront of his mind in book 1. But in books 2 and 3, Douglass indicates that at a very early age (approximately six years old), while still under the care of his grandmother (i.e. before he was removed from his grandparents' care and given over to the slave master), he contemplated thoughts of how slavery was unjust and evil and the various possibilities of escape.

Apparently such thoughts came to Douglass even before he learned to read. Consider the following passages from book 2 where Douglass (1855) gives voice to images of subjectivity. I quote these passages from Douglass at length to give the reader a substantive sense of what Douglass was experiencing emotionally:

THE heart-rending incidents, related in the foregoing chapter, led me, thus early, to inquire into the nature and history of slavery. Why am I a slave? Why are some people slaves, and others masters? Was there ever a time when this was not so? How did the relation commence? These were the perplexing questions which began now to claim my thoughts, and to exercise the weak powers of my mind, for I was still but a child, and knew less than children of the same age in the free states. As my questions concerning these things were only put to children a little older, and little better informed than myself, I was not rapid in reaching a solid footing. By some means I learned from these inquiries, that "God, up in the sky," made every body; and that he made white people to be masters and mistresses, and black people to be slaves. This did not satisfy me, nor lessen my interest in the subject. I was told, too, that God was good, and that He knew what was best for me, and best for everybody. This was less satisfactory than the first statement; because it came, point blank, against all my notions of goodness. It was not good to let old master cut the flesh off Esther, and make her cry so. Besides, how did people know that God made black people to be slaves? Did they go up in the sky and learn it? or, did He come down and tell them so? All was dark here. It was some relief to my hard notions of the goodness of God, that, although he made white men to be slaveholders, he did not make them to be bad slaveholders, and that, in due time, he would punish the bad slaveholders; that he would, when they died, send them to the bad place, where they would be "burnt up." Nevertheless, I could not reconcile the relation of slavery with my crude notions of goodness. Then, too, I found that there were puzzling exceptions to this theory of slavery on both sides, and in the middle. I knew of blacks who were not slaves; I knew of whites who were not slaveholders; and I knew of persons who were nearly white, who were slaves. Color, therefore, was a very unsatisfactory basis for slavery.

At such a young age, how does one account for the capacity of Douglass to "imagine" that slavery was not good while existing in an environment where the objectification of black bodies was normalized, socialized, legalized, and even worse, rendered as God's will? We also learn in this passage what Douglass was taught by society from early on about the ideology of the slavocracy: that it was by God's design that white people were to be masters and mistresses and that black people were to be slaves and submit to God's plan. Given the pervasiveness of such teaching, it is conceivable that there were very few, if any, objects that Douglass could have internalized or used as self-objects to aid him in his reflections. I suggest that more fundamental than drive fulfillment or object seeking is the *interior force of being* that is organic to the psychic structure of Douglass. This *force of being* enabled him at least to conceptualize self-hood and subjectivity in an extreme environment. Furthermore, I suggest that this capacity to imagine selfhood reflects a potency for life, is organic to selfhood, and exists interdependently with other subjectivities but is not necessarily dependent upon the empathic or affirmative recognition by the other subject(s) within the intersubjective milieu. From a theological anthropology perspective, the *interior force of being* suggests that the human spirit—crafted in the image and likeness of God—is not designed to be enslaved or oppressed. If the *interior space* of the person concedes to the demonic ideology of affirming enslavement or oppression, then such a position reflects a self-experience of negation, consequently reflecting varying degrees of neurosis, pathology, trauma, or spiritual sickness.

The psychological task that Douglass faced was enormous. The destructive psychosocial milieu in which Douglass existed was designed to underscore white subjectivity through the total suppression and/or obliteration of black selfhood. For Douglass to be able to imagine his own selfhood in the midst of extreme violence was truly noteworthy. William Jones (1998) recognizes this in his controversial project that addresses the proposition of whether or not God is a white racist. He problematizes the age-old axiom of God's goodness and challenges black liberation theologians to prove that God is not antagonistic toward black life in light of the radical evil that for centuries has been perpetrated on people of African descent. While Jones' project is not psychosocial in nature, his descriptive challenge presents a compelling psychologic and theodicy, crystalizes the psychosocial milieu Douglass was up against, and describes the extreme difficulties he encountered as he struggled for self-realization and self-imagination.

Jones describes the paradoxical question of divine racism using five key propositions that take seriously slavery and black suffering: (1) God constructs a two-category system with humans, an in-group and an out-group, and has greater concern for the in-group than the out-group; (2) the out-group suffers more than any person or group in the entire population; (3) if God's favor has created an in-group and out-group such that the out-group suffers more, then the suffering of the out-group must reflect God's will and also justify the acts of the architects and agents of slavery and black oppression, as they are simply carrying out God's will; (4) God's favor of the in-group over the out-group is connected with racial identity; and (5) because God favors the in-group and "wills" the suffering of the out-group, it must also be that God is a member of the in-group.

Building on these propositions, Jones offers up a biblical summation of the topic of suffering, suggesting that it can either reflect God's wrath, God's favor (which suggests that suffering is redemptive), or one could remain agnostic on the question of suffering. Yet, how could any individual or group know what their suffering represented (i.e. God's favor, God's wrath, or simply nothing)? Based on his review of biblical references on suffering, Jones argues that it is the "exaltation-liberation" event. The exaltation-liberation event is the relief from suffering and the restoration of wellness that effectively proves that one's suffering represents God's favor and redemption. For Jones, this "exaltation-liberation" event has never occurred for African Americans. To this end, he rounds out his argument by positing that black oppression is fundamentally driven by God's disdain for the ethnicity of the group based on the maldistribution of the suffering (i.e. suffering is disproportionately imputed to the minority race compared to the majority), its "negative quality" (meaning that the suffering serves no redemptive purpose to a greater good), its enormity (meaning the suffering affects a significant percentage of the group), and its "non-catastrophic" nature (meaning that the suffering is prolonged over centuries and generations as opposed to a catastrophic event that hits decisively and then retracts). Jones concludes that "it is my contention that the peculiarities of black suffering make the question of divine racism imperative; it is not my position that the special character of black suffering answers the question...what I do affirm is that black theology, precisely because of the prominence of ethnic suffering in the black experience, cannot operate as if the goodness of God for all mankind were a theological axiom" (p. 22).

I take this detour of describing Jones' work to demonstrate the ease with which Douglass could have conceded that slavery was sanctioned and justified by God and that his sole purpose was to exist to delight and serve white people. It would be easy to conclude that God does indeed commission and sanction the enslaved condition—as many plantation owners contended and tried to convince the enslaved. Daly (2002) demonstrates how southern Evangelicalism rationalized, moralized, and ultimately sacralized slavery. These ideological commitments represented the bed-rock of the slavocracy, effectively ossifying the moral compass of its design-ers and those who stood to benefit from the system. Daly argues that the "evangelical language of morality and concepts of power gave new life to the claim that good men could hold slaves... slaveholding was a traditional mark of success, and a moral defense of slavery was implicit whenever Americans who considered themselves good Christians held slaves" (p. 30). Such observations show what Douglass was up against.

Thus his capacity to question and counter well-established ideologies purporting the redemptive qualities of enslavement (without ever experi-encing freedom and self-determination, etc.) demonstrates his well-developed force of being. It is thanks to this force of being that, in Chap. 6 of book 2 entitled "Treatment of Slaves on Lloyd's Plantation," as he reconsiders his early childhood reflections on why he is enslaved, Douglass (1855) concludes

> It was not color, but crime, not God, but man, that afforded the true expla-nation of the existence of slavery; nor was I long in finding out another important truth, viz: what man can make, man can unmake. The appalling darkness faded away, and I was master of the subject. There were slaves here, direct from Guinea; and there were many who could say that their fathers and mothers were stolen from Africa—forced from their homes, and com-pelled to serve as slaves. This, to me, was knowledge; but it was a kind of knowledge which filled me with a burning hatred of slavery, increased my suffering, and left me without the means of breaking away from my bond-age. Yet it was knowledge quite worth possessing. I could not have been more than seven or eight years old, when I began to make this subject my study. It was with me in the woods and fields; along the shore of the river, and wherever my boyish wanderings led me; and though I was, at that time, quite ignorant of the existence of the free states, I distinctly remember being, even then, most strongly impressed with the idea of being a freeman some day. This cheering assurance was an inborn dream of my human nature—a constant menace to slavery—and one which all the powers of slavery were unable to silence or extinguish. (pp. 90–91)

Later, in book 3, the chapter in which he recounts this incident Douglass now renames "A Child's Reasoning," as if to emphasize how young was when engaging in such reflections on freedom and selfhood. Douglass posits that before he even knew there was a "free state," he knew what it was to be free. It was this that repeatedly prompted him to reimagine his subjectivity (or manhood) in the midst of the slavocracy. His interior force of being effectively resisted the threat of non-self. That these imaginations and experiences of subjectivity were with him in the woods, fields, and along the shores or wherever else his "boyish" wanderings led him suggest the power of sacred liminal spaces and play in propping up one's internal *force of being*. In another place in book 2, Douglass (1855) again recollects childhood thoughts about the evils of slavery and images of freedom, even though the materialization of such images was nonexistent in his environment:

> As I grew older and more thoughtful, I was more and more filled with a sense of my wretchedness. The cruelty of Aunt Katy, the hunger and cold I suffered, and the terrible reports of wrong and outrage which came to my ear, together with what I almost daily witnessed, led me, when yet but eight or nine years old, to wish I had never been born. I used to contrast my condition with the black-birds, in whose wild and sweet songs I fancied them so happy! Their apparent joy only deepened the shades of my sorrow. There are thoughtful days in the lives of children—at least there were in mine—when they grapple with all the great, primary subjects of knowledge, and reach, in a moment, conclusions which no subsequent experience can shake. I was just as well aware of the unjust, unnatural and murderous character of slavery, when nine years old, as I am now. Without any appeal to books, to laws, or to authorities of any kind, it was enough to accept God as a father, to regard slavery as a crime. (pp. 133–134)

Douglass' desire not to exist and his capacity to contrast his existence with that of the freedom of the black birds do not reflect neurosis or pathology but a sophisticated organic psychic structure. Object internalization does not speak adequately to what we witness in Douglass at such an early age. While Fairbairn (1946) allows for the internalization of both good and bad objects, such an explanation is inadequate to explain Douglass' selfhood at such an early age and would introduce psychodynamic and theological problems (to say the least). The plantation environment was ill-suited for the development of a libidinal ego and exciting object within Douglass (as conceptualized by Fairbairn) that would yield the kind of childhood imagination and reflections he is recollecting. According to Douglass, he was generating such thoughts even without knowledge of the existence of free states. From a theoretical perspective, to suggest that Douglass' redemptive imagination reflects internalized object relations of the plantation and slavocracy assigns redemptive qualities to the slavocracy: an assignment that would be morally indefensible and theologically bankrupt.

As I discuss further shortly, for Douglass, it was an interior force of being that compelled his childhood mind to argue that "God as a father" was sufficient for him to recognize that slavery was criminal. Yet how could he even have constructed an amicable God-image? While offensive to some, William Jones' challenge to black liberation theologians that they have to demonstrate that God is not a racist in light of the radical suffering black people have endured is compelling and logical. When viewed through the eyes of the one who is suffering, it is easy to concede that God does indeed favor the oppressor. While Jones is not a psychologist, his premise reflects a sound psychology. It stands to reason that the individual's past necessarily influences present relational patterns and object constructions.

And indeed, there were many victims of the slavocracy whose ego structure reflected the absolute colonization of psychic space and the psychological internalization of the tenets of the slavocracy. To the extent that Douglass (and his contemporaries) did not have access to sacred spaces of play and reflection was denied bodily redemption and the opportunity to create counter-narratives, his force of being and subjectivity would be depleted and overwhelmed by the psychic space created by the slavocracy leading to a kind of psychological or spiritual neurosis, pathology, or trauma. Douglass' healthy force of being prevented this assault on his subjectivity.

Contemporary psychoanalytic theory supports that in Douglass' context, a depleted *force of being* would then render the psychic structure vulnerable to form selfhood around such early negative experiences. Thus Gehrie (1996) argues that the aggression an analyst might experience in the transference during therapy does not necessarily reflect an empathic break on the side of the analyst, but could reflect the client's engagement of negative experiences during the formation of early psychic structures. For

> the self is formed around early experience, and the result of this process becomes the 'shape of the self' and the template through which the environment is subsequently experienced... Structure accrues from experience during the formative period regardless of its valence; its substance includes the internalized, subjectively organized early versions of experience that tend to remain relatively constant over time, and subsequently acts as a kind of template through which new experiences are processed". (p. 163)

Douglass' testimony about enslaved victims who believed that the condition of enslavement reflected divine will and purpose seems to support Gehrie's position of the effects of negative experiences in early character development. In book 2, after learning to read, Douglass (1855) recollects reading the *Columbian Orator*, a school book in which Douglass found various essays and speeches on liberty, emancipation, and freedom. After reading it, Douglass indicates that he wished he had remained as ignorant as some other victims of the slavocracy. He laments:

> *I have met many religious colored people, at the south, who are under the delusion that God requires them to submit to slavery, and to wear their chains with meekness and humility.* I could entertain no such nonsense as this; and I almost lost my patience when I found any colored man weak enough to believe such stuff. Nevertheless, the increase of knowledge was attended with bitter, as well as sweet results. The more I read, the more I was led to abhor and detest slavery, and my enslavers. "Slaveholders," thought I, "are only a band of successful robbers, who left their homes and went into Africa for the purpose of stealing and reducing my people to slavery." I loathed them as the meanest and the most wicked of men. As I read, behold! the very discontent so graphically predicted by Master Hugh, had already come upon me. I was no longer the light-hearted, gleesome boy, full of mirth and play, as when I landed first at Baltimore. Knowledge had come; light had penetrated the moral dungeon where I dwelt; and, behold! there lay the bloody whip, for my back, and here was the iron chain; and my good, kind master, he was the author of my situation. The revelation haunted me, stung me, and made me gloomy and miserable. As I writhed under the sting and torment of this knowledge, I almost envied my fellow slaves their stupid contentment.[8] (pp. 159–60)

Yet reading the *Columbian Orator* was not what precipitated Douglass' position on slavery and liberty. Douglass testified to having had a disdain for slavery long before he could read. Consequently, while literacy was definitely a formidable tool whereby Douglass enhanced his internal constitution, it was not necessarily foundational. Yet it did provide Douglass with additional talking points for a conclusion he had already reached: that slavery had nothing to do with God and that it was abominable.

Consequently, one is left with the question of how to account for Douglass' healthy psychic structure compared to that of other victims. I conclude that Douglass had access to circumstances that were conducive to the development of his interior space by: (1) engaging sacred spaces of play and interior reflection, (2) practicing agency over the body, and (3) crafting counter-hegemonic life stories that subverted the narrative of the slavocracy and white superiority. Yet I suggest that it was only after the force of being had been sufficiently cultivated and mobilized in Douglass that he was he able to use relationality and other self-objects in a way that was structure building.

In the previously mentioned passage where Douglass argues that without any appeal to books, laws, or other authorities, "God as father" was enough for him to understand the perversion of slavery, he demonstrates an ability to construct an amicable God-image conducive to the enhancement of his psychic space. Douglass' recollection of such God-talk early on in his life fits with both Rector (2001) and Holliman's (2002) contention that religious experience and a healthy God-image can facilitate the construction of a healthy subjectivity. For Rector, mystical experiences can potentially fulfill an idealizing self-object need and compensate for the lack of human idealizing subjects in one's environment. This compensatory function would seem especially to support certain areas of Douglass' psychic needs, especially in a slavocracy. Rector asserts that "the need to affiliate with perfection as a solution to the loss of one's sense of perfection is especially relevant to a psychological understanding of mystical experience...Certain forms of mysticism function as a form of 'fuzzy idealism' in which disappointment in the experience of human self-objects is avoided by appealing to a vague sense of perfection" (p. 192).

The following example captures this idea of fuzzy idealism. Douglass recollects an incident in his childhood in which Thomas Auld, his master in rural Maryland, sent Douglass to live with the master's brother, Hugh Auld, in Baltimore. In Baltimore Douglass learned to read from Sophia Auld, the wife of Hugh Auld. While this excerpt is taken from book 2, the way in which Douglass (1855) describes the event is similar to its mention in book 1. In essence, he attributes the move to Baltimore as a special favor endowed by God upon him, compared to all of the other children on the plantation:

> I may say here, that I regard my removal from Col. Lloyd's plantation as one of the most interesting and fortunate events of my life. Viewing it in the light of human likelihoods, it is quite probable that, but for the mere circumstance of being thus removed before the rigors of slavery had fastened upon me; before my young spirit had been crushed under the iron control of the slave-driver, instead of being, today, a FREEMAN, I might have been

wearing the galling chains of slavery. I have sometimes felt, however, that there was something more intelligent than chance, and something more certain than luck, to be seen in the circumstance. If I have made any progress in knowledge; if I have cherished any honorable aspirations, or have, in any manner, worthily discharged the duties of a member of an oppressed people; this little circumstance must be allowed its due weight in giving my life that direction. I have ever regarded it as the first plain manifestation of that "Divinity that shapes our ends, Rough hew them as we will." I was not the only boy on the plantation that might have been sent to live in Baltimore. There was a wide margin from which to select. There were boys younger, boys older, and boys of the same age, belonging to my old master—some at his own house, and some at his farm—but the high privilege fell to my lot. (pp. 138–139)

Douglass describes and attributes this incident to special divine favor and intervention in 1845 (book 1) and 1855 (book 2). At the time of these writings, the former just seven years after the escape from his master Thomas Auld and the latter just five years before the outbreak of war, Douglass was still in danger of either being recaptured or encountering violence for his abolitionist associations and anti-slavery publications. With very few idealizing self-objects to connect with for psychic and self-regulating purposes, Rector's mystical experiences seem to be an appropriate way in which to understand how Douglass narrates his move to Baltimore:

I may be deemed superstitious and egotistical, in regarding this event as a special interposition of Divine Providence in my favor; but the thought is a part of my history, and I should be false to the earliest and most cherished sentiments of my soul, if I suppressed, or hesitated to avow that opinion, although it may be characterized as irrational by the wise, and ridiculous by the scoffer. From my earliest recollections of serious matters, I date the entertainment of something like an ineffaceable conviction, that slavery would not always be able to hold me within its foul embrace; and this conviction, like a word of living faith, strengthened me through the darkest trials of my lot. This good spirit was from God; and to him I offer thanksgiving and praise. (pp. 139–140)

Douglass' ability to construct a favorable God-image reflects a force of being that resisted the internalization of the harmful experiences of the slavocracy. It allowed him to craft an idealizing self-object via his God-image that helped to replenish the depleted spaces in his self-structure. Indeed, "psychological structure [can] be accrued through experiences with a sacred other" (Rector (2001) (p. 192)). Holliman (2002) likewise argues that "religious experience can …prevent a person under extreme emotional stress from further decompensation" and that "religious experience can enhance development of the self" (pp. 200–201). Interestingly, in book 3, when Douglass describes his move to Baltimore, he does not mention the transition as being caused by divine intervention but simply attributes this move to a very fortunate happening. I suggest that this is evidence of an increase in Douglass' interior self-structure; with time, he depended less heavily on an altruistic God-image.[9]

Cultivating the Force of Being[10]

How did Douglass cultivate such a life-seeking force of being? One event that triggered its cultivation was his witnessing a scene of bodily redemption—a female victim named Nelly resisting an overseer that was attempting to flog her. The effect on Douglass was quite different to that of seeing his Aunt Hester being flogged. Hester did not resist. Nelly did.

Introduction to Bodily Redemption

Douglass had seen several similar atrocities by the time he witnessed the incident with Nelly. As Douglass (1881) describes it in book 3:

> The one of these which agitated and distressed me most was the whipping of a woman, not belonging to my old master, but to Col. Lloyd. The charge against her was very common and very indefinite, namely, "*impudence.*" This crime could be committed by a slave in a hundred different ways, and depended much upon the temper and caprice of the overseer as to whether it was committed at all. He could create the offense whenever it pleased him. A look, a word, a gesture, accidental or intentional, never failed to be taken as impudence when he was in the right mood for such an offense. In this case there were all the necessary conditions for the commission of the crime charged. The offender was nearly white, to begin with; she was the wife of a favorite hand on board of Mr. Lloyd's sloop and was besides the mother of five sprightly children. Vigorous and spirited woman that she was, a wife and a mother, with a predominating share of the blood of the master running in her veins. Nellie (for that was her name) had all the qualities essential to impudence to a slave overseer. My attention was called to the scene of the

castigation by the loud screams and curses that proceeded from the direction of it. When I came near the parties engaged in the struggle, the overseer had hold of Nelly, endeavoring with his whole strength to drag her to a tree against her resistance. Both his and her faces were bleeding, for the woman was doing her best. Three of her children were present, and though quite small, (from seven to ten years old I should think,) they gallantly took the side of their mother against the overseer, and pelted him well with stones and epithets. Amid the screams of the children "*Let my mammy go! Let my mammy go!*" the hoarse voice of the maddened overseer was heard in terrible oaths that he would teach her how to give a white man "*impudence.*" The blood on his face and on hers attested her skill in the use of her nails, and his dogged determination to conquer. (pp. 40–41)

Psychodynamically, I suggest that "impudence" is the crime of narcissistic injury incurred by white slave power. The ways in which Douglass describes Nelly's resistance are telling. Only in book 2 does Douglass' description of Nelly as nearly white (in skin complexion) and her high spirit and vigor suggest how he has entered the intersubjective space of what was occurring. It seems that he needs the courage and defiance that Nelly apparently possesses, but does not yet possess himself, thus triggering an experience of envy within Douglass:

> *There is no doubt that Nelly felt herself superior, in some respects, to the slaves around her.* She was a wife and a mother; her husband was a valued and favorite slave. Besides, he was one of the first hands on board of the sloop, and the sloop hands—since they had to represent the plantation abroad— were generally treated tenderly. The overseer never was allowed to whip Harry; why then should he be allowed to whip Harry's wife? *Thoughts of this kind, no doubt, influenced her; but, for what ever reason, she nobly resisted, and, unlike most of the slaves, seemed determined to make her whipping cost Mr. Sevier as much as possible.*[11] (pp. 93–94)

How does Douglass know that Nelly feels superior to him and the other slaves and therefore above being whipped? It is conceivable that Douglass envies Nelly's courage to fight back, a *redemption of her body* and an episode that was rarely seen on the plantation.

Klein (1975) understands envy as frustrated desire. The desire to influence the intersubjective space around him (through resisting the impositions of the slave power) was something for which Douglass longed, but during his early years he lacked the necessary ego strength and self-structure.

In speaking of envy in early childhood, Klein posits "envy is the angry feeling that another person possesses and enjoys something desirable—the envious impulse being to take it away or to spoil it...Moreover, envy implies the subject's relation to one person only." Yet Douglass himself, rumored to be the son of his master, felt that he was superior to the other slaves. The *force of being* that was resident in Douglass caused him to greatly desire (to the point of envy) the capacity for bodily redemption that Nelly exhibited:

> I watched, with palpitating interest, the course of the preliminary struggle, and was saddened by every new advantage gained over her by the ruffian. There were times when she seemed likely to get the better of the brute, but he finally overpowered her, and succeeded in getting his rope around her arms, and in firmly tying her to the tree, at which he had been aiming. This done, and Nelly was at the mercy of his merciless lash; and now, what followed, I have no heart to describe. The cowardly creature made good his every threat; and wielded the lash with all the hot zest of furious revenge. The cries of the woman, while undergoing the terrible infliction, were mingled with those of the children, sounds which I hope the reader may never be called upon to hear. When Nelly was untied, her back was covered with blood. The red stripes were all over her shoulders. She was whipped—severely whipped; but she was not subdued, for she continued to denounce the overseer, and to call him every vile name. He had bruised her flesh, but had left her invincible spirit undaunted. Such floggings are seldom repeated by the same overseer. They prefer to whip those who are most easily whipped. The old doctrine that submission is the best cure for outrage and wrong, does not hold good on the slave plantation. He is whipped oftenest, who is whipped easiest; and that slave who has the courage to stand up for himself against the overseer, although he may have many hard stripes at the first, becomes, in the end, a freeman, even though he sustain the formal relation of a slave. "You can shoot me but you can't whip me," said a slave to Rigby Hopkins; and the result was that he was neither whipped not shot. If the latter had been his fate, it would have been less deplorable than the living and lingering death to which cowardly and slavish souls are subjected. (pp. 94–95)

Nelly redeemed her body by fighting back, physically and verbally. Such resistance is also structure building for those who witness such scenes of bodily redemption, and it clearly influenced Douglass deeply.[12]

Douglass concludes this passage in book 3 (1881) by noting that "the slave who had the courage to stand up for himself against the overseer, although he might have many hard stripes at first, became while legally a slave virtually a freeman" (p. 42). It is this dialogical tension between being a legal slave and a virtual freeman that is central to the concept of the force of being, the psychological, spiritual, and emotional autonomy to transgress or implement a causal effect on the intersubjective milieu in which one is embedded. The state of the "virtual freeman" reflects the ability to impact the intersubjective space such that one's subjectivity is resurrected and reclaimed.

Even if one was not successful in securing one's material freedom, the act of resistance and affecting the slavocratic intersubjective milieu with one's agency and selfhood was structure building. Douglass' response to another incident reinforces this notion. Douglass testifies that knowledge of his Aunt Jenny and Uncle Noah successfully escaping from the slave plantation caused him to question the alleged divine mandate that blacks should be enslaved. Douglass (1881) recounts the thoughts of his childhood:

> Besides, I could not tell how anybody could know that God made black people to be slaves. Then I found, too, that there were puzzling exceptions to this theory of slavery, in the fact that all black people were not slaves, and all white people were not masters. An incident occurred about this time that made a deep impression on my mind. One of the men slaves of Captain Anthony and my Aunt Jennie ran away. A great noise was made about it. Old master was furious. He said he would follow them and catch them and bring them back, but he never did it, and somebody told me that Uncle Noah and Aunt Jennie had gone to the free states and were free. Besides this occurrence, which brought much light to my mind on the subject, there were several slaves on Mr. Lloyd's place who remembered being brought from Africa. There were others that told me that their fathers and mothers were stolen from Africa. This to me was important knowledge, but not such as to make me feel very easy in my slave condition. The success of Aunt Jennie and Uncle Noah in getting away from slavery was, I think, the first fact that made me seriously think of escape for myself. I could not have been more than seven or eight years old at the time of this occurrence, but young as I was I was already a fugitive from slavery in spirit and purpose. (pp. 39–40)

Similar to what he observed with Nelly, Douglass notes that in "spirit and purpose" he was already a fugitive based on what he learned about his Aunt Jennie and Uncle Noah successfully escaping. He transgresses his assigned role as an acquiescent slave and in so doing becomes more fully human.

NOTES

1. The healthy internalization of early childhood caregivers and/or significant others.
2. Psychical and emotional tasks as espoused by traditional psychodynamic theory, while arguably useful to analyze various narratives in Douglass' autobiographies, were secondary or tertiary at best. It is not that traditional psychodynamic paradigms lack explanatory power or hermeneutical relevancy. Indeed, in various pockets of existence, one could read the life of Douglass and other slave narratives through the lens of self-psychology, object relations, or relational theory. But any of the psychic tasks related to traditional psychoanalytic theories arguably would have been so severely undermined in the slavocracy that they would not yield significant discursive potentiality. Instead, I suggest that in the harsh context of the slavocracy whereby the larger psychosocial context denigrated and sought to destroy the humanity of an entire group of people, Douglass was fundamentally life seeking or in pursuit of what is defined in this project as the *force of being*.
3. My emphasis.
4. The contention that Douglass' internal *force of being* was constitutional from birth is not wholly inconsistent with a key proposition of the psychology of the self and the paradigmatic shift it makes in asserting that from birth, the individual does not have to progress through developmental stages to become a self-aware being but experiences subjectivity from birth. From a self-psychological perspective, Tolpin (1989) posits an autonomous psychological construction from birth, noting that the person "is born with complexly functioning, designed-in equipment that makes for being a separate psychic entity, and independent center of initiative, impressions, and experience" (p. 309). Wolf (1991) contends that from birth, outside of any developmental scheme, the child is capable of interacting with the environment in a reciprocal fashion. For Wolf, "the nervous system is from the very beginning not a closed circuit but an interactive system in dialogue with its environment...We can now study the very early—perhaps at birth—emergence of an infant as an independent center of initiative who actively seeks selfobject experiences via interactive transactions" (p. 127). The only difference in Wolf's and Tolpin's position from what this project offers up is that instead of the search for objects being the primary psychological task, when the external context compels existence in extremity, one is equipped from birth with an interior *force of being* that seeks to experience selfhood by stimulating or effecting the intersubjective milieu in which the subject exists—thereby constituting an experience of self. *In a cultural ecology that was constructed to dominate the sociopolitical,*

economic, religious, and theological imagination of the nation with the ideology of slavery (while simultaneously stifling black subjectivity), the conception of an organic force of being, outside of any developmental scheme or interaction with the environment, best explains Douglass' capacity to imagine and experience a selfhood that the broader environment rendered unimaginable.

5. My emphasis.
6. My emphasis.
7. Hyper-arousal is considered a key symptom of post-traumatic stress disorder. See Judith Herman (Herman, M.D. 1997).
8. My emphasis.
9. Another way of understanding this observation is to recognize the inverse relationship between a substantive interior force of being and the exterior grandiose usage of God-talk to explicate the mundane. That is to say, the more fortified one's interior self-structure is, the less likely they are to engage God-talk to casually reflect upon the commonplace aspects of their life.
10. The concept of an internal *force of being* begs the question of either a developmental trajectory or some other paradigm that explicates the nourishment of the human project that is fundamentally *life seeking*. What psychological events facilitate the laying down of psychic structures in a paradigm whereby the human project is conceived as fundamentally *life seeking*? For many object relations theorists, this reflects the internalization of enough "good objects" such that the central ego of a person is capable of being independent. For Winnicott, this reflects a facilitating environment and good-enough mothering that compels the person out of the illusion of omnipotence and into healthy object usage that ultimately leads toward independence. For Kohut and a psychology of the self, in the early formational years of the individual, the self is structured by psychically using caregivers (i.e. self-objects) for the purposes of self-affirmation or to calm internal anxiety by idealizing and associating with the caregiver. The ultimate goal of a psychology of the self is again, to become one's own center of initiative, independent of others. *However, in the paradigm of living life in the extremity, the individual's force of being is propped up by the engagement of sacred spaces of play and reflection, practicing agency over one's body, and the creation of counter-hegemonic life stories. To experience selfhood interdependently within one's intersubjective milieu is the principle psychical goal.* In Chap. 6 of books 2 and 3, Douglass' recollection of his early childhood thoughts on slavery and freedom were both precipitated by Douglass lamenting the brutal flogging of his aunt Hester (referred to in the previous chapter). Yet, I suggest that it was Douglass witnessing a scene of bodily redemption in the form of another female victim resisting an overseer (that was attempting to flog her) that triggered the internal *force of being* within Douglass' psychic

structure at such an early age and instigated his imagination of selfhood and freedom. As will be seen, the effect on Douglass after witnessing this female slave, Nelly, being flogged was far different from the chilling effect Aunt Hester's flogging had on Douglass' psyche. What was the difference between the two sites of violence? Nelly fought back and resisted. Aunt Hester did not resist.

11. My emphasis.

12. Klein (1975) goes on to distinguish the close alliance between greed and envy noting that "greed aims primarily at completely scooping out, sucking dry, and devouring...whereas envy not only seeks to rob in this way, but also to put badness, primarily bad excrements and bad parts of the self into the mother ... in order to spoil and destroy ... in the deepest sense this means destroying her creativeness" (p. 181). Summers (1994) goes further in describing the inner workings and practical effects of envy arguing that "envy goes beyond hatred to the desire to injure ... the most useful initial defense against envy is devaluation because denigration involves denial of the need for the object" (p. 81). Douglass' depreciating description of Nelly actually demonstrates his need, desire, and subsequently, envy for the psychic capacity she displayed. While he recollects this incident in both books 2 and 3, his conclusion of the incident in book 2 is slightly more detailed and reflects extent to which Douglass was psychically and spiritually invested in this violent intersubjective space.

BIBLIOGRAPHY

Altman, N. (2010). *The analyst in the inner city: Race, class, and culture through a psychoanalytic lens* (2nd ed.). New York: Routledge.

Aron, L. (1996). *A meeting of minds: Mutuality in psychoanalysis.* Hillsdale: The Analytic Press.

Daly, J. P. (2002). *When slavery was called freedom: Evangelicalism, proslavery, and the causes of the civil war.* Lexinton: The University Press of Kentucky.

Des Pres, T. (1976). *The survivor: An anatomy of life in the death camps.* Oxford: Oxford University Press.

Douglass, F. (1845). *Narrative of the life of frederick douglass, an American slave: Written by himself.* Boston: Published at the Anti-Slavery Office.

Douglass, F. (1855). *My bondage and my freedom.* New York: Miller, Orton & Mulligan.

Douglass, F. (1874). *Self-made men.* Carlisle: Indian Print, Indian Industrial School.

Douglass, F. (1881). *Life and times of frederick douglass: His early life as a slave, his escape from bondage, and his complete history to the present time.* Hartford: Park Publishing Company.

98 D. G. GIBSON

Fairbarin, W. R. (1946). Object-relationships and dynamic structure. *The International Journal of Psychoanalysis, 27,* 30–37.

Frie, R. (2012). On culture, history, and memory: Encountering the "narrative unconscious". *Contemporary Psychoanalysis, 48,* 329–343.

Gehrie, M. J. (1994). Discussion of Stolorow and Atwood's "the myth of the isolated mind". *Progress in Self Psychology, 10,* 251–255.

Gehrie, M. J. (1996). Chapter 9 empathy in broader perspective: A technical approach to the consequences of the negative selfobject in early character formation. *Progress in Self Psychology, 12,* 159–179.

Hartman, S. V. (1997). *Scenes of subjection: Terror, slavery, and self-making in nineteenth-century America.* New York: Oxford University Press.

Hegel, G. W. (1977). *Phenomenology of spirit* (A. V. Miller, Trans.). Oxford: Oxford University Press.

Herman, J. (1997). *Trauma and recovery: The aftermath of violence--from domestic abuse to political terror.* New York: Basic Books.

Holliman, P. J. (2002). Religious experience as selfobject experience. *Progress in Self psychology, 18,* 193–205.

Holliman, P. J. (2013, March 13). *Where is the other? Engaging in the space between.* Evanston: Garrett Evangelical Theological Seminary.

Jones, W. R. (1998). *Is God a white racist?* Boston: Beacon Press.

Klein, M. (1975). Envy and gratitude. In M. Masud & R. Khan (Eds.), *Envy and gratitude and other works 1946–1963* (pp. 1–346). London: The Hogarth Press and the Institute of Psycho-Analysis.

Oliver, K. (2004). *The colonization of psychic space.* Minneapolis: University of Minnesota Press.

Rector, L. J. (2001). Mystical experience as an expression of the idealizing selfobject need. *Progress in Self Psychology, 17,* 179–195.

Seeley, K. M. (2000). *Cultural psychotherapy: Working with culture in the clinical encounter.* Lanham: Rowman & Littlefield Publishers, Inc.

Stolorow, R. D. (1995). An intersubjective view of self psychology. *Psychoanalytic Dialogues, 5,* 393–399.

Stolorow, R. D., & Atwood, G. E. (1996). The intersubjective perspective. *The Psychoanalytic Review, 83,* 181–194.

Summers, F. (1994). *Object relations theories and psychopathology: A comprehensive text.* New York: Psychology Press.

Summers, F. (1996). Self psychology and its place among contemporary psychoanalytic theories. *Annual of Psychoanalysis, 24,* 157–171.

Tolpin, M. N. (1989). A prospective constructionist view of development. *The Annual of Psychoanalysis, 17,* 308–316.

Wolf, E. S. (1991). Advances in self psychology: The evolution of psychoanalytic treatment. *Psychoanalytic Inquiry,* 123–146.

CHAPTER 4

A New Birth: Agency Over One's Self and Body and Sacred Spaces of Play

The previous chapter ended by suggesting through Nelly's example that one can become more fully human in the context of extremity by engaging intentional practices. An incident in which Douglass himself attained this greater humanness is his fight with Covey "the nigger breaker." In book 1, Douglass (1845) prepares the reader by asserting "you have seen how a man was made a slave; you shall see how a slave was made a man" (pp. 65–66). After spending approximately seven years in Baltimore with the brother-in-law of his master where he learned to read, Douglass returned to the plantation of his birth, under the ownership of his master, Thomas Auld. As Douglass (1845) relates, after he returned to the plantation at around the age of 16, his master determined that Douglass "served no good purpose" and, as such, needed to be broken in. The task fell to a farmer by the name of Edward Covey, who was well known in the community and in the Methodist church as very religious and pious—and also as the "nigger-breaker."

This was the first time in his life that Douglass was a field worker. It was one of the darkest times of his life. During the first six months of being with Covey, he was stripped and beaten with cow skin on a weekly basis. To contrast the reputation Covey had in the slave community with the one he had in the Methodist church as a very religious and pious man, Douglass described in great detail how Covey purchased a black female slave for the sole purpose of "breeding." Douglass describes how Covey locked the

© The Author(s) 2018
D. G. Gibson, *Frederick Douglass, a Psychobiography*,
Black Religion/Womanist Thought/Social Justice,
https://doi.org/10.1007/978-3-319-75229-7_4

slave up nightly with another man until she conceived and gave birth. Of these first six months with Covey, Douglass (1855) writes:

> If at any one time of my life, more than another, I was made to drink the bitterest dregs of slavery, that time was during the first six months of my stay with Mr. Covey. We were worked all weathers. It was never too hot or too cold; it could never rain, blow, snow, or hail too hard for us to work in the field. Work, work, work, was scarcely more the order of the day than of the night. The longest days were too short for him, and the shortest nights were too long for him. I was somewhat unmanageable when I first went there; but a few months of this discipline tamed me. <u>Mr. Covey succeeded in breaking me</u>. I was broken in body, soul and spirit. My natural elasticity was crushed; my intellect languished; the disposition to read departed; the cheerful spark that lingered about my eye died; the dark night of slavery closed in upon me; and behold a man transformed into a brute ... I was sometimes prompted to take my life, and that of Covey, but was prevented by a combination of hope and fear. (p. 219)

Some resilience literature suggests that survivors of extreme atrocities have special characteristics that are almost moralistic in nature. Such suggestions run the risk of creating a special sub-class of human beings endowed with a special force or capacity to endure what others cannot, or of implying that had those who didn't survive garnered the resources that the survivors possessed, they too would have lived. Both interpretations cast the individual as being deficient, rather than the perpetrator as being evil. Instead of trying to discover what was special about Douglass, this project is about expanding the purview of anthropological subjectivity.

Fortunately, Womanist anthropological discourse already cautions against this propensity to idealize black bodies as unique and unbreakable, constructed in a way to withstand objectification, abuse, and traumatization. In her theological anthropology, Karen Baker-Fletcher and Garth Kasimu Baker-Fletcher (2002) challenges those who caricature black women as "superwomen" or "mammies" or as being in some way exceptional. Baker-Fletcher says that such caricatures "implies that they are not quite human (presumably more than human), which falls into the old trap of denying that women who do not fit into traditional categories are fully women...It is as sexist to suggest so-called nontraditional women are more than human as it is to suggest they are less than human" (p. 144). Similarly, to depict a person like Douglass as super-human would erroneously suggest that slavery couldn't have been that bad and that the problem was really not about heinous human atrocities but about black people who lacked the character and stamina that Douglass seemingly possessed. Indeed, Douglass himself indicates that he was broken. To be broken is to be human. Ontologically speaking, to suggest that someone cannot be broken diminishes their humanity. For Douglass, to be a "brute" meant to be "broken in body, soul, and spirit." His *desire* for creativity and imagination was successfully broken by Covey. His *interior force of being* was compromised. Douglass (1855) concedes:

> I shall never be able to narrate the mental experience through which it was my lot to pass during my stay at Covey's. I was completely wrecked, changed and bewildered; goaded almost to madness at one time, and at another reconciling myself to my wretched condition. Everything in the way of kindness, which I had experienced at Baltimore; all my former hopes and aspirations for usefulness in the world, and the happy moments spent in the exercises of religion, contrasted with my then present lot, but increased my anguish. I suffered bodily as well as mentally. I had neither sufficient time in which to eat or to sleep, except on Sundays. The over work, and the brutal chastisements of which I was the victim, combined with that ever-gnawing and soul-devouring thought—"I am a slave—a slave for life—a slave with no rational ground to hope for freedom"—rendered me a living embodiment of mental and physical wretchedness. (p. 221)

Indeed, human that he was, Douglass did not always feel hopeful.

THE FORCE OF BEING AND SACRED SPACES OF PLAY

So what did offer him hope? What were those occasional glimpses of goodness that sustained him? In all of his autobiographies, Douglass keenly recalls moments near the Chesapeake Bay in which he would reflect upon philosophical, religious, and theological themes to do with his experiences with Covey and his life as a slave. The sight of the boats moved by the wind across the bay precipitated Douglass' sense of "freedom," strengthened his force of being, and made him think of escaping to the north (1845):

> Our house stood within a few rods of the Chesapeake Bay, whose broad bosom was ever white with sails from every quarter of the habitable globe. Those beautiful vessels, robed in purest white, so delightful to the eye of freemen, were to me so many shrouded ghosts, to terrify and torment me

with thoughts of my wretched condition…The sight of these always affected me powerfully. My thoughts would compel utterance; and there, with no audience but the Almighty, I would pour out my soul's complaint, in my rude way, with an apostrophe to the moving multitude of ships…The glad ship is gone; she hides in the dim distance. I am left in the hottest hell of unending slavery. O God, save me! God, deliver me!

   Let me be free! Is there any God? Why am I a slave? I will run away. I will not stand it. Get caught, or get clear, I'll try it. I had as well die with ague as the fever. I have only one life to lose. I had as well be killed running as die standing. Only think of it; one hundred miles straight north, and I am free! Try it? Yes! God helping me, I will. It cannot be that I shall live and die a slave. I will take to the water. This very bay shall yet bear me into freedom. The steamboats steered in a north-east course from North Point. I will do the same; and when I get to the head of the bay, I will turn my canoe adrift, and walk straight through Delaware into Pennsylvania. When I get there, I shall not be required to have a pass; I can travel without being disturbed. Let but the first opportunity offer, and, come what will, I am off. Meanwhile, I will try to bear up under the yoke. I am not the only slave in the world. Why should I fret? I can bear as much as any of them. Besides, I am but a boy, and all boys are bound to some one. It may be that my misery in slavery will only increase my happiness when I get free. There is a better day coming." (pp. 64–65)

This sacred space by the Chesapeake Bay allowed Douglass to imagine and experience himself in a way that ran transgressed the intersubjective context in which he was embedded. After all, there were no other avenues for affirmation. There were no external objects, self-objects, relationships, or attuned intersubjective spaces that could validate Douglass. At bayside, he could envision and experience himself, imagine freedom, and construct escape scenarios. The interior force of being that resisted the pervasive threat of non-self in the slavocracy enabled Douglass to envision "a better day;" the free-moving boats enlivened his imagination for selfhood and agency.

   In her project examining the psychological effects of genocide on childhood survivors, Kaplan (2008) attempts to crystalize some of the psychological coping strategies and themes that arise from the testimonies. In particular, she observes from survivor recollections a tendency for the survivors to engage in what she has termed "space creating":

[Space creating] refers to a psychic room that an individual, as a child, creates according to his or her needs. This phenomenon can have a link to a real space where, for instance, they could hide for a short while… These experiences were probably a prerequisite for existing at all and constitute meaningful themes for human existence. To highlight these moments gives us a sense of how the interviewees may have used mental strategies...to fend off perforating and the fear of dying. Culture and religion may support this process ... Thinking/fantasizing and thinking/active are the phenomena that I see as the base for space creating. (p. 56)

We see something similar in the space Douglass created for himself at the Chesapeake Bay. The self-work that Douglass engaged in there strengthened his force of being and propped up his psychic structure and subjectivity. Kaplan also describes the way in which childhood survivors became attached to certain objects that to those on the outside may seem pointless and trivial. But to the survivors, small items or objects seemed to carry significant value:

During the war the children seem to have held on to something or to someone—the psychic support person who was available. I have perceived these phenomena as central in the children's space creating...the interviewees give, for example, recurring descriptions of the nature of the sleeping places—stumps for pillows, planks to lie on, and paper sheets—during the war and immediately after the liberation...these linking objects and linking efforts do not need to have a symbolic value, but they are still important because of the need for something supporting the self, a survival value. (p. 56)

Similarly, it seems that Douglass was mesmerized by the sight and movement of the sea vessels on the Chesapeake Bay. He speaks of the boats as if they were people who incited jealousy in him because of their capacity to move freely about the bay while he could not.

Another incident of sacred space that contributed to Douglass' subjectivity and psychic structure can be found in his characterization of early childhood in book 2. In describing the first years of his life with his grandmother, Douglass (1855) recollects a kind of fantasy room in which he was free from the expectations of others. In this childhood sacred space, Douglass experiences himself more authentically than he is ever able to until he escapes the plantation and travels abroad as an adult:

The slave-boy escapes many troubles which befall and vex his white brother. He seldom has to listen to lectures on propriety of behavior, or on anything else. He is never chided for handling his little knife and fork improperly or awkwardly, for he uses none. He is never reprimanded for soiling the table-cloth, for he takes his meals on the clay floor. He never has the misfortune, in his games or sports, of soiling or tearing his clothes, for he has almost none to soil or tear. He is never expected to act like a nice little gentleman, for he is only a rude little slave. Thus, freed from all restraint, the slave-boy can be, in his life and conduct, a genuine boy, doing whatever his boyish nature suggests; enacting, by turns, all the strange antics and freaks of horses, dogs, pigs, and barn-door fowls, without in any manner compromising his dignity, or incurring reproach of any sort. He literally runs wild; has no pretty little verses to learn in the nursery; no nice little speeches to make for aunts, uncles, or cousins, to show how smart he is; and, if he can only manage to keep out of the way of the heavy feet and fists of the older slave boys, he may trot on, in his joyous and roguish tricks, as happy as any little heathen under the palm trees of Africa...In a word, he is, for the most part of the first eight years of his life, a spirited, joyous, uproarious, and happy boy, upon whom troubles fall only like water on a duck's back. And such a boy, so far as I can now remember, was the boy whose life in slavery I am now narrating. (pp. 41–42)

In this relatively unique (in the slavocracy) childhood experience with his grandmother, Douglass begins the process of actively developing his interior space, cultivating an internal *force of being* that enables him to question the veracity of his enslaved condition at an early age, even when the intersubjective milieu suggested to him that slavery was his God-given role and destiny. What Douglass describes seems to be consistent with Winnicott's (1971) notion of play, creativity, and the individual's search for the self. For Winnicott, it was the psychic space that existed between a person's capacity to imagine/create and the boundaries of social and cultural compliance/conformity that proved critical for selfhood and individual thriving. It was in this play space that reality testing was suspended in favor of individual creativity and imaging. For Winnicott, "it is in playing and only in playing that the individual child or adult is able to be creative and to use the whole personality, and it is only in being creative that the individual discovers the self" (p. 73).

Douglass describes the first years of his childhood in this manner. Such freedom to engage in play was structure building for him and is helpful in understanding how he may have developed a capacity for imagining selfhood, subjectivity, and even a God-image while yet embedded in an all-encompassing slavocracy. In his conception of play and the search for selfhood, Winnicott warns that "the self is not really to be found in what is made out of products of body or mind, however valuable these constructs may be in terms of beauty, skill, and impact" as "the finished creation never heals the underlying lack of sense of self" (p. 73). Winnicott's clarification of where "self" is to be found aligns well with the *force of being* that is conceptualized in this project, as Douglass and his contemporaries who existed in the extremity of the slavocracy could not find meaning necessarily in the productions of body or mind, productions that in the slavocracy were in service to the architects of a demonic system. The few life-giving productions were suppressed in the lived realities of plantation life. Selfhood was found in liminal spaces of play.

In their project to understand the connection between self-reflection and resilience in adolescents, Barkai and Hauser (2008) suggest that the individual's capacity for resilience in the face of hardships is positively correlated with their ability to be self-reflective. For the authors, "self-reflection is related to human agency (the ability to exercise control over one's experience) and self-efficacy (the beliefs underlying this competence), among the individuals assets conferring resilience" (p. 116). Douglass' multiple references to his internal meanderings were not inconsequential, and may have enabled his escape in 1838. For Barkai and Hauser then, in a context of adversity or hardship, a developed and sustained capacity for self-reflection functions:

> through motivational, cognitive, and affective processes" and "reduces vulnerability to stress and strengthens resistance to the effect of adversity via the belief that one can effect change, potentially generating favorable and averting disadvantageous circumstances. Psychoanalytic theory similarly **links self-reflection to personal agency** as a core feature of human adaptation and associates **deficits in personal agency to psychopathological outcomes**. (p. 121)

The slavocracy made it difficult for Douglass to imagine himself outside of it.

THE NEW BIRTH: FREDERICK DOUGLASS AND BODILY REDEMPTION

The most obvious turning point in Douglass' early life came when he engaged in a physical fight with Covey, an act of bodily agency that empowered Douglass' force of being. Douglass describes this event as being akin to a resurrection and says that it resulted in him becoming a man. Approximately six months into his one-year term with Edward Covey, Douglass buckled under fatigue and heat exhaustion. In response, Covey began to beat and kick him. Toward the end of this savage assault, with Douglass unable to comply with repeated commands to return to work, Covey struck Douglass on the head with a sharp object making him profusely. As Covey walked away from him, Douglass somehow mustered the strength to escape and return to his master, Thomas Auld, to protest the brutal treatment he had received from Covey over the past six months.

As this climatic incident with Covey begins to unfold, we see the beginnings of a radical theological and spiritual transformation in Douglass. He finally turns his back on the common southern *evangelistic assumption* of the time that the cultural and social order of the South (i.e. the slavocracy) reflected God's divine will and begins to question seriously how southern religious convention interpreted divine sovereignty. Douglass (1855) recalls that "after lying there about three quarters of an hour, brooding over the singular and mournful lot to which I was doomed, my mind passing over the whole scale or circle of belief and unbelief, from faith in the overruling providence of God, to the blackest atheism, I again took up my journey toward St. Michael's" (p. 228), the home of Thomas Auld.

Douglass knows that running away from Covey could cost him his life if he is unable to convince Thomas Auld (the plantation owner) that he was brutalized by Covey. After arriving at the plantation, standing before him with his head, face, and clothing covered in blood, Douglass (1855) recollects his slave master's response in the following manner:

> At first, master Thomas seemed somewhat affected by the story of my wrongs, but he soon repressed his feelings and became cold as iron. It was impossible—as I stood before him at the first—for him to seem indifferent. *I distinctly saw his human nature asserting its conviction against the slave system, which made cases like mine possible; but, as I have said, humanity fell before the systematic tyranny of slavery.* He first walked the floor, apparently much agitated by my story, and the sad spectacle I presented; but, presently, it was his turn to talk. He began moderately, by finding excuses for Covey, and ending with a full justification of him, and a passionate condemnation of me. "He had no doubt I deserved the flogging. He did not believe I was sick; I was only endeavoring to get rid of work. My dizziness was laziness, and Covey did right to flog me, as he had done." After thus fairly annihilating me, and rousing himself by his own eloquence, he fiercely demanded what I wished him to do in the case! (p. 229)

This interaction with master Thomas marked a turning point and altered Douglass' self-structure over the ensuing days. Interesting in this recounting of the story is Douglass' observation of Thomas Auld's internal struggle with the atrocities of the slave system. Both in last line of the above passage as well as in another place during this interaction, Auld inquires of Douglass what to do about the situation. It seems as if Thomas Auld is internally split and engages in a series of secondary defense processes that included repression and isolation of affect. Such defenses are common when an individual experiences cognitive dissonance related to moral or religious inconsistency. In order to alleviate the anxiety related to the dissonance, the individual—in this case Thomas Auld—will isolate or repress disruptive emotions (such as guilt) in order to effectuate a decision or action that is inconsistent with what one may perceive at a deep level to be immoral. Hence, within this intersubjective milieu, Douglass experiences his slave master's attempt to resolve the cognitive dissonance—a dissonance created by the slave owner's own internal conscience, the mangled appearance of Frederick Douglass, and the slave ideology that dominated and arrested the imagination of the American South. Douglass (1855) notes his failed attempt to appeal to his master in the following manner:

> With such a complete knock-down to all my hopes, as he had given me, and feeling, as I did, my entire subjection to his power, I had very little heart to reply. I must not affirm my innocence of the allegations which he had piled up against me; for that would be impudence, and would probably call down fresh violence as well as wrath upon me. The guilt of a slave is always, and everywhere, presumed; and the innocence of the slaveholder or the slave employer, is always asserted. The word of the slave, against this presumption, is generally treated as impudence, worthy of punishment. "Do you contradict me, you rascal?" is a final silencer of counter statements from the lips of a slave. (p. 230)

Douglass attempts to convince Thomas Auld that if he returns to Covey (especially after fleeing to complain about him), Covey will probably kill him. Auld, appealing to Covey's reputation as an *upstanding Christian*, immediately dispelled Douglass' hopes that Auld will help him. He is forced to return to Edward Covey's farm and complete the remaining six-month term of service, Auld warning Douglass he will punish him himself if he does not do so.

In order to fully appreciate the dilemma and intersubjective matrix in which Douglass is enthralled, a hermeneutic of affective attunement is useful. Epistemologically speaking, it is vital to grasp the sense of desperation and futility that Douglass experienced, as none of his options represented any sort of reprieve from his terror. Similar to how a pastoral psychotherapist uses empathy and affect to understand a client, as the reader, we can similarly use empathy to examine this particular incident with Douglass.

There is relatively little to be found in trauma and resilience literature regarding individuals whose entire life—from birth to death—reflects an existence in extremity. The closest and most substantive psychodynamic work that has been done in this regard are resilience and trauma studies related to the Holocaust and various other twentieth-century human atrocities. Nevertheless, whether considering the preponderance of trauma literature or the subcategory of unique literature related to victims of prolonged forms of trauma, the literature tends to assume a point of normalcy before the trauma and a possible point of reprieve and assistance after the trauma. Douglass had neither.

Douglass thus departs from his master, Thomas Auld, and returns to Edward Covey. As he approaches Covey's farm, Douglass spots Covey running toward him with a rope and cowskin in hand. Fearful for his life and imminent torture, Douglass successfully retreats into the woods and evades Covey's pursuit for the entire day, a Saturday. In book 2, Douglass (1855) laments, "I had no friend on earth, and doubting if I had one in heaven" (p. 234). At this point we continue to see a build-up of affect within Douglass (and the entire intersubjective milieu) that will play a critical role in the intersubjective space that will be constructed between him and Covey and also between Douglass and Sandy (a good-Samaritan slave who comes to Douglass' aid while he is hiding in the woods). The following recollection of Douglass brings us into his mind and into the terror that enveloped him as he hid:

> I am clear of Covey, and of his wrathful lash, for the present. I am in the wood, buried in its somber gloom, and hushed in its solemn silence; hid from all human eyes; shut in with nature and nature's God, and absent from all human contrivances. Here was a good place to pray; to pray for help for deliverance—a prayer I had often made before. But how could I pray? Covey could pray—Capt. Auld could pray—I would fain pray; but doubts (arising from my own neglect of the means of grace, and partly from the sham

religion which everywhere prevailed, cast in my mind a doubt upon all religion, and led me to the conviction that prayers were unavailing and delu-
sive) prevented my embracing the opportunity, as a religious one. Life, in
itself, had almost become burdensome to me. All my outward relations were
against me; I must stay here and starve, (I was already hungry,) or go home
to Covey's, and have my flesh torn to pieces, and my spirit humbled under
the cruel lash of Covey. This was the painful alternative presented to me.
The day was long and irksome. My physical condition was deplorable. I was
weak, from the toils of the previous day, and from the want of food and rest;
and had been so little concerned about my appearance, that I had not yet
washed the blood from my garments. I was an object of horror, even to
myself. Life, in Baltimore, when most oppressive, was a paradise to this.
What had I done, what had my parents done, that such a life as this should
be mine? That day, in the woods, I would have exchanged my manhood for
the brutehood of an ox. (pp. 234–235)

Douglass' option was to starve to death in the woods, to be viciously
tortured and beaten by Covey, or to be killed. As Douglass recalls this
critical event in his life, the emotions and affective state that are triggered
within him evoke theological and religious reflections and existential questions about life itself and the purpose of his existence. There in the woods,
he questioned the efficacy of prayer and the legitimacy of religion. From a
psychology of religion perspective, Douglass' tenuous circumstances and
the pain experienced in his broken body served as a point of departure for
a kind of "twice-born" experience as conceived by James (1902).
Comparing the twice-born experience to the once-born where the individual lacks a capacity to incorporate radical evil into her meaning-making
system, James asserts that conversely, "in melancholiacs there is usually a
similar change, only it is in the reverse direction...the world now looks
remote, strange, sinister, uncanny...when disillusionment has gone as far
as this, there is seldom a restitution ad integrum ... one has tasted of the
fruit of the tree, and the happiness of Eden never comes again"
(pp. 151,156). The culmination of this twice-born experience and its
impact on Douglass' theology and religious experience is crystalized the
morning of Douglass' (1855) fight with Covey when he makes the
following resolution:

for I had brought my mind to a firm resolve, during that Sunday's reflection,
viz: to obey every order, however unreasonable, if it were possible, and, if
Mr. Covey should then undertake to beat me, to defend and protect myself

to the best of my ability. My religious views on the subject of resisting my master, had suffered a serious shock, by the savage persecution to which I had been subjected, and my hands were no longer tied by my religion. Master Thomas's indifference had severed the last link. I had now to this extent "backslidden" from this point in the slave's religious creed; and I soon had occasion to make my fallen state known to my Sunday-pious brother, Covey. (p. 241)

This *slave's religious creed* that Douglass mentions is consistent with the colonial logic offered up by William Jones (in Chap. 2) that suggests the evil imposed on black bodies signals Divine prerogative. A body-epistemology[1] (both physical persecution and Master Thomas' indifference to violence imposed on black bodies) seems to have obliterated the hold that the slave's religious creed had over Douglass. In another passage, subsequent to his fight with Covey and just prior to a failed escape attempt by Douglass and several other slaves, Douglass asserts that he was

quite **free from slave-holding priestcraft**. It was in vain that **we had been taught from the pulpit at St. Michael's**, the duty of obedience to our masters; **to recognize God as the author of our enslavement**; to regard running away an offense, alike against God and man; to deem our enslavement a merciful and beneficial arrangement; to esteem our condition, in this country, a paradise to that from which we had been snatched in Africa; to consider our hard hands and dark color as God's mark of displeasure, and as pointing us out as the proper subjects of slavery; that the relation of master and slave was one of reciprocal benefits; that our work was not more serviceable to our masters, than our master's thinking was serviceable to us. I say, it was in vain that the pulpit of St. Michael's had constantly inculcated these plausible doctrines. **Nature laughed them to scorn**. For my own part, I had now become altogether too big for my chains. (pp. 275–276)

Redemption of the body, as evidenced in Douglass' refusal to be further abused by Master Thomas or Edward Covey, strengthened his interior force of being and psychic structure and precipitated a twice-born event on the eve of his epic battle with Covey.

To understand the full significance and shift in Douglass' thinking, compare this twice-born experience with a much earlier experience when Douglass (1855) speaks of his religious awakening through the preaching of a Methodist minister named Hanson. Around the age of thirteen, Douglass recalls needing God as a "father and protector." Through the mentorship of a black man named Charles Lawson, Douglass claims "I saw the world in a new light ... I seemed to live in a new world, surrounded by new objects, and to be animated by new hopes and desires ... I loved all mankind—slaveholders not excepted...my great concern was, now, to have the world converted" (pp. 166–167). As the reader has seen (and will see even further), this earlier "healthy-minded" thinking by Douglass (healthy minded as conceived by William James) changes drastically as a result of Douglass' experience with Covey.

Douglass' refusal to accept that the abuse to his body was God-sanctioned seems to have precipitated his ensuing thoughts and actions and reinforced his force of being, the result being a subjectivity prepared to defy and resist Thomas Auld and Covey. This twice-born phenomenon caused Douglass to abandon the so-called slave's religious creed and resolve to defend and reclaim his body. His body was all to which he reasonably had access. Consequently, *any act of redeeming the body from being acted upon by the slave-powers was structure building for Douglass and his contemporaries.* In describing the transition from a "healthy-minded" individual to the "sick-soul" subjectivity, James' (1902) description of the new person is consistent with how Douglass will view the world:

> The happiness that comes, when any does come—and often enough it fails to return in an acute form, though its form is sometimes very acute—is not the simple ignorance of ill, but something vastly more complex, including natural evil as one of its elements, but finding natural evil no such stumbling-block and terror because it now sees it swallowed up in supernatural good. The process is one of redemption, not of mere reversion to natural health, and the sufferer, when saved, is saved by what seems to him a second birth, a deeper kind of conscious being than he could enjoy before. (p. 157)

While hiding from Covey in the woods on Saturday, at some point in the night, Douglass stumbles across Sandy, a fellow enslaved human being traveling through the woods to visit his wife (who apparently was free). In his autobiographies, Douglass describes Sandy as having a reputation among the slaves as being good natured and religious. After Douglass explains to Sandy the events of the previous two days, Sandy insists that Douglass come home with him for the evening. There, Douglass is able to eat and to care for his wounds for the first time in several days. Douglass understood that Sandy and his wife took him in at great risk to their own lives, as any slave caught harboring another runaway slave could be severely beaten. Up to this point, Douglass was overwhelmed with terror and a sense of hopelessness. Now, he is presented with a counter-effect of compassion and attunement from Sandy and his wife. In another place, Douglass (1855) indicates that the strength he summoned to return to Covey was because he had poured his "griefs into Sandy's ears, and got him enlisted in my behalf, having made his wife a sharer in my sorrows, and having, also, become well refreshed by sleep and food, I moved off, quite courageously, toward the much dreaded Covey's" (p. 240). Sandy and his wife created an empathic, life-giving attuned intersubjective space thanks to which Douglass' psychic structure and personhood entered a phase of repair and restoration and was unknowingly prepped for a radical transformation.

After dinner, Sandy discusses with Douglass his options with regard to Covey. After concluding that escape was virtually impossible, Sandy, in earnest fashion, tells Douglass that he has no alternative but to return to Covey. But before leaving, Sandy advises Douglass about a particular herb to be found in the woods. Sandy admonishes Douglass that if he should carry this particular herb on his right side (or in his right pocket), neither Covey or any other white man would be able to "whip" Douglass again. In book 1, Douglass indicates that he outright rejected Sandy's proposition but took the herb in order to please Sandy. In books 2 and 3, Douglass recollects that he initially rejects Sandy's proposition because of Douglass' disbelief in such "divination" and that for Douglass (1881), "it was beneath one of my intelligence to countenance such dealings with the devil as this power implied" (p. 134). Sandy's response was concise and compelling: all of Douglass book-learning still had not kept Covey from beating him. It was Sandy, a slave that could not read, who suggested that Douglass' selfhood could not be separated from his body. For far too long, western psychoanalytic thinking has erroneously bifurcated the body from selfhood and subjectivity. It was Sandy who enlightened Douglass to the importance of bodily redemption. In books 2 and 3, Douglass concedes that Sandy's logic was compelling. Douglass also intimates that "the hand of the Lord" was possibly involved in Sandy's suggestion. As Douglass tells the story, because he considered Sandy to be an upstanding person, Douglass complied with Sandy's request and placed the herb in his right pocket.

Douglass had already resolved to obey any reasonable request from Covey but to defend himself from any physical abuse. That Sunday morning as he approached the property, Douglass (1855) spotted Covey and his wife on their way to church and was stunned by Covey's response:

The manner of Covey astonished me. There was something really benignant in his countenance. He spoke to me as never before; told me that the pigs had got into the lot, and he wished me to drive them out; inquired how I was, and seemed an altered man. This extraordinary conduct of Covey, really made me begin to think that Sandy's herb had more virtue in it than I, in my pride, had been willing to allow; and, had the day been other than Sunday, I should have attributed Covey's altered manner solely to the magic power of the root. I suspected, however, that the Sabbath, and not the root, was the real explanation of Covey's manner. His religion hindered him from breaking the Sabbath, but not from breaking my skin. He had more respect for the day than for the man, for whom the day was mercifully given; for while he would cut and slash my body during the week, he would not hesitate, on Sunday, to teach me the value of my soul, or the way of life and salvation by Jesus Christ. All went well with me till Monday morning; and then, whether the root had lost its virtue. (pp. 240–241)

Douglass' intuition served him well. We read that on Monday morning, Covey viciously attacks Douglass, knocking him to the floor and attempting to tie his legs. Without warning, Douglass fights back, astonishing Covey and all of those around. Douglass recalls that "the fighting madness had come upon me" (p. 242). I suggest that this "fighting madness" is Douglass' internal force of being at work. Surprised and disheartened by Douglass' response, Covey calls out for help from his cousin Hughes and two other slaves in the vicinity. Douglass kicks Hughes in the stomach, incapacitating him and discouraging him from further involvement. The other two slaves refuse to get involved. Similar to the violent episode that Douglass witnessed with Nelly in his early years, he was now likewise involved. Douglass' actions transgressed the normative practices and narrative of the intersubjective milieu. Everyone, including Douglass, was astonished. Hughes and the slaves' refusal to get involved, and Douglass' decision to fight, were all actions that were significantly contrary to convention. The intersubjective milieu that Douglass transgressed influenced all those around. His decision to resist, driven by a *force of being*, enabled him to affect the intersubjective space between him and Covey in a way that was affirming for Douglass' subjectivity, even in a space where the other architects of the slavocracy failed to acknowledge his humanity. Douglass recollects that he and Covey fought for approximately two hours. At the end of the fight, Douglass notes that a very exhausted Covey suggested to Douglass that he wouldn't have been as harsh on Douglass if Douglass had not resisted. But more importantly,

Douglass reports in his autobiographies that for the remaining six months he was contracted out to Covey, Covey never laid a hand on him again.

This event was arguably the most formative experience of Douglass' early life and had a tremendous impact on his philosophical and theological worldviews. In several of his autobiographies, he refers to it as a resurrection event in his life. Douglass was dumbfounded as to why Covey never turned him over to the local authorities to be severely punished for fighting and resisting. While Douglass speculated that Covey didn't want his reputation as a "negro-breaker" to be compromised by a 16-year-old boy, perhaps Douglass' act of bodily redemption transformed the intersubjective space between him and Covey such that Covey, apparently, could no longer arbitrarily act upon Douglass' body as an object.

However, for the purposes of this project, it is sufficient to note that the drive to exist, or the force of being, is fundamental to the human enterprise. This fundamental task reflects the agency and capacity to imagine and experience one's subjectivity and body interdependently within the intersubjective milieu in which one is embedded. The *force of being* enacted by Douglass reflected the autonomy to exert a causal effect on the intersubjective milieu of the slavocracy. His enactment of agency enabled him to influence and agitate the intersubjective space between himself and Covey such that it changed both of them. Douglass (1855) defines this event as a resurrection for him and a pivotal moment in his life. The meaning he attributes to it is worth quoting at length:

Well, my dear reader, this battle with Mr. Covey,—undignified as it was, and as I fear my narration of it is—was the turning point in my "life as a slave." *It rekindled in my breast the smouldering embers of liberty;* it brought up my Baltimore dreams, and revived a sense of my own manhood. *I was a changed being after that fight. I was nothing before; I WAS A MAN NOW.* It recalled to life my crushed self-respect and my self-confidence, and inspired me with a renewed determination to be A FREEMAN. *A man, without force, is without the essential dignity of humanity.* Human nature is so constituted, that it cannot honor a helpless man, although it can pity him; and even this it cannot do long, if the signs of power do not arise.

He only can understand the effect of this combat on my spirit, who has himself incurred something, hazarded something, in repelling the unjust and cruel aggressions of a tyrant. Covey was a tyrant, and a cowardly one, withal. After resisting him, I felt as I had never felt before. *It was a resurrection from the dark and pestiferous tomb of slavery, to the heaven of comparative freedom.* I was no longer a servile coward, trembling under the frown of a

brother worm of the dust, but, my long-cowed spirit was roused to an attitude of manly independence. I had reached the point, at which *I was not
afraid to die. This spirit made me a freeman in fact, while I remained a slave
in form.* When a slave cannot be flogged he is more than half free. He has a
domain as broad as his own manly heart to defend, and he is really "a power
on earth." While slaves prefer their lives, with flogging, to instant death,
they will always find christians enough, like unto Covey, to accommodate
that preference. From this time, until that of my escape from slavery, I was
never fairly whipped. Several attempts were made to whip me, but they were
always unsuccessful. Bruises I did get, as I shall hereafter inform the reader;
but the case I have been describing, was the end of the brutification to
which slavery had subjected me.[2] (pp. 246–247)

Yet, what Douglass failed to capture in any of his autobiographies is
that no matter how preposterous thought Sandy's idea to place an herb
on his right side for protection, from that day forward, Douglass internalized Sandy's belief that no other white man would be able freely to beat
Douglass henceforth. In the brief interaction between Sandy, his wife,
and Douglass, the intersubjective space created was saturated with such
intense affect that Douglass' interior space was transformed. He seemingly
internalized Sandy as a psychic object in a manner that traditional object
relations theory postulates can only occur over a period of years. After this
fight with Covey, he never again allowed himself to be handled or beaten
by any slaveholder. Douglass (1881) may have snubbed Sandy's suggestion and course of action as beneath his dignity and intelligence, but as
his ideological worldview going forward, Sandy's proposition to Douglass
that he would become a man that "no white man could whip" (p. 134)
turned out to be a governing manifesto in Douglass' personal philosophy.

The level of affect and affection was robust in the intersubjective space
between Douglass and Sandy, as Sandy was empathically attuned to
Douglass in one of the darkest moments in his life. Contrary to a traditional developmental scheme that suggests the build-up of psychic structure evolves over a period of years, in a context of extremity it is conceivable
that one could internalize an affirming object in a much shorter period of
time. Sandy was Douglass' good Samaritan. Their interaction stands out
in all of Douglass' autobiographies and represents a pivotal, life-changing
event for Douglass.

Here, Stolorow's (2007) conception of ontological unconscious is useful regarding the ego enhancement and structure-building potential of

affect-laden events. In his chapter on ontological unconscious, Stolorow uses a poem he wrote about his daughter from his second marriage entitled "Emily Running." The poem speaks of his joy of walking his daughter to school, offset immediately by a shadow of darkness as they part ways after reaching the school. With this in mind, Stolorow develops his conception of ontological unconsciousness by recalling the trauma of finding his first wife, Dede, dead in their bed on February 23, 1991, having succumbed to a recently diagnosed bout with lung cancer. In March 1993, he remarried and had a daughter, Emily, in June 1995 by Julia Schwartz. Stolorow recalls how grief over the death of his first wife so overwhelmed him that his second wife, a psychoanalyst herself, could no longer tolerate his grief, as it made her feel estranged from him.

During the Christmas season of 2004, more than 13 years after the death of his first wife, Stolorow tells how he was periodically retraumatized by the painful memory of Dede no longer being able to jog with him during the Christmas season prior to her death because of her failing health. At this time in 2004, Julia (the second wife) was better able to tolerate Stolorow's grief over the death of his first wife. Julia suggests to Stolorow that the title of the poem he wrote about their daughter, "Emily Running," symbolizes the empathic activity in which his first wife could no longer engage because of her failing health. Upon hearing this interpretation, Stolorow says that he cried without restraint several minutes, suggesting to him that "Julia's interpretive comment was a key that unlocked the full force of my emotional devastation, which now found a relational home with her...[W]hen I finally did go jogging on Christmas morning [in 2004], I felt a sense of vitality and aliveness that had been profoundly absent during the prior Christmases since Dede's death [over 13 years before]" (p. 26). Stolorow describes ontological unconscious as "a loss of one's sense of being...when my traumatized states could not find a relational home, I became deadened, and my world became dulled... when such a home became once again present, I came alive, and the vividness of my world returned" (p. 26). Countering the Descartian axiom "I think therefore I am," Stolorow offers up his own postulate of "I feel, therefore I am" (p. 29) and characterizes his Christmas 2004 renewal experience as a somatic-linguistic integration. He concludes that "it is in the process of somatic-symbolic integration, the process through which emotional experience comes into language, that the sense of being is born[;] linguisticality, somatic affectivity, and attuned relationality are constitutive aspects of the integrative process through which the sense of being takes form (p. 30)."

In light of this, I suggest that the intersection of certain life events with an affect-laden intersubjective milieu necessarily modifies the ego and self-structure in a way that is transformative for the remainder of one's life. Just as an individual's psyche can be negatively impacted—in a life-changing way—from a trauma that overwhelms one's emotional capacity, what we witness between Douglass and Sandy is the exact opposite. Douglass' psychic structure is propped up as his self-structure is overwhelmed by Sandy's empathic attunement to Douglass' traumatic experience. This interaction causes Douglass to internalize Sandy's proposition that with the possession of this herb, no white man can "whip" Douglass again. A transformation or structural enhancement that human developmental theory suggests can only occur over a period of years in one's early childhood years seems to have occurred with Douglass through a rare, affect-laden intersubjective space.

A THEORETICAL DISCUSSION OF BODILY REDEMPTION: DOUGLASS VS. COVEY

O my body, make of me always a man who questions! (Frantz Fanon)

Douglass' engagement with Covey was an episode of bodily redemption. This redemption enhanced Douglass' internal force of being, and this in turn fundamentally enhanced his self-experience and subjectivity. Douglass characterizes the fight with Covey as a "resurrection" in which he became a man as opposed to existing as a non-being prior to the conflict. Based on Douglass' testimony, it was resisting with his body (and not necessarily being victorious) that precipitated the resurrection of a new subjectivity. When Douglass (1855) surmises that a "man without force, is without the essential dignity of humanity" (p. 246), contextually speaking, his body was fundamentally all to which he had access within the slavocracy. Consequently, every effort Douglass made to enhance the dignity of his body increased his internal force of being, which in this context was the most fundamental psychological task of a person living in extremity. From this moment forward, he experienced himself as a "freeman in fact," even though he was a "slave in form." For Douglass, the body, though distinguishable from the spirit, was inseparable from the human spirit. Contrary to western psychodynamic convention, for Douglass, the body was an essential part of his subjectivity.

Douglass' testimony suggests that though in the slavocracy freedom was not a material reality for many, that there is the creation of a space within the intersubjective milieu of oppression where one can exist—or be—until the material reality of freedom is realized. The therapeutic space created by Douglass was precipitated in part by his violent act of resisting the encroaching spectacle of death imposed by Covey and the entire slavocracy. In this environment, the law, social contracts, theology, and religious experience all suggested that black bodies were at the sadistic disposal of white desire and pleasure. Instead of desire and pleasure, for Douglass and many of his contemporaries, to experience their bodies in the extreme environment of the slavocracy was to experience the negation of selfhood. When Douglass asserts that "a man without force is without the essential dignity of humanity," the force of which he speaks is a potential for life consistent with the notion of an *interior force of being*. In extremity, a potential for life compels the individual to seek out opportunities for bodily redemption. Conversely, acts of bodily redemption are organically structure building, sustaining the individual's internal force of being and psychic structure.

Psychodynamic literature's relative silence on the body (and until very recently, race) is very conspicuous. This silence reflects the obstinate privileging afforded to the bodies of psychoanalytic theorists who cannot conceive of contemporary and historical narratives in which their own bodies have been objectified and brutalized. Western theological reflection tends to reflect the same tendencies. Since western history has hailed the *imago* of the white male body as the standard, the impact of the body on the psyche has been largely overlooked in psychodynamic literature. Psychodynamic theory has taken for granted how the European bodily image (which has not been brutalized and objectified historically) props up the psychic structure of those who have traditionally existed on the top side of modernity. This oversight created the disembodied subject in psychodynamic theory. Mills (1997) observes the racial contract's propensity to ignore the body, arguing "the reality is that one can pretend the body does not matter only because a particular body (the white male body) is being presupposed as the somatic norm ... but as feminist theorists have pointed out, the body is only irrelevant when it's the (white) male body" (p. 53). The history of radical evil and sadistic violence imposed on black bodies does not allow for the disembodied subject when reflecting upon African heritage. Through the lens of black history and black existence, psychodynamic theory must take a different course.

In his endeavor to undermine the colonial project, Frantz Fanon (1952) accentuates the black body, both materially and metaphorically, as a central tenet for understanding the colonial logic and the psychology of the colonized and the colonizer. To describe how the colonized incorporates the values and subsequent inferiority imposed by the French colonizers, Fanon coined the term the epidermalization of inferiority. The racist values that subjugate the colonized are conceived as permeating the outermost surface of one's body and then attacking the innermost parts of the psyche. Under the burden of what he characterizes as the white gaze, Fanon asserts that "in the white world, the man of color encounters difficulties in elaborating his body schema ... the image of one's body is solely negating" (p. 90). In what he has recognized as a bodily curse, Fanon argues that the black man's identity is not organic but always juxtaposed to that of the white man. Consequently, Fanon understands inferiority as "how the wretched black man could whiten himself and thus rid himself of the burden of this bodily curse" (p. 91). In another place where he emphasizes the body by contrasting the racial oppression toward Jews and the black man, Fanon asserts:

> No anti-Semite, for example, would ever think of castrating a Jew. The Jew is killed or sterilized. The black man, however, is castrated. The penis, symbol of virility, is eliminated; in other words, it is denied...The Jew is attacked in his religious identity, his history, his race, and his relations with his ancestors and descendants... But the black man is attacked in his corporeality. It is his tangible personality that is lynched. It is his actual being that is dangerous. The Jewish peril is replaced by the fear of the black man's sexual power. (pp. 140–142)

In a well-known passage, Fanon refers to an incident on a train in which a white child sees him and exclaims to his mother, "Mama, look, a Negro; I'm scared!" (p. 91). Fanon succinctly captures this perverse dialectic between the glorified white body and the debased "gazed-upon" black body, saying

> I couldn't take it any longer, for I already knew there were legends, stories, history, and especially the historicity ... as a result, the body schema, attacked in several places, collapsed, giving way to an epidermal racial schema...I was responsible not only for my body but also for my race and my ancestors. I cast an objective gaze over myself, discovered my blackness, my ethnic features; deafened by cannibalism, backwardness, fetishism, racial stigmas, slave

traders...my body was returned to me spread-eagled, disjointed, redone, draped in mourning on this white winter's day. (pp. 92–93)

Fanon describes the dire psychic effects and self-loathing of the fetishized black body who does not contest such objectification and his self-state in response to his body being gazed upon

> Disoriented, incapable of confronting the Other, the white man, who had no scruples about imprisoning me, I transported myself on that particular day far, very far, from myself, and gave myself up as an object. What did this mean to me? Peeling, stripping my skin, causing a hemorrhage that left congealed black blood all over my body. Yet this reconsideration of myself, this thematization, was not my idea. I wanted quite simply to be a man among men. (p. 92)

Fanon suggests that the uncontested objectification of the black body results in a kind of psychic incapacitation. Such incapacitation renders one unable to impact the surrounding intersubjective milieu. While it is unclear from his description whether the characterizations of bodily mutilation are self-imposed or caused by another, the results to the selfhood and subjectivity are devastating.

Consequently, acts of redeeming or resisting the objectification of one's body or resisting one's body from being inscribed upon by the fetishes and phobias of the broader intersubjective milieu bolster one's potential for life and psychic structure. The bodily redemption of which I speak was not unfamiliar to Douglass and his contemporaries. For Douglass, bodily redemption occurred when he fought Covey. Bodily redemption occurred for Nelly when she resisted her overseer (and also for Douglass as he witnessed the violent encounter). Douglass testified that while she was badly beaten, because of her bodily resistance she was not broken. Likewise, in her biography of Harriet Jacobs, Yellin (2004) narrates the incident in which a young Jacobs had to deal with the reality not of *whether* she would be raped and molested by her master (Dr. James Norcom) but of *when* the brutalization would occur. To avert this, in an act of bodily redemption, she became the mistress of Samuel Tredwell Sawyer, a single young lawyer in the town who had shown Jacobs a level of attention and kindness which modestly impressed her. According to social contract, Jacobs knew that if she became Sawyer's mistress and become pregnant, her own master, James Norcom, could not touch her. Jacobs' exercise of agency over her body (i.e. bodily redemption), no matter how mundane, was edifying to her psychic structure and internal force of being.

In her project on the bodies of enslaved women in the plantation south, Camp (2002) calls attention to the bodies of slaves, in particular black women, not only as sites of domination and terror but also as sites of politics and resistance through enactments of pleasure. No matter how mundane or short-lived the efforts or activities, Camp shows how various uses and displays of the enslaved black female body constituted acts of resistance and agency. For Camp then, "studying the body through a framework of containment and transgression grants us access to new perspectives on resistance" (p. 540). The multiple social bodies that slaves possess are central to Camp's work. For Camp, slaves possessed three social bodies: (1) a body that was a site of sadism, terror, and domination that was acted upon by the slavocracy; (2) a body in which the slave experienced his or her own body as negation, as a nonentity, and as loathsome, all of which represent elements crafted and imposed by the colonial logic; and (3) the outlawed body, the body that sought to exist outside of the boundaries of the colonial imagination:

> And yet, within and around the plantation, enslaved people's bodies were a hotly contested terrain of struggle. Again and again, enslaved people violated plantation boundaries of space and time; in the spaces they created, runaway partygoers celebrated their bodies and did what they could to reclaim them from planter control and view. This reclaimed body, this outlawed body, was the bond person's third body: the body as site of pleasure and resistance. For enslaved women, whose bodies were so central to the history of black bondage, the third body was significant in two ways. First, their third body was a source of pleasure, pride, and self-expression... Second, bondwomen's third body was a political site: it was an important symbolic and material resource in the plantation South, and its control was fiercely contested between owner and owned. Just as exploitation, containment, and punishment of the body were political acts, so too was enjoyment of the body. (p. 544)

What Camp describes as a third body parallels what I have suggested is bodily redemption in this project: scenes and acts which seek to redeem the body from the colonial logic and slavocratic imaginary and, as such, underwrote Douglass' internal force of being and psychogenic enterprise.

In his examination of death camp survivors from the Holocaust, Des Pres (1976) brings attention to survivor testimony regarding forced habitation among human excrement, bodily fluids, the smell of decaying flesh, and the odor of bodies being burned in crematories. Des Pres asserts "there was no end to this kind of degradation. The stench of excrement mingled with the smoke of the crematoria and the rancid decay of flesh. Prisoners in the Nazi camps were virtually drowning in their own waste, and in fact death by excrement was common" (p. 58). What Des Pres observes in the survivor testimony is an example of bodily redemption that props up the psychic structure. The survivors themselves began to recognize that any effort either to remain clean or to purify their body contributed to their will to survive. For the camp survivors, bodily redemption was structure building and helped them survive. For Des Pres, the degradation of the bodies of the death camp inhabitants was not simply a by-product of the war but was intentional and methodical, reflecting a perversion that is the outcome of absolute power. Des Pres concludes:

> Washing, if only in a ritual sense—and quite apart from reasons of health—was something prisoners needed to do. They found it necessary to survival, odd as that may seem, and those who stopped soon died...another survivor describes the initial disappearance of concern for his appearance, and the gradual realization that without such care he would not survive...by passing through the degradation of the camps, survivors discovered that in extremity a sense of dignity is something which men and women cannot afford to lose. (pp. 63–64)

Des Pres' observations about Shoah survivors have parallels with the key theme of this project in that bodily redemption contributes to one's internal force of being and overall psychic structure. Survivor testimony reveals that in extremity, the western divide between body and psyche is problematic. When the body is all that one possesses, any act to redeem the body from the desecration imposed by radical evil contributes to psychological health and subjectivity.

TRAUMA AND THE FORCE OF BEING

Taking up the issue of trauma in the slavocracy presents significant problems, both psychologically and ethically, many of which go beyond the scope of this project. One of the primary issues is how trauma itself is conceptualized. Many definitions of trauma are located in a paradigm in which an element of "normalcy" is disrupted by a tragic event that overwhelms the boundaries of an individual or group. In this paradigm, one begins with a baseline or element of normalcy, followed by a violent disruption and a presumed return to "normalcy" in which an element of basic trust can be restored. Yet in a slavocracy, one is born into slavery. Violence to one's body and selfhood is normative in such a society, but not normative for the individual suffering the infliction. Moreover, in the slavocracy, there was little if any reprieve from the violence. The individual was born, lived, and died in an environment of violence.

In her feminist critique of how the definition of trauma is aligned with white male experience, Brown (1995) chides those who understand traumatic experiences as being outside of normative human experiences. While definitions of trauma may differ, there is usually an element of a non-normative or extraordinary event—as defined by an individual, group, or society—that contributes to overwhelming the psychological, emotional, and spiritual faculties. The critical question then becomes: whose experience is in mind when we think of trauma? For example, in the fifth edition of the *Diagnostic and Statistical Manual of Mental Disorders*, the definition of trauma includes someone being exposed to death, death being threatened, the materialization of threat of injury, or direct or indirect sexual violence. Yet there are many other experiences that in absolute or potential terms can repress or destroy the human spirit such that mental and emotional faculties are irreparably altered. The assumption is that the non-normative experiences that underwrite trauma definitions mainly reflect the experiences of a white male power structure.

It seems then that Brown's critique is fitting for black experience and is indicative of why slavery is hardly mentioned in the canons of traumatology literature: the extreme experience of slavery is outside of normative white experience and so has never been conceptualized as non-normative. It is only the benefits of slavery—executed on the backs and lives of black people in the western democratic project—that is taken for granted in white normative experience.

At this point, the reader should be able to see why most contemporary understandings of trauma, while useful in certain instances, are nevertheless woefully inadequate to interpret the experiences of black people in the slavocracy. If the violation of what is considered normal in a western context is a prerequisite for trauma, then the experience of Frederick Douglass and his cohorts was not traumatic. This could be a key reason why the reality and horrors of slavery remain a repressed flashpoint in the American psyche: the experience is outside of democratic idealism and is contradictory to what is perceived as a normal human experience in the political ideology of American freedom and life. In deconstructing traditional conceptions of trauma, Brown observes that "the range of human experience becomes the range of what is normal and usual in the lives of men of the dominant class; white, young, able-bodied, educated, middle-class, Christian men ... Trauma is thus that which disrupts these particular human lives, but no other" (p. 101). For Brown then, psychopathology is imputed upon those whose history and life experience are outside of white male experience. Those on the underside of history are responsible for the atrocities they suffered. The culpability of the perpetrators is erased or ignored.

Consequently, this project suggests that a possible beginning point for addressing this dilemma is to divorce the conception of trauma from a strict material understanding of normalcy and to understand it both from the perspective of material reality, the interior force of being, and from the intersubjective milieu. Thus, trauma reflects an internal force of being that is so severely compromised that the individual forced to exist in extremity can only experience him/herself as negation. In this conception, trauma reflects the inability to resist the encroaching threat of non-self. Because of the radical evil that seeks to destroy the human spirit, trauma reflects the lack of drive, desire, and agency to experience selfhood interdependently in the intersubjective milieu in which one is embedded, thus rendering the individual or group impotent to influence or transgress the intersubjective space. Countermeasures to structures of hegemony within the intersubjective milieu are virtually nonexistent. Traumatology in this paradigm reassigns human subjectivity to a masochistic state or, to use Douglass' terminology, a "brute" state. The causes for this disruption could be a bodily or material assault to an individual, but could also be symptomatic of radical evil and structural or ideological oppression that the majority is unable to see or understand because it falls "outside" of their conception of normal human experience. I therefore propose that the point of departure for trauma be expanded to include the capacity of the internal force of being to effectuate the intersubjective matrix of the individual.

This proposed paradigm of trauma is consistent with Holliman's (2013) conception of relational intersubjectivity. For Holliman, it is only within relationality constituted in the intersubjective space that we can truly understand reality. By extension, to locate reality in the intersubjective space better positions us to understand when the other is traumatized, as we are not only co-creators of human experience and life but also develop a capacity to be co-experiencer (in some small part) of the suffering and oppression of those at the margin. For Holliman then, it is developing the capacity to *relinquish the narcissistic internal need to understand the other* that enables the person to enter into the subjective space of the other. Complete understanding of the other, especially the subaltern, is not a prerequisite for empathy and cooperation with shalom. Selfhood is not predicated on being understood by the other but on being able to influence the intersubjective milieu that we all share. To impede one's internal force of being and incapacitate one's ability to influence or transgress the intersubjective milieu is necessarily traumatic, as selfhood is annihilated. The offshoot of this is that trauma is now not necessarily limited to bodily harm, but includes the inability to imagine or reimagine one's selfhood. Winnicott (1971) captures this in his observation about individuals exposed to prolonged political suffering and the impact it has on their creativity:

> When one reads of individuals dominated at home, or spending their lives in concentration camps or under lifelong persecution because of a cruel political regime, one first of all feels that it is only a few of the victims who remain creative. These, of course, are the ones that suffer ... It appears at first as if all the others who exist (not live) in such pathological communities have so far given up hope that they no longer suffer, and they must have lost the characteristic that makes them human, so that they no longer see the world creatively. (p. 91)

With this proposed reconsideration of how we might understand trauma for those who exist on the underside of the democratic experiment, the next chapter reflects on how trauma is manifested and the group and cultural level. Specifically, we will gain better insight into the importance of narratives, cultural artifacts, and life stories sustaining one's interior force of being and how Frederick Douglass writing four autobiographies over his lifetime reflected a counter-hegemonic strategy that was ego-accretive and beneficial to his agency and subjectivity.

NOTES

1. I use this term to challenge a common approach to epistemology that prioritizes "ways of knowing" via cerebral or noetic conceptions. In this instance, Douglass' deconstruction of the slave religious creed seems to have emanated from the persecution his body incurred. The implications for practical theology and the related praxis is significant for marginalized/victimized persons and groups whose bodies have been abused, marred, or ostracized due to interpersonal or structural evil and oppression.
2. My emphasis.

BIBLIOGRAPHY

Baker-Fletcher, K., & Baker-Fletcher, G. K. (2002). *My sister, my brother: Womanist and xodus God talk*. Eugene: Wipf and Stock Publishers.

Barkai, A. R., & Hauser, S. T. (2008). Psychoanalytic and developmental perspectives on narratives of self-reflection in resilient adolescents explorations and new contributions. *The Annual of Psychoanalysis, 36*, 115–129.

Brown, L. S. (1995). Not outside the range: One feminist perspective on psychic trauma. In C. Caruth (Ed.), *Trauma: Explorations in memory* (pp. 100–112). Baltimore: The Johns Hopkins University Press.

Camp, S. M. (2002). The pleasures of resistance: Enslaved women and body politics in the plantation south, 1830–1861. *The Journal of Southern History, 68*, 533–572.

Des Pres, T. (1976). *The survivor: An anatomy of life in the death camps*. Oxford: Oxford University Press.

Douglass, F. (1845). *Narrative of the life of Frederick Douglass, an American slave: Written by himself*. Boston: Published at the Anti-Slavery Office.

Douglass, F. (1855). *My bondage and my freedom*. New York: Miller, Orton & Mulligan.

Douglass, F. (1881). *Life and times of Frederick Douglass: His early life as a slave, his escape from bondage, and his complete history to the present time*. Hartford: Park Publishing Company.

Fanon, F. (1952). *Black skin, white masks*. Paris: Editions du Seuil.

Holliman, P. J. (2013). *Where is the other? Engaging in the space between*. Evanston: Garrett Evangelical Theological Seminary.

James, W. (1902). *The varieties of religious experience*. New York: Dover Publications, Inc.

Kaplan, S. (2008). *Children in genocide: Extreme traumatization and affect regulation*. London: The International Psychoanalytical Association.

Mills, C. W. (1997). *The racial contract*. Ithaca: Cornell University Press.

Stolorow, R. D. (2007). *Trauma and human existence*. New York: Routledge.

Winnicott, D. W. (1971). *Playing and reality*. New York: Routledge.

Yellin, J. F. (2004). *Harriet Jacobs: A life*. New York: Basic Civitas Books.

CHAPTER 5

The Force of Being, Life Stories, and Counter-Narrative: A Brief Comment on Cultural Trauma and Resiliency

As argued in the previous chapter, when forced to exist under oppression, effectuating one's interior force of being is the fundamental psychological and spiritual human task. The force of being is described as the interior motivation, desire, and agency to imagine and experience self-hood interdependently within the intersubjective milieu in which one is embedded and the autonomy to influence or transgress such space. A healthy force of being enables one to experience herself in a life-giving, counter-hegemonic way that defies how one otherwise may have experienced oneself in a violent and oppressive intersubjective milieu. One develops and cultivates one's internal force of being by (1) engaging sacred spaces of play or contemplation, (2) witnessing or enacting scenes of bodily redemption or agency, and (3) bearing witness (throughout life) of one's experiences and selfhood through life stories, testimonies, or counter-narratives. Such bearing witness of one's experiences and selfhood through life stories Douglass most certainly did, not once, but in four autobiographies.

Why write four autobiographies? I suggest that Frederick Douglass did so as an act of resilience to prop up his internal *force of being*, as he existed in extremity, both antebellum and postbellum. Douglass' ongoing passion to craft a counter-narrative over and against the overarching narrative of white supremacy and black subjugation is clear in his repeated efforts to write down the story of his existence and selfhood. These efforts built the

© The Author(s) 2018
D. G. Gibson, *Frederick Douglass, a Psychobiography*,
Black Religion/Womanist Thought/Social Justice,
https://doi.org/10.1007/978-3-319-75229-7_5

structures of his self, both psychologically and spiritually. His internal force of being compelled him to offer up his life story, and the construction of this biographic material in turn aided in establishing and sustaining his internal force of being.

My argument highlights the extent to which dominant psychodynamic theories fail to capture how culture shapes the individual psyche (or even the psychodynamic theories). Meaning-making symbols and artifacts that have been consciously or unconsciously formulated through contemporary and historical narratives, or inferred meanings that reflect derivatives of social contract, *necessarily* support the benefactors of any given culture and further undermine the oppressed and marginalized of the same culture. Thus, because historical and social narratives of western progress and ideologies of whiteness propped up the selfhood and psychic structure of whites in the intersubjective milieu of the slavocracy and postbellum America, through biographing his own life and inserting his own counter-narrative into the same intersubjective milieu, Douglass nourished his interior force of being and psychic structure.

In his conception of the human mind, Bruner (1990) highlights its capacity for meaning making and how the construction of meaning is situated in the dictates of culture. Brunner coins the term "folk psychology" to describe unconscious, taken-for-granted *ways of being* that any culture has adopted. The totality of these meanings and processes that unconsciously determine how individuals exist and interact among each other within a culture also create an unwritten canon that exposes those who are noncompliant, hence creating *the other* or the *subaltern*. This folk psychology is then determinative of the individual psyche. Consequently, for Bruner, psychology stands to benefit "when it comes to recognize that the folk psychology of ordinary people is not just a set of self-assuaging illusions, but the culture's beliefs and working hypotheses about what makes it possible and fulfilling for people to live together...folk psychology needs explaining, not explaining away" (p. 32).

Important for our task is understanding the effect on a person in a hegemonic intersubjective milieu when folk psychology is operationalized in a way that renders subjectivities and bodies abject. For Douglass, testifying about his life story, or imposing a counter-hegemonic narrative into the intersubjective milieu of the slavocracy, was spiritually additive and ego-accretive to his psychic structure and internal force of being. Bruner maintains that "culture is also constitutive of mind ... meaning [that it] achieves a form that is public and communal rather than private and autistic ... only by replacing this transactional model of mind with an isolating individualistic one have Anglo-American philosophers been able to make Other minds seem so opaque and impenetrable" (pp. 33–34). Like me, Bruner suggests that the broader culture does indeed prop up or sustain the individual mind.

Overarching social and cultural narratives, whether formed by history and memory and the manner in which it is articulated and depicted, or grand narratives formed by social contract, prejudices, and so on, all influence the way in which group and individual psyches are constructed and sustained. In his article on the importance of culture and history on the individual psyche, Thomas A. Kohut (2003) begins by recounting a personal incident in which, during a walking tour of Brussels with a family friend who was also a Holocaust survivor, this particular friend had a panic attack as the group passed a hole in the pavement of a construction site. This friend's reaction apparently stemmed from such familiar sites during the Holocaust. Kohut indicated that his father, who was also a Holocaust survivor, would have a similar reaction. But more critically to the impact of history and culture in the individual psyche, Kohut emphasized that although he was born in a successive generation and was not a part of the Holocaust, he would have enacted a similar reaction as well, because he somehow had internalized his father's life story. Kohut uses this personal story to demonstrate "the powerful influence of history on the psyche, an influence that exerts itself over generations ... here I serve as an example, for I have internalized the historically determined reaction of my father ... I have come to the conclusion that the influence of history on the psyche is as at least as significant as the influence of the psyche on history" (p. 226).

As a psycho-historian, Kohut highlights the traditional methodological approach of identifying salient historical events or people, and then tracing the psychological background of the progenitors of such events as a way of decoding possible motivations. Said differently, as a mode of interpretation, psychology has traditionally envisioned the individual psychologic as preceding cultural and historical phenomenon. However, after conducting a research project for which he interviewed 62 Germans who were adolescents in the First World War, Kohut examined the effect history had on the interviewees and the effect they had on history. I quote him at length, as his findings are relevant to this project:

We need to recognize that the inner world is shaped through experience of the outer world, that human beings are historical, and that we cannot deeply or truly know the psyche if we ignore the creative power of history...philosophically, a failure to appreciate the fact that psychoanalysis is historically determined and that analytic theory and practice reflect a particular cultural moment will render it unable to adapt to changing historical circumstances. Conservative and dogmatic, psychoanalysis will remain frozen in time, becoming increasingly anachronistic. Clinically, ignorance of the historically determined environment will cause analysts to miss crucial cultural influences on their analysands and, as a result, to misunderstand them. Creatively, a gaze that is focused exclusively on the clinical situation will cause analysts to overlook a vital source for understanding human beings. Just as theory exposes the clinician to a large number of patients and to the knowledge and experience of colleagues past and present who have worked with them, so knowledge of history and culture exposes the psychoanalyst to the vast psychological universe beyond the consulting room, the world where people actually live out their lives. It can hardly be an accident that those who have contributed the most to psychoanalysis were steeped in the European, classical, humanistic tradition. Widely read and deeply learned, they not only "applied" analysis to society, culture, and history; even more they *learned* from society, culture, and history. It seems highly unlikely that Freud came to the concept of the Oedipus complex exclusively from the clinical situation. (pp. 234–235)

In contrast to Kohut, Bruner's position is unidirectional. Instead of conceptualizing a reciprocal relationship between culture and the individual, he asserts that "it is culture, not biology, that shapes human life and the human mind, that gives meaning to action by situating its underlying intentional states in an interpretive system" (p. 34).

Consequently, history and the social narratives that it constructs are not simply topics to be discussed arbitrarily, but indeed form not only the deep structures of society, but also the psychic structures (i.e. people) that are embedded in such cultures. Groups and individuals whom the grand narratives are designed to benefit and advance are typically oblivious to the psychic, spiritual, and ego-enhancing potency that history and narrative supply to the individual psyche and self-structure. Those who are not a part of the *benefiting group* create counter-narratives in an effort to survive an existence in extremity. For Douglass, this came in the form of four autobiographies. These counter-narratives provided Douglass with the agency and opportunity to construct a selfhood and identity that transgressed the role assigned to him in a slavocracy.

In their work to understand the resiliency of children in war and how they subsequently respond to the trauma incurred in war, Cyrulnik and Causa (2008) identify the capacity to make meaning out of what has occurred as a key component of resiliency. The authors note that "by structuring his or her story, the narrator enables both self and audience to relate to one another" (p. 26). And indeed this was the case for Douglass, as he sought to relate to the world on his own terms. The autobiography allowed Douglass to be the agent of his own subjectivity, as opposed to being the object of another's pleasure or purpose. This was not only the case in the slavocracy, but even among the northern abolitionist who Douglass befriended after he escaped from the south. As Douglass (1881) joined various anti-slavery apologists on the lecture circuit, he found himself being depicted and presented as a kind of circus object, in that he was a runaway slave that could read and write. Douglass found himself in situations in which he was encouraged to communicate only the kinds of stories that both abolitionists and kindred audiences wanted to hear, in particular voyeuristic specifics about the everyday life of slavery, but not moral, religious, philosophical, or theological themes as they pertained to his past experiences:

During the first three or four months my speeches were almost exclusively made up of narrations of my own personal experience as a slave. "Let us have the facts," said the people. *So also said Friend George Foster, who always wished to pin me down to my simple narrative. "Give us the facts," said Collins, "we will take care of the philosophy." Just here arose some embarrassment.* It was impossible for me to repeat the same old story, month after month, and to keep up my interest in it. It was new to the people, it is true, but it was an old story to me; and to go through with it night after night, was a task altogether too mechanical for my nature. "Tell your story, Frederick," would whisper my revered friend, Mr. Garrison, as I stepped upon the platform. I could not always follow the injunction, for I was now reading and thinking. New views of the subject were being presented to my mind. *It did not entirely satisfy me to narrate wrongs; I felt like denouncing them.* I could not always curb my moral indignation for the perpetrators of slaveholding villainy, long enough for a circumstantial statement of the facts which I felt almost sure everybody must know. Besides, I was growing, and needed room. *"People won't believe you ever was [sic] a slave, Frederick, if you keep on this way," said friend Foster. "Be yourself," said Collins, "and tell your story."* "Better have a little of the plantation speech than not," it was said to me; "it is not best that you seem too learned." These excellent friends were actuated by the best of motives, and were not altogether wrong in their advice; and still I must speak just the word that seemed to *me* the word to be spoken *by* me.[1] (pp. 218–219)

The highlighted portions above demonstrate how even his northern advocates denigrated Douglass' subjectivity. Such objectification retraumatized Douglass; the hearers denied him the voice to construct his own narrative. And this is precisely the issue that Cyrulnik and Causa (2008) raised when they describe the importance of narrative in fostering resiliency in children of war. While they may have had the best of intentions, through their own undiagnosed racism and objectification of Douglass the northern abolitionists were effectively silencing him. For Cyrulnik and Causa, "to remain mute or to deny is a way to avoid a painful memory … being mute or denying is a protective factor but not a resilient one…the resilient narrative of the trauma integrates and reframes the painful past in order to create a shared experience" (p. 27). Douglass expresses the embarrassment he incurred when he was told to provide just facts and leave the philosophy to others. This embarrassment and retraumatization is consistent with what Cyrulnik and Causa (2008) suggests occurs when the subaltern subject is denied the agency to give voice to their own experience. Ostensibly speaking from personal experience, the authors stress the importance of narrative when they assert that:

> the scenario I imagine in my inner world of what happened to me constitutes my narrative identity … the other's account of what happened to me establishes my 'niggerness,' the way you think of my traumatism … and the history, myth, stereotype, and even prejudice structure the verbal world imprinting in my soul, be it a feeling of shame or of pride, consistent with your rhetoric. (p. 27)

We see the formational influence of contemporary and historical grand narratives on a group intersubjective milieu and on the individual psyche in Douglass' fourth and last autobiography. This version of his story includes a lengthy addendum to the third autobiography (written in 1881) and was penned by Douglass in 1892, largely in response to the Supreme Court decision of 1883 which struck down the Civil Rights law of 1875, effectively ending the symbolic promise of progress, equality, citizenship, and personhood heralded by Reconstruction. In the following passage, while we do not see Douglass (1892) engaging in explicit discourse on the impact of history and psychology, his concern is forceful, as he laments the impact of the revisionist history imposed by southern Democrats the further removed in time the country was from the Civil War:

> In further illustration of the reactionary tendencies of public opinion against the black man and of the increasing decline, since the war for the Union, in the power of resistance to the onward march of the rebel States to their former control and ascendency in the councils of the nation, the decision of the United States Supreme Court, declaring the Civil Rights law of 1875 unconstitutional, is striking and convincing. *The strength and activities of the malign elements of the country against equal rights and equality before the law seem to increase in proportion to the increasing distance between that time and the time of the war.* When the black man's arm was needed to defend the country; when the North and the South were in arms against each other and the country was in danger of dismemberment, his rights were well considered. *That the reverse is now true, is a proof of the fading and defacing effect of time and the transient character of Republican gratitude. From the hour that the loyal North began to fraternize with the disloyal and slaveholding South; from the hour that they began to "shake hands over the bloody chasm;" from that hour the cause of justice to the black man began to decline and lose its hold upon the public mind, and it has lost ground ever since. The future historian will turn to the year 1883 to find the most flagrant example of this national deterioration.* Here he will find the Supreme Court of the nation reversing the action of the Government, defeating the manifest purpose of the Constitution, nullifying the Fourteenth Amendment, and placing itself on the side of prejudice, proscription, and persecution.[2] (pp. 652–653)

For Douglass, what he believed to be evidence of national deterioration—namely, a Republican change in gratitude toward blacks who fought in the Civil War and a decline in drive and passion for achieving the philosophical goals of Reconstruction—were all attributable to the effect of revisionist history that shifted the South from being recognized as rebel states, to fellow brethren whose state's rights were superior to the rights and humanity of blacks. For Douglass, the change in how history was interpreted and understood, whether because of the passage of time or because of deliberate acts to revise a national story, all had a direct impact on the psychosocial landscape of the nation and the individual psyches of both whites and blacks.

Blight (1989) chronicles Douglass' tenuous effort to encourage his fellow black Americans to embrace an authentic historicity of the Civil War and slavery. Recognizing a generational transition in which blacks with firsthand accounts of slavery and the war were slowly passing away and being replaced by a new generation of African Americans that knew little to nothing of the actual history and plight of the previous generation, Douglass was concerned about the adverse psychosocial effects of historical ignorance. Blight notes that Douglass was accused by many to be living in the past (an allegation of which many are accused even in the twenty-first century if they engage topics around slavery). Important to this project, however, is Blight's focus on Douglass' anxiety about the psychosocial effects of forgetting the war. Speaking of Douglass, Blight says that "around the pledge to 'never forget,' Douglass organized his entire postwar effort to shape and preserve the legacy of the Civil War" (p. 1160). Although he does not explicitly address it, Douglass recognizes how forgetting about the war and slavery props up the ego and psyche of the former southern confederate constituents and how remembering the war and slavery was structure building to African American subjectivity. Blight claims that "by intellectual predilection and by experience, Douglass was deeply conscious that history mattered ... Douglass deeply understood that peoples and nations are shaped and defined by history. He knew that history was a primary source of identity, meaning, and motivation" (p. 1160).

Douglass' fear of losing history and its impact on the collective psyche of the nation, and in particular African Americans, is captured succinctly in Eyerman's (2004) conception of cultural trauma. Unlike more traditional understandings of trauma that highlight psychic or bodily shock or the overwhelming of mental capacities, Eyerman situates cultural trauma in the "dramatic loss of identity and meaning, a tear in the social fabric, affecting a group of people that has achieved some degree of cohesion" (p. 61). In his project, Eyerman is concerned with progression of African American identity formation from the end of the Civil War through the Civil Rights era. Exploring multiple theories of individual and collective memory, Eyerman explicates how memory is not just a function of individual faculties, but represents the collective, multigenerational process of the larger group regarding the interpretation of symbols and historical events. Created from these large group interpretations are various deep structures of society that include unconscious philosophical, religious, and political genres. For Eyerman then, collective memory is not an academic category and is to be distinguished from transcribed history. Borrowing from Halbwach, Eyerman argues that collective memory is dynamic and accretive to group identity. Transcribed history primarily reflects the documentation of past events that is generally known to a particular group or culture, whereas collective memory references data points from transcribed history and makes interpretations of it consistent with the psychosocial needs of the group:

> Collective memory is conceived as the outcome of interaction, a conversational process within which individuals locate themselves, where identities are described as the different ways individuals and collectives are positioned by, and position themselves, within narratives. This dialogic process is one of negotiation for both individuals and for the collective itself. It is never arbitrary. From this perspective, the past is a collectively articulated, if not collectively experienced, temporal reference point that shapes the individual more than it is reshaped to fit generational or individual needs. (pp. 66–67)

What Eyerman explicitly argues in his work on black identity formation is what Frederick Douglass implicitly understands in his fourth autobiography, the high-stakes game of how the history of slavery and the Civil War will be constructed and used in collective memory. The victors of this negotiation in history and collective memory benefit from a master narrative that underwrites both the psychosocial intersubjective milieu and the individual psychic and self-structure. The victors of this negotiation in historicity will experience selfhood in a more robust way than those who lose the transaction. Those who exist on the underside of modernity and whose story is mute are confronted with a traumatizing annihilation anxiety in which they experience a fragmentation and decompensation in self-structure and identity. This loss of collective identity is what constitutes cultural trauma for Eyerman. Douglass intuitively understood the ramifications of revisionist history and lost memory. But Douglass (1892) also understood the potential of testimony and the counter-narrative to foster a life-giving collective memory and to bolster one's internal force of being. He suggests as much when he gives his rationale for penning the revised edition of this third autobiography just two years before his death:

> I write freely of myself, not from choice, but because I have, by my cause, been morally forced into thus writing. Time and events have summoned me to stand forth both as a witness and an advocate for a people long dumb, not allowed to speak for themselves, yet much misunderstood and deeply wronged... Fifty years have passed since I entered upon that work, and now that it is ended, I find myself summoned again by the popular voice and by what is called the negro problem, to come a second time upon the witness

stand and give evidence upon disputed points concerning myself and my emancipated brothers and sisters who, though free, are yet oppressed and are in as much need of an advocate as before they were set free. (p. 620)

Moreover, the revisionist history against which Douglass was fighting was white people's denial of the atrocities committed against generations of black people in the American democratic experiment. This denial and repression is not only something that Douglass battled in the wake of the Reconstruction era; it is still grappled with in virtually every aspect of contemporary American democracy. To deny the material reality of the slavocracy and its ongoing legacy in the western democratic experiment, or to deny the historical reality of crimes against humanity or the present reality of structures of evil, is to deny the humanity of those who have been victimized, the humanity of survivors, and the memory of those who succumbed to the instantiation of radical evil. In short, whether we are speaking of individual trauma, collective trauma, or cultural trauma, the efforts of benefactors and perpetrators to repress, trivialize, or deny their acts of cruelty, violence, death, genocide, or *ambivalent gazing* not only (re)traumatizes those who were directly affected by evil but also successive generations who engage in the process of meaning making for the sake of individual and collective identity formation, as well as psychological and spiritual thriving.

The social denial and repression of the evil that precedes trauma seems to be part and parcel of the trauma process that those who have been victimized are forced to endure. Sitting on a panel to discuss the 25th anniversary of her seminal work *Trauma and Recovery*, Judith Herman observes that communal denial is a common feature that cannot be overlooked in any discourse on traumatology and that in many cases hampers the reintegration process that is crucial for trauma recovery.[3] While not using the terminology of trauma, Frederick Douglass seems to have anticipated the ill effects that the collusion of constituents in the North and South would have on the soul of a nation—a collusion that, according to Douglass, revised the story of the Civil War from that of an illegal rebellion driven in large part by a desire to preserve the slavocracy as a story of romanticized patriotism based on states' rights. In such a revision, the reality of the evil of slavery is all but eradicated from the minds and hearts of the collective society and expelled from the story of American democracy. Such a narrative process is inherently dehumanizing to generations of black people, for it enhances white supremacy and depletes black subjectivity.

Jessica Benjamin recognizes this dynamic. In what she refers to as the "moral third," Benjamin (2011) argues for spaces that recognize and acknowledge the suffering of all human beings. Moreover, such recognition must precede any life-giving restorative actions in the wake of human atrocity and trauma, she says. For Benjamin, "certain historical traumas are precisely in need of being linked up with their origins and meaning... this holds true more obviously when one has been a perpetrator but is equally true where one has been a victim and the failure of witness has led to the demise of a lawful world...actual Holocaust survivors in Israel did not...receive the kind of recognition that allowed them to find a way to socially express and mark their suffering in a way that reestablished their dignity" (p. 212). Narratives that do not give voice to suffering are by definition dehumanizing.

Through the lens of cultural trauma, one can more easily discern why Douglass felt compelled to write four autobiographies: the exercise of biographing builds up both his spiritual and psychological structure and, fundamentally, his *interior force of being*. The act of biography is at once a witness to his humanity and personhood and also an outright defiance of violence and hegemony that was (and remains) inherent in the western democratic experiment. The very act of writing one's biography was an act of resistance against the pervasive threat of non-self that existed both in the slavocracy and its latent and ubiquitous legacy. Douglass' autobiographies were a counter-hegemonic strategy that transgressed or defied what the benefactors and bystanders of the slavocracy (i.e. the slave powers, onlookers, and the anti-slaveholding community) *thought or expected Douglass should have been doing* as a black male body within the intersubjective milieu. The mere fact that his biographing triggered virtually every constituent within the American democracy, whether or not they affirmed his humanity, in and of itself built up his selfhood and his *interior force of being*. For who or what else in the milieu of the slavocracy could have had a significant positive effect on the personhood of Frederick Douglass.

Two of Frederick Douglass' autobiographies were written antebellum, and two were written postbellum. Each, I believe, was written to inject a counter-narrative into an intersubjective milieu that sought to denigrate black subjectivity through the western narratives that were propped up by particular biased transcriptions of history and collective memory. Each of his works was in the service of propping up his internal force of being and black subjectivity. At the end of his book 1, written just seven years after his escape from slavery, Douglass (1845) issues a forceful rebuke of a

Christian theology and tradition that validated slavery. In an effort to clarify what many would interpret as an atheist stance he asserts,

> What I have said respecting and against religion, I mean strictly to apply to the *slaveholding religion* of this land, and with no possible reference to Christianity proper; for, between the Christianity of this land, and the Christianity of Christ, I recognize the widest, possible difference—so wide, that to receive the one as good, pure, and holy, is of necessity to reject the other as bad, corrupt, and wicked. (p. 118)

Indeed, Douglass refuses to allow a pro-slavery interpretation of the Christian faith to have the last word in the governing narrative that informs the intersubjective matrix he inhabits.

At the end of book 2, published just five years after the Fugitive Slave Act of 1850 (which legalized slavery throughout the entire country and further built up and denigrated white and black subjectivity, respectively), Douglass (1855) concludes the work with a commitment to fight the onset of nihilism within his black contemporaries. In an effort to enhance the internal force of being in himself and other blacks, Douglass insists that "progress is yet possible" (p. 405). In a slew of appendages to the autobiography (that includes excerpts from his speeches, lectures, letters, etc.), Douglass again imposes a counter-narrative to the implied white superiority that undergirds the fugitive slave act. This autobiography ends most famously with an open letter to his former master, Thomas Auld, in which Douglass publically scolds him for the hypocrisy of being an alleged Christian slaveholder. Douglass publicly demands to know the condition of his grandmother and sisters. He publicly poses a rhetorical question to his former master of how he would feel if Douglass stole and treated his daughters as his former master treated Douglass' mother and sisters. His counter-narrative is one that seeks to subvert the normalization of evil that runs roughshod throughout the nation. The absence of countermeasures against hegemonic master narratives that prop up oppressive systems precipitates cultural trauma.

The critical role that controlling narratives play in personal and community subjectivity and identity formation cannot be overstated. The argument being made for cultural trauma in the context of Frederick Douglass, and the importance that life-giving narratives play in the emotional well-being of individuals, can be said of any culture—including western European culture. Perhaps a contemporary example can be seen in the very public (and private) discussions about the appropriateness of institutions displaying the Confederate flag or Confederate monuments or of professional athletes kneeling during the singing of the national anthem. For some sectors of the society, the removal (or even consideration of removal) of Confederate flags and monuments is cause for great consternation, anger, rage, and vitriol, both individually and collectively. No matter how *recorded history* connects these symbols to the right to enslave, violate, or destroy an entire people, a master narrative of a *Christianized American democracy* as evidenced in the prioritizing of individual and State's rights, privacy, individualism, or wealth accumulation and ownership seems to best the reality of the radical structures of evil and oppression that propped up the slavocracy—the actual historical period in which the Confederacy emerges. This is to say, regardless of historically objective facts, when we consider individual and collective identity formation and emotional well-being, controlling narratives play a critical role. No matter how professional athlete-protestors (and their backers) may argue that kneeling during the singing of the national anthem is not meant to insult military veterans, or that freedom to protest is an inherent American democratic value, there remains a significant part of the American population that becomes vehemently outraged at the sight of such protests. In short, a controlling narrative that mistakenly equates an unqualified salutation to a symbol (i.e. nationalism as opposed to patriotism) as love and respect for a country seems to trump any other rational argument that seeks to explicate democracy and patriotism.

Through this example I simply want to highlight the intensity of anger, vitriol, or rage that people experience when they perceive certain narratives or symbols are under attack. In part, the impassioned reactions are less about an ethical or moral response to what one perceives as disrespectful and more about individual and group annihilation anxiety. The hermeneutics behind any action, symbol, or narrative would largely be moot if such materials were irrelevant to individual and collective subjectivity. But such is not the case. *Cultural symbols and narratives do matter and are accretive to the interior structures of self and one's force of being.* The way the story or narrative is told and understood props up—or degenerates—the constituents of any given intersubjective milieu. Just as certain governing narratives or symbols can serve as *spiritual and psychic structure-building* inputs that prop up individual and group subjectivity at the center—for members in the majority western culture the absence of truth-telling narratives that reflect the oppression of those victimized at the margin is the essence of cultural trauma. The annihilation anxiety that members of the western majority experience when narratives of a Christian America, moral superiority, or American innocence are challenged, those at the margin similarly experience when the reality of oppression and its history are denied. Similar to what Jessica Benjamin has observed in relation to the survivors of the Holocaust, the denial of the atrocities inflicted on those forced to exist on the underside of modernity is by definition dehumanizing and, as such, culturally traumatizing. As it relates to cultural trauma then, Alexander (2004) does not recognize the etiology of the traumatic in any particular event per se but in how the collective makes meaning of the event in relation to their sense of group identity. For Alexander, "trauma is not the result of a group experiencing pain...it is the result of this acute discomfort entering into the core of the collectivity's sense of its own identity...to represent social pain as a fundamental threat to their sense of who they are, where they came from, and where they want to go" (p. 10). Stories, heritage, history, and the interpretation of such do indeed matter.

NOTES

1. My emphasis.
2. My emphasis.
3. Judith Herman was part of a panel co-sponsored by the Moral Injury and Recovery in Religion, Society and Culture group and the Psychology, Culture, and Religion Group at the 2017 American Academy of Religion conference in Boston, MA. The panel was convened to reflect on the impact of Herman's work in trauma since the publication of her book *Trauma and Recovery* in 1992.

BIBLIOGRAPHY

Alexander, J. C. (2004). Toward a theory of cultural trauma. In J. C. Alexander, R. Eyerman, B. Giesen, N. J. Smelser, & P. Sztompka (Eds.), *Cultural trauma and collective identity* (pp. 1–30). Berkeley: University of California Press.

Benjamin, J. (2011). Acknowledgment of collective trauma in light of dissociation and dehumanization. *Psychoanalytic Perspectives, 8*(2), 207–214.

Blight, D. W. (1989). "For something beyond the battlefield": Frederick Douglass and the struggle for the memory of the Civil War. *The Journal of American History, 75*(4), 1156–1178.

Bruner, J. S. (1990). *Acts of meaning.* Cambridge: Harvard University Press.

Cyrulnik, B., & Causa, H. (2008). Children in war and their resiliences. In H. Parens, H. P. Blum, & S. Akhtar (Eds.), *The unbroken soul: Tragedy, trauma, and resilience* (pp. 21–36). Lanham: Jason Aronson.

Douglass, F. (1845). *Narrative of the life of Frederick Douglass, an American slave: Written by himself.* Boston: Published at the Anti-Slavery Office.

Douglass, F. (1855). *My bondage and my freedom.* New York: Miller, Orton & Mulligan.

Douglass, F. (1881). *Life and times of Frederick Douglass: His early life as a slave, his escape from bondage, and his complete history to the present time.* Hartford: Park Publishing Company.

Douglass, F. (1892). *Life and times of Frederick Douglass written by himself: His early life as a slave, his escape from bondage, his complete history to the present time.* Boston: De Wolfe, Fiske & Company.

Eyerman, R. (2004). Cultural trauma: Slavery and the formation of African American identity. In J. C. Alexander, R. Eyerman, B. Giesen, N. J. Smelser, & P. Sztompka (Eds.), *Cultural trauma and collective identity* (pp. 60–111). Berkeley: University of California Press.

Kohut, T. A. (2003). Psychoanalysis as psychohistory or why psychotherapists cannot afford to ignore culture. *The Annual of Psychoanalysis, 31,* 225–236.

CHAPTER 6

A Constructive Theology of Deliverance: Redeeming the Internal Force of Being

*I did not, when a slave, understand the deep meanings of those rude, and apparently incoherent songs. I was myself within the circle, so that I neither saw nor heard as those without might see and hear. They told a tale which was then altogether beyond my feeble comprehension; they were tones, loud, long and deep, breathing the prayer and complaint of souls boiling over with the bitterest anguish. Every tone was a testimony against slavery, and a prayer to God for **deliverance from chains***
Frederick Douglass (1855, p. 99)
*With all other blessings sought at the mercy seat, I always prayed that God would, of His great mercy, and in His own good time, **deliver me from my bondage.***
Frederick Douglass (1855, p. 169)

A THEOLOGY OF DELIVERANCE

In the courses I teach on historical instances of Christian complicity or ambivalence such as the transatlantic slave trade, slavery, the Native American genocide, and the Holocaust, I often ask students to consider what has changed within Christian discourse and praxis that makes such acts wrong or feel wrong today, though apparently they were not deemed to be wrong nor felt to be wrong and perhaps were even considered perfectly alright when they were being carried out.[1] I deliberately use emotive terminology in this question to signal that cognitive faculties alone are

© The Author(s) 2018
D. G. Gibson, *Frederick Douglass, a Psychobiography*,
Black Religion/Womanist Thought/Social Justice,
https://doi.org/10.1007/978-3-319-75229-7_6

inadequate in responding to this question. In short, if the biblical text has not changed and major theological categories have not changed, then how do we account for the change in Christian thought that today views slavocracy as clearly wrong, but did not consider it to be so in years gone by? If neither biblical text nor major theological categories or creeds have undergone significant shifts, then we might be justified in concluding that Christian praxis at the time was somehow severely corrupted in its engagement and deployment of Christian texts, symbols, and tradition. There must be a better contemporary assessment tool than hindsight, which tends to occur on the backs of the subaltern.

I propose that a *pastoral theology of deliverance* points toward a more redemptive trajectory. In this chapter, I demonstrate that the performance of the faith devoid of a pastoral theology of deliverance (i.e. un-actualized in the flesh), ultimately leads to degenerative theologics, doctrines, and ecclesial praxis, that collaborate in perpetuating the death and destruction of bodies, such as witnessed in the slavocracy. Furthermore, I demonstrate that across generations, the absence of a pastoral theology of deliverance prepares individuals and groups to engage in radical evil. It conditions the church and community to tolerate evil. Paul Tillich's construal of the demonic will be useful for understanding how the church was able to participate actively in the slavocracy and its ongoing legacy in the western democratic experiment.

In constructing a practical theology through the lens of Frederick Douglass' life and using his terminology of the ultimate concern, I suggest that a pastoral theology of deliverance is critical to understanding Christian complicity in the slavocracy. For Christianity's texts and symbols were used as ideological currency to legitimate an oppressive system. A pastoral theology of deliverance challenges two principles: (1) the practice of forming and universalizing theologies, ethics, and praxis with cognitive faculties alone, and (2) forming such theologics in a culturally homogeneous environment. Pentecost turns both commonly enacted principles on its head. Moreover, as I will demonstrate in this chapter, Frederick Douglass understood how both practices led to Christian complicity in the slavocracy. The Enlightenment's turn to the subject, along with modernity's objective to universalize human experience, has in part provided the social, religious, and ideological currency for such practices, practices that history has shown to be deadly for those forced to exist at the margin. When the church adopts this communal practice of reducing theology and religion to culturally homogenous mental exercises, it becomes inherently dangerous. While occasionally it yields neutral or progressive results, more often than not those results are destructive to those that lack the religious and sociopolitical power to engage in ideological resistance.

The proposed pastoral theology of deliverance is Pentecostal in nature because Pentecost recognizes and honors that engagement with all of humanity is necessary for the creation of life-giving and redemptive theological and pastoral ethics and praxis. On the day of Pentecost, Divine disclosure was not disseminated through one culture to all of humanity. Instead, Divine disclosure came directly to all. Additionally, the outpouring of the Spirit at the Pentecost event involved more than cognition but engaged body, soul, and mind. Consequently, God-talk and praxis that begins with any one culture or group must be in constant conversation with the entirety of God's creation, as it takes all of creation to better appreciate who God is and what it means to be human. That is to say, any formulation of theology and praxis that is delimited to any one tradition or culture, or is delimited to cognition without regard for individual and communal affect and emotion, or is delimited to cognition without regard to the material effects on bodies is a theological formulation that is necessarily incomplete and inherently dangerous. Christian complicity in the slavocracy—as evidenced in the autobiographies of Frederick Douglass—provides ample evidence of what is being argued here.

The question being addressed in this chapter is inherently pastoral. For it seeks to address not only the care of souls of victims but the corruption of souls in the perpetrators, enablers, and bystanders. While the church traditionally emphasizes the end-result theological reflections and constructs, seldom does it reflect theologically on the human and communal process by which it derives and constructs its doctrines and confessions. How is it that Frederick Douglass, using the same Christian literature and symbols, so clearly sees the evil, degradation, destruction, and hypocrisy inherent in the slavocracy, while his captors who engage the same Christian literature and symbols reach a far different, death-dealing conclusion that the slavocracy is divinely sanctioned? The proposed pastoral theology of deliverance addresses this question. Disembodied theological and biblical frameworks (along with the communities they engender) are deceptive. Their theologies feel so right: they cater to the most primal human need to believe that our existence and worldviews represent the center of God's creation and the Divine priority and that the difficult and complex Pentecostal requirement for intercultural dialogue and communion is simply a luxury and suggestion rather than a requirement for communal survival and a biblical mandate. For Douglass then, a pastoral theology of deliverance reflected a counter-hegemonic theology for his soul and intra-psychic space: a theological repertoire that redeemed his internal force of being. The proposed pastoral theology of deliverance deduces its constructive and hermeneutical currency from theological tradition, biblical narrative, and Douglass' embodied experiences. Its goal is the redemption of body, soul, and spirit from the demonic grip of the slavocracy and other structures of radical evil. Such a pastoral theology of deliverance is about redeeming the soul of the democracy experiment from the bondage of the slavocracy and drawing it closer to the heart of God, which entails justice, freedom, shalom, and a radical love for neighbor.

The language of "deliverance" was not only used in the hush-arbor God-talk that Douglass employed but has remained in common usage in black church theology throughout the twentieth century. This theology of the oppressed has not been given significant attention or respect in the academy, though it is rich with healing and redemptive possibilities. A pastoral theology of deliverance is Pentecostal in that it recognizes the necessity of a multiplicity of voices to encounter the Divine more fully. Conversely, disembodied theology seeks out the shelter of cultural and social homogeneity. In the multiplicity of many voices, human oppression, violence, abuse, rape, torture, terror, death, and destruction (all ubiquitous components of the slavocracy) can no longer be interpreted as normative to human experience and reflective of Divine sovereignty. Douglass (1855) understood this well. On one occasion while in Baltimore, away from the southern plantation, he notes "slavery dislikes a dense population, in which there is a majority of non-slaveholders. The general sense of decency that must pervade such a population, does much to check and prevent those outbreaks of atrocious cruelty, and those dark crimes without a name, almost openly perpetrated on the plantation" (pp. 147–148). Moreover, in a reception speech given at Finsbury Chapel in Moorfields, England, in 1846, when asked about why he thought it necessary to expose the evils of American slavery to the British public, his response was rich with Pentecostal sensibilities:

> Slavery is the common enemy of mankind, and all mankind should be made acquainted with its abominable character. My next answer is, that the slave is a man, and, as such, is entitled to your sympathy as a brother. All the feelings, all the susceptibilities, all the capacities, which you have, he has. He is a part of the human family. He has been the prey—the common prey—of christendom for the last three hundred years, and it is but right, it is but just,

it is but proper, that his wrongs should be known throughout the world...
It requires the humanity of christianity, the morality of the world to remove
it. (pp. 416–17)

This kind of Pentecostal sensibility remains present in contemporary
understandings of a pastoral theology of deliverance in certain black
church experiences when, at the invitation of a worship leader, individuals
approach the altar to receive a prayer of deliverance. The evil which
oppresses and destroys people in isolation and deludes them into thinking
that such victimization is normative loses its grip once the victim's humanity is placed in solidarity with the humanity of the collective. Whereas
perpetrators of human atrocity are more easily able to justify their vile acts
as normative and divinely inspired in the isolation of social enclaves, the
collective voice as a more robust expression of humanity is able to contra-
dict such degenerative theology. A pastoral theology of deliverance insists
that any form and manifestation of theology that assumes slavocracy and
oppression to be normative is necessarily bankrupt.

A pastoral theology of deliverance likewise recognizes that human
oppression and soteriology cannot be part of a life-giving community.
Thus, any Christian community that justifies and integrates human-
sponsored evil, violence, or oppression into its ecclesial praxis and theological framework is fraudulent and those who are victimized by its
practices should resist it. Even in the absence of material deliverance, freedom, or justice, *resistance in and of itself is redemptive, as it prevents the
internalization of such oppression as being divinely directed.*

Nowhere is this better seen than in the conclusion of Douglass' epic
fight with Covey, the Negro-breaker. Although he was still enslaved at the
conclusion of the fight, Douglass claimed that he was now *a man*, a man
with a rekindled determination to realize actual freedom. After the battle,
he claims that he experienced a resurrection and that he was now "free in
fact" although still enslaved in form. He juxtaposes his new position to the
Christianity of Covey that had oppressed him. Clearly, Douglass' words
are existential and spiritual in nature and reflect a kind of new birth consistent with his prayers of deliverance. The distinction that Douglass makes
with free in fact vs. enslaved in form marks a move toward redeeming his
interior force of being. He makes an honest assessment that while evil will
not have the last word eschatologically, on this side of the eschaton it will
exact material damage. Frederick Douglass' move toward extricating his
interior experience of freedom from the instantiation of material evil in the

slavocracy anticipates Howard Thurman's similar move in the twentieth century. In his examination of Thurman's philosophy on the relationship between the individual, God, and society, Fluker (1990) highlights Thurman's focus on the interior sense of freedom as a condition precedent to a healthy fight for material liberty in society. According to Fluker, Howard Thurman's understanding of freedom "refers to a quality of being and spirit: freedom is located within; its locus is the human will... 'liberty,' on the other hand, refers to external prerogatives, privileges, and grants that are conferred upon the individual from a social arrangement or context" (p. 40).

Lastly, a pastoral theology of deliverance honors the entirety of the human project, not just cognition. A pastoral theology of deliverance engages context, cognition, affect, body, spirit, and aesthetics, recognizing that the Divine can enter human experience at any point. Disembodied theology suppresses the fullness of human experience in the service of cognitively produced propositions that deny the fullness of humanity and the heart of God (i.e. even the demons believe).[2] Recall how, moments before his epic fight with Covey, Douglass describes how his feelings, downtrodden affect, and his tortured body all changed his theology:

> My religious views on the subject of resisting my master, had suffered a serious shock, by the savage persecution to which I had been subjected, and my hands were no longer tied by my religion. Master Thomas's indifference had severed the last link. I had now to this extent "backslidden" from this point in the slave's religious creed; and I soon had occasion to make my fallen state known to my Sunday-pious brother, Covey. (p. 241)

Douglass understood deliverance to be incarnational. Such a pastoral theology of deliverance does not devalue the body, nor the behavioral, affective, and emotional elements of the human condition. It engages equally bodily experience and condition, affect and emotion, as well as cognition in its theological constructs, tenets, confessions, axioms, and ethics. If engagement of the entire human project were unnecessary for life-giving theology, then we should also have to question the necessity of the Word becoming flesh and dwelling among humanity (a core tenet of the Council of Chalcedon which—at least on paper—is a foundational element of most Protestant theologies and communities). Instead, a pastoral theology of deliverance is Eucharistic in that we are called to be partakers in each other's suffering.

Religious practice and theological reflection that is limited to cognitive and speculative faculties alone is inherently dangerous, as it has not been formulated and conditioned by body, soul, and affect. Such theology that has not been shaped by the entirety of human experience and a Pentecostal multiplicity of communities risks perpetrating or facilitating violence toward *the other* and promoting death-dealing practices. The work of Kelly Brown Douglass (2005) is useful in this regard. She shows how decontextualized and disembodied theologies collude to hide and disown Christian complicity in human atrocities. Using as her example the terrorism of lynching black bodies, which in many instances was condoned by Christian churches, Brown postulates how abusive power, as well as Christian tradition grounded in Platonism and Stoicism, contributed to Christian complicity in the reign of terror witnessed in lynching.

Especially as it relates to the context of Frederick Douglass and the slavocracy, one might understandably believe that brute force alone is what preserved slavery in the west for centuries. And indeed, physical violence played a fundamental role. But there was also another form of power that preserved the slavocracy: the power of self-discipline instigated by the gaze of pure evil. The gaze-like effect of evil has the potential to compel its victims to cooperate with its death-dealing objectives. Using a Foucauldian lens, Douglass explicates the nonphysical elements of power that are just as destructive as brute force. According to her, power is both productive and disciplinary, and history shows both of these elements colluded to make Christians oblivious to their complicity in heinous acts.

In its disciplinary form, power governs interpersonal relationships. It governs how we experience and feel about ourselves as well as others in our context. In its disciplinary form, power is seductive in that it compels individuals to cooperate with their own oppression and destruction, seduced into feeling that such oppression and destruction is not only divinely oriented but conducive to personal and communal well-being. Such power produces the gaze-like component of evil, coaxing individuals and collectives into believing that evil and oppression is normative and something that we cannot do without. Disciplinary power was foundational to the slavocracy and remains a core ingredient of the legacy of slavery and the democratic experiment. Frederick Douglass refers to this form of power as *priestcraft*—a possible reference to the gaze and seductive elements of slave power. In several instances, Douglass (1881) alludes to how some enslaved victims succumbed to disciplinary power. In one place he laments, "I have met many good religious colored people at the south, who were under the delusion that God required them to submit to slavery and to wear their chains with meekness and humility…and I quite lost my patience when I found a colored man weak enough to believe such stuff" (p. 77).

In its productive form, Kelly Brown Douglass (2005) contends that power is self-generative. For it endeavors to be self-sufficient by being monopolistic in the production of power, preferring monologue over dialogue, paternalism over mutuality. Power generates knowledge specifically designed to justify, sacralize, and underwrite its death-dealing objectives, as we see in the slavocracy.[3] Brown Douglass observes:

> Christian theology is an essential component of discursive power…but perhaps Christianity's more dangerous involvement in human oppression is implicit…the Christian theological tradition has contributed to a certain collective theological consciousness that allows for, if not sanctions, unrelenting oppression of various human beings. What the most notable and influential Christian theological tradition both emphasizes and does not emphasize provides a theological framework for Christian men and women to participate in attacks as vile as lynching. This theological tradition is disseminated most prominently in Christian institutions through the hymns people sing, the creeds they recite, and/or the sermons they hear. (p. 9)

While it is easier to see how the productive form of power was manifested in the Church's pro-slavery arguments, its implicit power to prop up white supremacy can even be seen among the anti-slavery and abolitionist groups as they endeavor to control both Frederick Douglass (1881) and their production of knowledge by limiting what he was allowed to say in speeches during meetings sponsored by northern abolitionists. Even among well-intending constituents, the objectification of black bodies was ingrained in the mindset of the slavocracy:

> During the first three or four months my speeches were almost exclusively made up of narrations of my own personal experience as a slave. "Let us have the facts," said the people. So also said Friend George Foster, who always wished to pin me down to my simple narrative. "Give us the facts," said Collins, "we will take care of the philosophy." Just here arose some embarrassment…"tell your story, Frederick," would whisper my revered friend, Mr. Garrison…"People won't believe you ever was a slave, Frederick, if you keep on this way," said friend Foster. "Be yourself," said Collins, "and tell

your story." "Better have a little of the plantation speech that not," it was said to me; "it is not best that you seem too learned." (pp. 218–219)

Frederick Douglass' experiences in London at the World's Evangelical Alliance and the World's Temperance convention in 1846 represents a more brazen example of corrupt power's drive to control knowledge production and discourse. Delegates from America were greatly vexed by the presence of Douglass at the conventions, ostensibly believing that he had no place or was not entitled to be in such a setting—evidence that they were mentally transporting the intersubjective milieu of the slavocracy across the Atlantic. Individuals such as Rev. Samuel Hanson Cox, D.D. and other American delegates attempted to deny Douglass the opportunity to speak at the conventions but to no avail. They were terrified at the prospect that information about American slavery would be made public at a global convention. The American delegates wanted to control the discourse. However, being in London, they were in a different intersubjective matrix. Cox was indignant that Douglass would raise the issue of slavery, wailing that "it is a streak of meanness! It is abominable...as if he had been our school-master, and we his docile and devoted pupils; and launched his revengeful missiles at our country without one palliative...I came here his sympathizing friend: I am such no more" (pp. 251–252).

We find another nineteenth-century example of Christianity's use of discursive power in a document produced by Samuel B. How, D.D. (1856) for the General Synod of the Reformed Protestant Dutch Church in October of 1855. The document, entitled *Slaveholding Not Sinful: Slavery, The Punishment of Man's Sin, Its Remedy, The Gospel of Christ*, was produced by Samuel How in response to a synodical vote about whether to grant the request of the North Carolina Classis of the German Reformed Church for an "ecclesiastical connection" with the Reformed Protestant Dutch Church. The two central objections to receiving the classis from North Carolina—both focusing on the issue of slavery—were (1) that the question about slavery was so contentious that some individuals felt simply entertaining the topic would be too disruptive to the well-being of the church and (2) that slavery was a sin and the church shouldn't be in communion with churches involved with slavery. In terms of the first objection, such an attitude seemed to reflect the general mood in the north, an attitude which had evidently become pervasive when in 1854 the Missouri Compromise (which prevented the spread of slavery in the Louisiana Territory) was repealed by the Kansas-Nebraska Act. In light of the repeal of the Missouri Compromise, Douglass (1881) observed that "the people of the North had been accustomed to ask, in a tone of cruel indifference, 'What have we to do with slavery?' and now no labored speech was required in answer...slaveholding aggression settled this question for us" (p. 299). While the Reformed Protestant Dutch synod eventually voted to receive the classis from North Carolina (50 affirmative votes to 47 no votes), the German Reformed classis (which apparently was a slaveholding community) ultimately declined, offended by that fact that the synodical vote was so close.

It was in conjunction with this event that Samuel How produced the document in question, offering up a detailed apologetic that slaveholding was not sinful. This he based in no small part on the logic that "our Lord repeatedly spoke of slaves, especially in several of his parables, without the slightest intimation that he condemned slavery, and in such a way as plainly showed that he considered it lawful" (p. 24). Said differently, since Jesus didn't explicitly forbid slavery, he plainly supported it. Such logic was common. In 1846, while attending the World's Evangelical Alliance and World's Temperance Convention in London, Douglass encountered a Dr. Cunningham who offered a Christian defense on behalf of the Free Church of Scotland to receive monetary contributions from American slaveholders. Douglass' observation of Cunningham's defense is nearly identical to the one put forth to on the floor of the synod at the General Synod of the Reformed Protestant Dutch church in 1855. Douglass asserts, "the Doctor proceeded with his speech—abounding in logic, learning, and eloquence, and apparently bearing down all opposition; but at the moment—the fatal moment—when he was just bringing all his arguments to a point, and that point being that 'neither Jesus Christ nor his holy apostles regarded slaveholding as a sin'" (p. 257).

Critical to How's argument was also the dehumanization and stereotyping of African peoples, ostensibly designed to suggest that their enslavement was beneficial. How asserts:

> The inhabitants of Western Africa are somewhat above the savage state... their religion consists of the worst forms of idolatry...their religion sheds no purifying or elevating influences over their minds, but cherishes and strengthens every impure and debased passion...universally ignorant, without any moral restraint, and ruled by the worst passions whose sway is uncontrolled, they know not what good government is...contemplated from any point of view, this portion of Africa "presents little else to the eye of humanity than one vast continent of sin, misery, and superstition. (pp. 75–77, 83–84)

Believing that slavery is evidence of God's judgment, How concludes that, "Christianity, while it civilizes the slave, improves him in all parts of his character...it takes away piecemeal the mass of barbarian ignorance, superstition, and corruption...it is advantageous to their whole physical, intellectual, and moral nature...it makes the slaves better, more intelligent... better men...better servants of God" (p. 46). Again, in the context of anthropology and human subjectivity, from a pastoral perspective, we are compelled to ask how this attitude has been passed down intergenerationally and manifests itself in latent and unconscious forms of missiological and evangelical bigotry. It is undeniable that racism has been foundational in many western discourses on theological anthropology. While many western theologians will use philosophers such as Immanuel Kant or David Hume in developing their arguments, Hopkins (2005) reminds us that, "Usually ignored or covered up are these thinkers' views of Africans and darker-skinned humans. The key issue here is to realize that all of these writings by the so-called brilliant philosophers of Europe privileged upper-class white men" (p. 138).

Even among abolitionists, Frederick Douglass experienced this ingrained bigotry when they encouraged him not to come across in his public speaking as being too educated or too well read. While often overlooked in the discourse of theological anthropology, Hopkins observes that both Immanuel Kant and David Hume conclude that "by natural development or biological creation, white folk are superior in their intellect, their aesthetics, and their right to power over darker-skinned peoples globally" (p. 139). Indeed, Brown Douglass' observation of the discursive and productive elements of power inherent in western Christian thought cannot be overstated in terms of how it underwrote the slavocracy.

This detour to assess the nonphysical aspects of the power of the slavocracy does not minimize the terror and trauma of the material effects of the slavocracy. The terror inflicted upon generations of black bodies and psyches was substantial and far reaching. But to assume that military and police power alone is what constitutes power and oppression is misguided. The focus on the disciplinary and productive aspects of the corrupt power that has underwritten the slavocracy and the democratic experiment is helpful in uncovering how it continues to exist in the legacy of slavery, the ongoing marginalization of subaltern bodies at the hands of white supremacy, and how Christian thought and praxis continue to underwrite structures of oppression. Subjectivity (whether individual or group) is anthropological in nature. How we experience others—especially the marginalized and downtrodden—in contemporary intersubjective milieus has its antecedents in the history of the American democratic experiment. The way we experience each other is passed down intergenerationally.

Thus, we cannot overstate how disciplinary and productive aspects of power inform contemporary Christian discourse. This is because Christian thought and persuasion did not eradicate slavery. A bloody civil war served that purpose. In an antebellum personal reflection on John Brown[4] and Sojourner Truth, Frederick Douglass is all too clear about this point. While he begins with an assumption that persuasion and conversion could end slavery, Douglass ends in a far different place. In speaking of John Brown, Douglass recalls: "when I suggested that we might convert the slaveholders, he became much excited, and said that could never be, 'he knew their proud hearts and that they would never be induced to give up their slaves, until they felt a big stick about their heads'" (p. 281). Douglass admits the impact his interactions with John Brown had on his personal disposition about the efficacy of persuasion alone. When he presents his doubts to Sojourner Truth, he notes, "I was suddenly and sharply interrupted by my good old friend Sojourner Truth with the question, 'Frederick, is God dead?' 'No.' I answered, and 'because God is not dead slavery can only end in blood'" (p. 282).

Western Christianity has far too long taken too much misplaced credit about its role in justice, shalom, and a desire for reconciliation. It often has a misplaced understanding of reconciliation that is divorced from justice, repentance, and lament. If disembodied theologies are children of Platonism and Stoicism, then modernity and the American democratic experiment played a formidable role in raising them. The purpose of such disembodied theology is not to redeem, heal, or save but to control mind(s) for the purposes of the power structure, to prop up evil, and to promote the purposes of its architects. And this remains the legacy of disembodied theology: to sacralize structures of oppression and to conflate Christian praxis and ethics with these elements of the democratic experiment. Carter G. Woodson aptly assesses the telos of disembodied theology by noting that:

> If you can control a man's thinking you do not have to worry about his action. When you determine what a man shall think you do not have to concern yourself about what he will do. If you make a man feel that he is inferior, you do not have to compel him to accept an inferior status, for he will seek it himself. If you make a man think that he is justly an outcast, you do not have to order him to the back door. He will go without being told; and if there is no back door, his very nature will demand one. (Woodson 1933)

Throughout his biographies, when Frederick Douglass appeals to God to "deliver him" from his bondage, he is recognizing that salvation of body, soul, and spirit are inseparable and by extension that redemption of the soul but enslavement of the body are not the divine will. It is only through a disembodied theology, through religious and spiritual reflection that is not in conversation with a pastoral theology of deliverance, that the architects and perpetrators of the slavocracy can rationalize that the enslavement of bodies is consistent with legitimate theological ethics.

CHRISTIAN PARTICIPATION, THE SLAVOCRACY, AND THE DEMONIC

For Douglass then, a pastoral theology of deliverance functioned as soul care and preserved his personhood in an environment in which Christian complicity—both ideologically and materially—represented a key component in the underwriting of the slavocracy. This pastoral theology of deliverance provided Douglass (1845) with the intellectual, spiritual, and emotional currency to say (in the appendix of his first autobiography): "what I have said respecting and against religion, I mean strictly to apply to the slaveholding religion of this land, and with no possible reference to Christianity proper; for, between the Christianity of this land, and the Christianity of Christ, I recognize the widest, possible difference—so wide, that to receive the one as good, pure, and holy, is of necessity to reject the other as bad, corrupt, and wicked" (p. 118).

This theology of deliverance is pastoral in nature because its concern is both for the care of the soul of the one who is suffering or victimized and for the corruption of souls: the souls of individuals and groups whose interior spiritual and psychic space is divided such that radical evil and awareness of the Divine are able to coexist with little to no cognitive, religious, or spiritual dissonance. Such dissonance in a healthy soul should arguably guide the inner and communal moral compass to a radical love, justice, and freedom, both for those existing at the center as well as the subaltern subject. A pastoral theology of deliverance therefore begs a key question: how is it that the heinous acts perpetrated in the slavocracy seemed so right and felt so right to their architects and actors? Toleration of radical evil is degenerative to the human spirit for both victim, direct perpetrators, and bystanders. While the deleterious effects on those victimized in the slavocracy are readily grasped, seldom do we consider the deleterious religious, spiritual, and emotional effects that the slavocracy and its legacy has on the soul of a whole nation: the American psyche.

In no way do I suggest that perpetrators and bystanders in the slavocracy incurred similar harm. Yet we also cannot assume that the only soul-degenerative effects of slavery occurred with its victims and their descendants. While there is a growing amount of commendable literature that reflects upon the traumatic legacy of slavery on African Americans, it seems to be taken for granted that the psychosocial and soul condition of those existing at the center—along with the democratic experiment itself and Christianity too—was untouched by the evil of the slavocracy.

In a speech at Finsbury Chapel in Moorfields, England, Frederick Douglass (1855) exposed the hypocrisy and paradoxes revealed by Christian complicity in the slavocracy.[5] Apparently there are some that fear Douglass' strong public rebuke of American Christianity will somehow undermine the institutional church and the Christian cause—as it the fear of exposing Christian complicity in the slavocracy was greater than the concern for bodies being broken and destroyed. For perpetrators and bystanders, the attraction to a form or appearance of godliness is both irresistible and intoxicating, but it anesthetizes individuals and groups to the felt power of the Divine both individually and collectively—all the fruit of disembodied theology or the absence of a pastoral theology of deliverance.[6] Thus the corrupting power of the slavocracy was total and complete. Before his British audience in Moorfields, Douglass was clear in proclaiming: "slavery is a system of wrong, so blinding to all around, so hardening to the heart, so corrupting to the morals, so deleterious to religion, so sapping to all the principles of justice in its immediate vicinity, that the community surrounding it lack the moral stamina necessary to its removal" (pp. 416–417). The toleration of the slavocracy and its ubiquitous violence necessarily ossifies the capacity of the human heart and soul to grieve and lament the material outcome of violence, evil, and suffering. The toleration of pure evil such as the slavocracy compromises, distorts, and ultimately deadens individual and collective capacities necessary to engender mercy and compassion that leads to embodied morality and justice and pastoral or theological ethics that underwrite the operationalization of Divine shalom. In such a condition, the individual and communal practice of constructing theologies and Christian praxis is necessarily flawed and corrupted.

In courses about human suffering and trauma, I tell my students that not all suffering is redemptive, no matter how contemporary church discourse romanticizes the docile sufferer. If we are to maintain a sense of integrity in theological reflection, we have to be clear that persons would have been better off had they not incurred the violence that led to their suffering. This category of suffering is what I refer to as suffering without agency. Suffering without agency necessarily degenerates the human spirit. But it also degenerates the spirit of those who are aware of, witness, or hear about the plight of those who suffer without agency and yet do not participate in, witness, or call for the liberation and justice of those who are oppressed. In doing nothing, they become a little less human. While it can in no way be reasonably argued that the victimizer or perpetrators of the slavocracy suffered to that of the victimized, the soul condition of both degenerated. The toleration of radical evil leaves no part of human existence untouched. The slavocracy thus also affects those generations who came long after it ended. This legacy is manifested mostly in an enterprise of disembodied theologies in the church and the academy that show little courage, coherence, competence, or basic interest and desire to engage and dismantle structures of evil and to care for and uplift the least of these among us. Such theologies are instead infatuated with a politic of assimilation or the latent nature of cultural enclaves that prioritize cognitive virtuoso of doctrines, creeds, and confessions, along with a corresponding (and sometimes culturally required) emotional celebration of such mastery, all under the illusion that such practices are inherently salvific (as opposed to them being simply religious symbols, practices, or means that may or may not be redemptive). The twentieth century is rife with examples of the church remaining silent about evil and oppression of those at the margins. Such ecclesial paralysis and pastoral ineptitude fails to make the life-giving embodied connection between religion, theology, and the lived experiences of those outside of the walls of organized religion. And it is not the first time such paralysis has occurred. In the biblical story of the good Samaritan[7] (a representative of the subaltern subject), one wonders whether this was the first time that the priest or Levite passed by someone in need. Passing by on the other side seems to have been done with such muscle memory and absence of thought that we can imagine it was a well-worn practice of disembodied theology.

The toleration of evils such as the slavocracy ultimately leads the realm of demonry—for both individuals and the accommodating society. It has contaminated and ultimately undermined the very idea of the democratic experiment in, both in American history and contemporary idealism. The individual and collective soul condition observed by Frederick Douglass that inspired the power brokers of slavocracy to appeal to Christian scripture and symbolism to underwrite its diabolical schemes is best understood in the sphere of the demonic, as postulated by Paul Tillich (1936). According to Tillich, concern for the demonic was not about spirits per se (as commonly depicted in media) but about the spiritual realm within the human project. Discourse about the demonic tends to be easily dismissed within the academy believing that it somehow leads to conversation that absolves human beings from culpability—especially as it relates to atrocities. But for Tillich, the freedom and the capacity to self-determine and maintain power over oneself are never compromised. Instead, the demonic is reflected what he referred to as a cleavage: a destructive contradiction in the personality of individuals and collective societies. That is to say, possession is not about crazed acts depicted in movies or the absolution of personal culpability and responsibility. Possession reflects divided personhood, whereas spiritual health is a sign of an integrated spiritual consciousness. In this paradigm, the demonic is a distortion of spirit: it doesn't outright eliminate the image of the God in human experience, but it does disfigure and falsify the Divine. In the slavocracy, it misnames radical evil as Divine sovereignty or manifest destiny. It misnames power and domination as Divine election. Frederick Douglass (1855) recognizes this sort of distortion initiated by the demonic and refers to it as priestcraft (presumably a play on witchcraft), suggesting that he and his contemporaries (with the exception of one individual) were free from its slaveholding effects:

> It was in vain that we had been taught from the pulpit at St. Michael's, the duty of obedience to our masters; to recognize God as the author of our enslavement; to regard running away an offense, alike against God and man; to deem our enslavement a merciful and beneficial arrangement; to esteem our condition, in this country, a paradise to that from which we had been snatched in Africa; to consider our hard hands and dark color as God's mark of displeasure, and as pointing us out as the proper subjects of slavery; that the relation of master and slave was one of reciprocal benefits; that our work was not more serviceable to our masters, than our master's thinking was serviceable to us. I say, it was in vain that the pulpit of St. Michael's had constantly inculcated these plausible doctrines. Nature laughed them to scorn. For my own part, I had now become altogether too big for my chains. (pp. 275–276)

Examples of the perversion wrought by the cleavage of spiritual consciousness and personality are manifold through Douglass' autobiographies. In one instance, Douglass (1855) describes the vicious change and demeanor in personality of the plantation owner Master Thomas—precipitated by a conversion to Christianity. According to Douglass, Master Thomas became all the more brutal, even using scripture during his brutalization of bodies, after his Christian transformation:

> I saw in him all the cruelty and meanness, after his conversion, which he had exhibited before he made a profession of religion. His cruelty and meanness were especially displayed in his treatment of my unfortunate cousin, Henny...I have seen him tie up the lame and maimed woman, and whip her in a manner most brutal, and shocking; and then, with blood-chilling blasphemy, he would quote the passage of scripture, "That servant which knew his lord's will, and prepared not himself, neither did according to his will, shall be beaten with many stripes."[8] (pp. 200–201)

In another frightening example of the demonic cleavage of consciousness, Douglass describes the atmosphere in the house of Edward Covey, known for his ability not only to break in enslaved victims but also for his supposed stringent religious devotions and commitment to a so-called good Christian life. The intensity of his alleged Christian worship and commitment seemed to have had no bearing on his desire to purchase a female victim of the slavocracy for the sole purpose of having her raped in order to bear subsequent generations of enslaved victims. This example again is given to highlight the demonic realm evidenced in the divided soul. Douglass observes of Covey that "the voice of praise, as well as of prayer, must be heard in his house, night and morning...his religion was a thing altogether apart from his worldly concerns...he knew nothing of it as a holy principle, directing and controlling his daily life, making the latter conform to the requirements of the gospel" (p. 217).

Thus Christian complicity and collaboration underwrote the religious and sociopolitical structures that propped up the system of evil and was a manifestation of the demonic: a spiritual sickness that reflects the absence of a pastoral theology of deliverance. Over the long run, the toleration of slavery—whether by perpetrators or bystanders—necessarily precipitates the demonic state. As an example of the long-term degenerative effects even on bystanders, in characterizing Miss Sophia (the wife of one of his enslavers) Douglass (1881) expresses his fondness of her because of her kind affections toward him when he first arrived in Baltimore, as well as the fact that she initially began to teach him how to read. But he is clear about what he perceives to be the long-term effects of the slavocracy even on bystanders, "for slavery could change a saint into a sinner, and an angel into a demon" (p. 68). Miss Sophia's desire to teach Frederick Douglass how to read slowly dissipated when Hugh Auld, her husband, strongly discouraged it as an inappropriate practice. Her disposition didn't change suddenly, but over time the environment of the slavocracy degenerated her personhood:

> The fatal poison of irresponsible power, and the natural influence of slave customs, were not very long in making their impression on the gentle and loving disposition of my excellent mistress. She regarded me at first as a child, like any other. This was the natural and spontaneous thought; afterwards, when she came to consider me as property, our relations to each other were changed, but a nature so noble as hers could not instantly become perverted, and it took several years before the sweetness of her temper was wholly lost. (p. 69)

Understood in this light, it is easy to conceptualize how the history and legacy of slavery in the United States represents the heritage of the demonic and pure evil. The demonic captures the individual and collective depth of human depravity and provocation in a way that cannot be conceptualized by psychological categories. In describing the horrific events of June 7, 1998, in which John William King and two accomplices lynched (via dragging behind a car) and ultimately decapitated James Byrd Jr., Baker-Fletcher (2006) uses the category of the demonic:

> Although some view King as a monster, he is more accurately a fallen human being who rejects divine grace in a fallen world...While King may be a human being, he did act monstrously. Or, in the language of Paul Tillich, he allowed himself to be motivated by "the demonic," a condition in which a finite individual or social structure claims divinity. The demonic suppresses obedience to structures of truth and distorts humanity. King chose inhumane devolution, rather than an ascent into the humanity of God ... to reject God's prevenient, justifying, and sanctifying grace is to descend into inhumanity ... King, in his descent into demonic rage, rejected the divine call to realize full humanity in God. (p. 115)

While some in academics may trivialize or dismiss the category of the demonic as dualism, Cooper-White (2003) warns against the automatic tendency to dismiss the existence of evil. She observes that "the vast majority of survivors of trauma have not read Augustine, and are unfamiliar with scholarly arguments about theodicy...they do, however, present themselves to us as legitimate experts on the experience of suffering, and the sense of personal acquaintance with evil" (p. 72).

DELIVERANCE AND BLACK LIBERATION THEOLOGY

The theology of deliverance I am proposing aligns closely with twentieth-century black neo-Pentecostal and charismatic traditions. With its focus on the interior space and inner spirituality, it is not that dissimilar from the goals and objectives of black liberation theology. Examined through the life of Frederick Douglass, it is conceivable that the theological tasks of liberation theology and the interior-focused theology of various black neo-Pentecostal and charismatic traditions are not mutually exclusive. They can be simultaneously embodied in one person. In his observation of black theology and Pentecostalism in the twentieth century, Ray (2009) argues that Classical Pentecostalism and Black Theology (which takes black experience as its point of departure) are more similar than dissimilar given their commitments to Christian discourse and its response to the systematic oppression of peoples of color. In speaking of Classical Pentecostalism, Ray suggests "given its emergence during what many scholars call the nadir of Black existence in the twentieth century and given its explicit rejection of the idolatrous mythology of Anglo-Saxonism and Aryanism which had defiled much of the Christian faith in the United States during that period, it is relatively easy to see the corollaries between Classical Pentecostalism and Black theology" (p. 5).

A pastoral theology of deliverance, which I consider to be a variation on the theme of liberation, encompasses the reality that here in the temporal realm radical evil will often prevail in the oppression or outright destruction of bodies. In the face of few material alternatives, a theology of deliverance seeks to protect the soul and psychic space from being overwhelmed by the evil (which in this case was the slavocracy) that permeates the intersubjective milieu. The Pauline epistle speaks to this construct in the second letter to the Corinthians when the writer notes that "we do not lose heart...[for] though our outer nature is wasting away, our inner nature is being renewed day by day."[9] Given the inescapable external affliction, the focus is on internal healing and protection of the soul.

Various Womanist theologians capture well how to protect the inner soul from suffering and healing as they expose how external structures of evil in society and in the black church have wreaked harm and suffering upon black women and their experience of selfhood. In her article examining a theology of suffering, Copeland (2011) focuses on the internal turmoil wrought by structural evil. She notes: "I understand suffering as the disturbance of our inner tranquility caused by physical, mental, emotional, and spiritual forces that we grasp as jeopardizing our lives, our very existence" (p. 136). While she does not say it explicitly, what Copeland describes is suffering that is intrapsychic, a peril that damages selfhood and soul. This is precisely the concern of a pastoral theology of deliverance. In a theological and religious approach that to many appears as an overextended focus on spirituality, for the sufferer, deliverance for the inner self represents a major liberation objective. It is an internal suffering that is precipitated by the same perpetrators of external structures of evil that black liberation theology addresses. Copeland concludes that "womanist theology claims the experiences of Black women as proper and serious data for theological reflection … a womanist theology of suffering is rooted in and draws on Black women's accounts of pain and anguish, of their individual and collective struggle to grasp and manage, rather than be managed by their suffering" (p. 139). Addressing this internal struggle is part of the liberation agenda.

WHERE DOES DOUGLASS SITUATE HIMSELF THEOLOGICALLY?

The following two passages from Douglass on theology and religion may seem to reflect distinct theological poles in his life. In the first passage, Douglass (1855) recounts his religious awakening as a child and his religious mentor, a black man referred to as Uncle/Father Lawson, who was the instigator of Douglass' conversion:

> I was not more than thirteen years old, when I felt the need of God, as a father and protector … I consulted a good colored man, named Charles Johnson; and, in tones of holy affection, he told me to pray, and what to pray for. I was, for weeks, a poor, broken-hearted mourner, traveling through the darkness and misery of doubts and fears. I finally found that change of heart which comes by "casting all one's care" upon God, and by having faith in Jesus Christ, as the Redeemer, Friend, and Savior of those who diligently seek Him. After this, I saw the world in a new light. I seemed to live in a new world, surrounded by new objects, and to be animated by new hopes and desires. I loved all mankind—slaveholders not excepted;

though I abhorred slavery more than ever. My great concern was, now, to have the world converted. The desire for knowledge increased...While thus religiously seeking knowledge, I became acquainted with a good old colored man, named Lawson. A more devout man than he, I never saw...This man not only prayed three times a day, but he prayed as he walked through the streets, at his work—on his dray—everywhere. His life was a life of prayer, and his words, (when he spoke to his friends,) were about a better world...becoming deeply attached to the old man, I went often with him to prayer-meeting, and spent much of my leisure time with him on Sunday. The old man could read a little, and I was a great help to him, in making out the hard words, for I was a better reader than he. I could teach him "the letter," but he could teach me "the spirit;" and high, refreshing times we had together, in singing, praying and glorifying God (pp. 166–167)

The God-talk that Douglass employs here intimates the tasks of a theology of deliverance, such as internal piety and renewal, and was consistent both with hush-arbor slave religion and also with many twentieth-century black neo-Pentecostal and charismatic traditions. That he uses language of "the spirit" and "glorifying God" while still enslaved seems to be deliberate and expresses his objective and his force of being, namely, to claim the agency to imagine and experience one's subjectivity and body interdependently within the intersubjective milieu in which one is embedded. Compare the previous passage with the following one Douglass (1881) included at the end of book 3, and that reads like a preamble to black liberation theology. In speaking of his black contemporaries, Douglass stresses:

That neither institutions nor friends can make a race to stand unless it has strength in its own legs; that there is no power in the world which can be relied upon to help the weak against the strong—the simple against the wise; that races like individuals must stand or fall by their own merits; that all the prayers of Christendom cannot stop the force of a single bullet, divest arsenic of poison, or suspend any law of nature. In my communication with the colored people I have endeavored to deliver them from the power of superstition, bigotry, and priest-craft. In theology I have found them strutting about in the old clothes of the masters, just as the masters strut about in the old clothes of the past. The falling power remains among them long since it has ceased to be the religious fashion of our refined and elegant white churches. I have taught that the "fault is not in our stars but in ourselves that we are underlings," that "who would be free, themselves must strike the blow." I have urged upon them self-reliance, self-respect, industry, perseverance, and economy—to make the best of both worlds—but to make the best of this world first because it comes first, and that he who does not improve himself by the motives and opportunities afforded by this world gives the best evidence that he would not improve in any other world. Schooled as I have been among the abolitionists of New England, I recognize that the universe is governed by laws which are unchangeable and eternal, that what men sow they will reap, and that there is no way to dodge or circumvent the consequences of any act or deed. My views at this point receive but limited endorsement among my people. They for the most part think they have means of procuring special favor and help from the Almighty, and as their "faith is the substance of things hoped for and the evidence of things not seen," they find much in this expression which is true to faith but utterly false to fact. (pp. 487–488)

While one may not be in agreement with every point raised by Douglass in this passage, its focus on self-reliance and exclusive support from within the black community, its strong urging to focus on things of this world, and the characterization of procuring "special favor" from the "Almighty" as a limited faith are very characteristic of some arguments put forth by black liberation theologians. Such theologians note the undue theological emphasis on internal spirituality, personal piety, and life after death, at the expense of overlooking or dismissing the critical needs of oppressed black people in the temporal realm. This is particularly the case as regards justice and liberation in the face of structural evil and oppression that Christians and others who exist at the center often ignore or deny, though these real and material oppressive structures are foundational to the American democratic experiment.

In his reflection on this silence of the church on racism and oppression, Cone (2012) is clear about the corrective moral mandate when he writes, "I urge white theologians, ministers, and other morally concerned persons to break their silence…it is immoral to see evil and not fight it. As Rabbi Prinz put it: 'Bigotry and hatred are not the most urgent problems. The most urgent, the most disgraceful, the most shameful and most tragic problem is silence'" (p. 152). As such, the critique of both Douglass and various strands of black liberation theology are valid and is very useful in deconstructing how productive and discursive power can undermine the efficacy of black church experience. But are the two theological expressions we see in the previous passages from Frederick Douglass truly different? How do we interpret such seemingly divergent theological perspectives in Douglass? I suggest that they reflect two variations on a constant theme of liberation.

It is common for many scholars who study Frederick Douglass to conclude that there was a significant evolution in his religious perspectives, that he somehow experienced a seismic shift in his theological framework from a heavenly or otherworldly focus to one that was more temporally situated to attend to the needs of black people in the nineteenth century. Interpretations of Douglass along this line are not necessarily wrong, as reading passages such as the ones previously outlined to some extent signify an evolving religious hermeneutic. However, through the lens of a pastoral theology of deliverance that redeems the internal force of being, I raise three alternative considerations:

First, I suggest that what we witness in Douglass' thought is not a theological evolution but more of a variation on the very complex and multidimensional theme of liberation. Douglass' encounter with the religion of those victimized by the slavocracy earlier in his life was just as salvific to his personhood as what appeared to be a move toward a liberation theology later in his life. The variation that seems like a shift could also reflect theological adaptation based on context. Second, a focus on inner spirituality or otherworldliness does not *necessarily predispose* a person or group to passivity as it relates to liberation any more than a formal adoption of a liberation hermeneutic *necessarily predisposes* one to a liberation praxis. Thirdly, Frederick Douglass' early God-talk can conceivably be conceptualized as a theology of deliverance that focused on the liberation of psychic space. Again, the proposed pastoral theology of deliverance for Douglass emerged in a context of existing in extremity, where liberation via a literal escape from the southern plantation system was unrealistic due to the physical constraints and power of the slavocracy. As such, in this third proposed alternative argument, the decision to attempt a physical escape was necessarily determined by the person and the context. When physical escape was not feasible, he sought *liberation in fact* as opposed to *liberation in physical form*. While it is undeniable that Douglass underwent an evolution of faith, this interpretation alone is insufficient. His context also affected his faith. The construction of Douglass' theology, whether internally or externally focused, was in large part a derivative of intersubjective matrix, agency, and subjectivity that was propped up by an interior force of being (i.e. his theology as a free man took on a different tone from when he was enslaved) but still reflected in each instance a liberation agenda.

Over the course of four autobiographies that spanned nearly 50 years, Douglass never speaks about his earlier life in a way that suggests he either regrets or views his theology (while victimized on the southern plantation) as flawed. Though he had ample opportunity to do so over the course of his writings, he never goes back on his early God-talk. I believe this is the case because fundamentally, his theology was beneficial to survival and to cultivating his interior force of being. When reflecting on his own thoughts during the time of his enslavement about the alleged conversion of his master Thomas Auld, Douglass (1855) makes the following observations:

> "If he has got religion," thought I, "he will emancipate his slaves; and if he should not do so much as this, he will, at any rate, behave toward us more kindly, and feed us more generously than he has heretofore done." Appealing to my own religious experience, and judging my master by what was true in my own case, I could not regard him as soundly converted, unless some such good results followed his profession of religion...But in my expectations I was doubly disappointed; Master Thomas was Master Thomas still. The fruits of his righteousness were to show themselves in no such way as I had anticipated. His conversion was not to change his relation toward men—at any rate not toward BLACK men—but toward God. There was something in his appearance that, in my mind, cast a doubt over his conversion...Slaveholders may, sometimes, have confidence in the piety of some of their slaves; but the slaves seldom have confidence in the piety of their masters. "He can't go to heaven with our blood in his skirts," is a settled point in the creed of every slave; rising superior to all teaching to the contrary, and standing forever as a fixed fact. The highest evidence the slaveholder can give the slave of his acceptance with God, is the emancipation of his slaves. This is proof that he is willing to give up all to God, and for the sake of God. Not to do this, was, in my estimation, and in the opinion of all the slaves, an evidence of half-heartedness, and wholly inconsistent with the idea of genuine conversion. (pp. 194–196)

Not only was there a crystalized and sound theological framework in hush-arbor religion, it also guided victims of the slavocracy in terms of praxis (i.e. authentic evidence of conversion). The above words reflect his mode of thinking and also the thinking of all those who were enslaved. This capacity to reject slaveholder religion, underwritten in large part by his own theology, protected Douglass' internal force of being and selfhood from being overrun by the ideologies that undergirded the slavocracy. The religion and theology of the enslaved victims protected them from internalizing the theology of the colonizer. We see this again when Douglass (1855) declares "I shall here make a profession of faith which may shock some, offend others, and be dissented from by all" (p. 190). In the following profession of faith, Douglass is reacting to the context of extremity to which he and other slaves were exposed, and he offers a theological-ethical construct that can only victims of the slavocracy can understand:

> The morality of free society can have no application to slave society. Slaveholders have made it almost impossible for the slave to commit any crime, known either to the laws of God or to the laws of man. If he steals, he takes his own; if he kills his master, he imitates only the heroes of the revolution. Slaveholders I hold to be individually and collectively responsible for all the evils which grow out of the horrid relation, and I believe they will be so held at the judgment, in the sight of a just God. Make a man a slave, and you rob him of moral responsibility. Freedom of choice is the essence of all accountability. But my kind readers are, probably, less concerned about my opinions, than about that which more nearly touches my personal experience; albeit, my opinions have, in some sort, been formed by that experience. (p. 191)

These theological tenets are born out of Douglass' earlier experiences within slave religion. His encounter with "traditional" religion was conducive to the liberation agenda, a liberation of the psyche and soul. Within the context of the slavocracy, the greatest act of liberation would have been to speak out against slavery, to encourage slave revolt and escape, or to enact a slave revolt or escape. In several places where Douglass reflects on his thoughts of escape and freedom, he attributes his capacity and courage to act on his convictions largely to the instruction, theology, and God-talk he amassed in slave religion under the tutelage of his mentor, Uncle Lawson. Much of this description is strikingly similar to and consistent with contemporary God-talk in black church theology and black neo-Pentecostal circles:

> But my chief instructor, in matters of religion, was Uncle Lawson. He was my spiritual father...The good old man had told me, that the "Lord had a great work for me to do;" and I must prepare to do it; and that he had been shown that I must preach the gospel. His words made a deep impression on my mind, and I verily felt that some such work was before me, though I could not see how I should ever engage in its performance. "The good Lord," he said, "would bring it to pass in his own good time," and that I must go on reading and studying the scriptures. The advice and the suggestions of Uncle

Lawson, were not without their influence upon my character and destiny. He threw my thoughts into a channel from which they have never entirely diverged. He fanned my already intense love of knowledge into a flame, by assuring me that I was to be a useful man in the world. When I would say to him, "How can these things be—and what can I do?" his simple reply was, "Trust in the Lord." When I told him that "I was a slave, and a slave FOR LIFE," he said, "the Lord can make you free, my dear. All things are possible with him, only have faith in God." "Ask, and it shall be given." "If you want liberty," said the good old man, "ask the Lord for it, in faith, AND HE WILL GIVE IT TO YOU." (pp. 168–169)

The liberal sprinkling of "spiritual" talk here indicates a theology of deliverance. It provides the individual with the requisite God-talk and sin talk to free one's internal force of being and selfhood for a liberation agenda. For those who existed in extremity and have long subsisted on the underside of modernity, spiritual talk represents a major theological resource, especially when one has few or no other resources from which to pull. On the eve of his first (although failed) escape attempt, Douglass describes in detail a theology of deliverance that echoes slave theology but outright contradicts what was preached from the Methodist pulpit. This enabled Douglass and his contemporaries to enact a liberation agenda of escape. But more tellingly, Douglass recalls the "prophecies" of Father Lawson and suggests that based on his childhood prophecies (received in traditional slave religion), he could no longer remain enslaved:

We were all, except Sandy, quite free from slave-holding priestcraft. It was in vain that we had been taught from the pulpit at St. Michael's, the duty of obedience to our masters; to recognize God as the author of our enslavement; to regard running away an offense, alike against God and man; to deem our enslavement a merciful and beneficial arrangement; to esteem our condition, in this country, a paradise to that from which we had been snatched in Africa; to consider our hard hands and dark color as God's mark of displeasure, and as pointing us out as the proper subjects of slavery; that the relation of master and slave was one of reciprocal benefits; that our work was not more serviceable to our masters, than our master's thinking was serviceable to us. I say, it was in vain that the pulpit of St. Michael's had constantly inculcated these plausible doctrines. Nature laughed them to scorn. For my own part, I had now become altogether too big for my chains. Father Lawson's solemn words, of what I ought to be, and might be, in the providence of God, had not fallen dead on my soul. I was fast verging toward man hood, and the prophecies of my childhood were still unfulfilled. (pp. 275–276)

Clearly, the religion of those victimized by the slavocracy did possess a rich theology, and this spiritual theology of deliverance had a liberation agenda. Douglass and his contemporaries understood that the sin was not in disobeying their masters but in accepting and internalizing the death-laden preaching coming from the pulpits in the slavocracy. Such slave theology emanates from a dialogue between biblical narrative and the embodied experiences of enslaved black women and men. This theology is then deeply inscribed in oral tradition and community rather than the written word. And why not? After all, in western church history, usage of the written text did little to deter a Native American genocide, centuries of African slave trade and enslavement, or even a twentieth-century Holocaust. The consistency of oral tradition reflects the ministry of the Holy Spirit in community. The writer of 1 John 2:26–27 (ESV) contends "I write these things to you about those who are trying to deceive you. But the anointing that you received from him abides in you, and you have no need that anyone should teach you. But as his anointing teaches you about everything—and is true and is no lie, just as it has taught you—abide in him." In short, in the context of deception and the slavocracy, Douglass and his contemporaries did not have to depend on the teaching of their slave masters. Instead, the Holy Spirit would lead them to the truth.

The religion of black people victimized in the slavocracy and a theology of deliverance derive its currency from the function of Spirit. This emphasis on the Spirit Baker-Fletcher (1997) captures in her piece "The Strength of My Life" where she posits that for many black women, the Spirit represents the driving source of power and strength in every area of their lives. The Spirit is not clearly demarcated as the third person in the Trinity but "is the all-encompassing, inclusive force in which God/Creator, Jesus, and all of creation are inextricably enwombed" (p. 124). In another place, Baker-Fletcher and Baker-Fletcher (2002) takes care to emphasize that the Spirit in womanist discourse in not about inert exercises in affect and emotion. Instead "it involves head and heart, reason and feeling ... we name and see God daily in small ways by giving witness to the palpable Spirit of God who touches humankind and all of creation through our own daily acts of struggle for justice, love, peace, and respect of others" (p. 35). In her work on theological anthropology, Copeland (2010) likewise connects the work of Spirit to emotional wholeness and well-being. Copeland conceptualizes the embodiment of spirit when she asserts that "incarnate spirit refuses to be bound...[E]scaping to freedom, purchasing one's own freedom or that of a loved one, fighting for freedom, offering up one's own body for the life and freedom of another, and dying for freedom were acts of redemption that aimed to restore black bodily and psychic integrity" (p. 46). When speaking of the importance of the Holy Spirit in a theology of deliverance, the reliance on Spirit does not represent an arbitrary free-for-all where one is unable to distinguish between that which does and does not emanate from the Spirit of God. Townes (1995) connects knowing the Holy Spirit to knowing love, loving God, and loving others. For Townes, "knowing the Spirit is to use both heart and head ... it is to lean into God's word as both salvation and challenge ... it is to allow ourselves to experience and live out of the experience of being wrapped in God's love and peace ... it is to witness out of the hope we grow into with the Spirit" (p. 143). It was this power of the Spirit that underwrote slave religion, and it is this power that continues to underwrite a theology of deliverance.

The suggestion that a religious framework which focuses on personal piety and internal spirituality renders persons passive to a life-giving liberation agenda is not without merit. However, as a practical theologian, I believe such a position reflects a zero-sum construct whereby the agenda of liberation and a theology of deliverance (or traditional slave religion or black neo-Pentecostalism) are needlessly mutually exclusive. black church theology that focuses on internal spirituality and piety does not necessarily predispose one to be inattentive to the agenda of liberation any more than embracing the tenets of liberation theology necessarily predisposes one to enact objectives of liberation. An individual or group could decide that they are better off by living in a way that benefits from evil power structures instead of working to dismantle the oppressive power structures that construct class/caste systems. Such an argument seems to scapegoat individuals who hold alternative conceptions about how best to achieve the liberation of the community.

The prime case in point is Frederick Douglass himself. In the context of nineteenth-century slavery, far before Douglass began to refine his theological arguments, he enacted the ultimate goal of liberation; he made the decision to attempt an escape from the southern plantation system. This liberation agenda of escape was fueled in large part by his existing religious framework at the time. It was only *after* Douglass had escaped from slavery and found himself in the company of other abolitionists that he formally began to refine his theological positions to more of what some scholars view as liberative. *But it is important to note that the context changed for Douglass at this point. While his environment in the north was not without its perils, it was definitely more conducive to safety and theological reflection than the southern slavocratic environment.* Andrews' (2002) warns against the propensity of black theology to denigrate or judge the internally focused spirituality of many black churches and denominations:

> Reliance upon the spiritual resources of the tradition does not necessarily indicate a defeated drive for equality. Contrary to many black theologians' assertions, black churches turned to these spiritual resources in the very pursuit of liberation. Hampered by the lack of political and economic power, black churches possessed few resources beyond the spiritual and moral dimensions of their religious faith...One cannot condemn a people's struggle for survival...What is at stake, here, is the role of refuge in the hermeneutics of liberation. (p. 55)

Lastly, what appears to be a shift in Douglass' theological position to more liberative purposes derived largely from his context, agency, and subjectivity. Recall the effect it had on Douglass to witness Nelly resisting being flogged by her overseer. Douglass subsequently argued that when enslaved victims possess the courage to stand up against the overseer, they become free persons even though her material reality may remain unchanged. I believe such a position is a by-product of a pastoral theology of deliverance, as the inner person was protected and secured while the external situation remained tenuous. Can we truly judge or dismiss Douglass' position by arguing that his notion of a "virtual" freeman or a freeman in "spirit" was not misplaced or lacked an authentic liberation heartbeat and that only those who successfully escaped or chose revolt were truly enlightened? A focus on internal spirituality does not necessarily represent a weaker position on the liberation front. I suggest that instead of only resisting structures of evil and oppression, the black liberation agenda must be expanded to include living, persevering, building, and creating, for the ones we love and for the sake of love itself—regardless of those who hate us and seek to destroy us.

Notes

1. Clearly it is recognized that even today, suggesting that historical atrocities such as slavery are viewed as clearly wrong by most contemporary religious leaders and scholars is—dare I say—relatively presumptuous, as there remains a multitude of interpretations regarding Christian complicity in what may now be viewed historically as crimes against humanity.

2. James 2:19.
3. This observation cannot be overstated regarding the brand of Christian discourse that underwrote the slavocracy and other crimes against humanity that have been instrumental in conducting the American democracy experiment. Such memories and histories are elements that the discursive power of occidental Christianity seeks to erase from its religious practices and theological reflections.
4. John Brown is known as the architect of the raid on the US arsenal at Harpers Ferry, Virginia. He is credited by many scholars as being among the progenitors of the Civil War.
5. Frederick Douglass delivers a reception speech on May 12, 1846 in Moorfields, England, at the Finsbury Chapel.
6. Adapted in connection with 2 Timothy 3:5.
7. Luke 10:25–37.
8. The degree of destruction manifested by the demonic reflects nothing short of human innovation in the design and imposition of suffering and oppression. Tillich (1936) postulates, "the possessed state, however, is cleavage of personality...the demonic is visible only when the cleavage of the ego has an ecstatic character, so that with all its destructiveness, it is still creative... thus...do the possessed in evangelical history recognize Christ as Christ" (p. 87).

   The demonic, evidenced in the cleavage of personality, speaks to the capacity for a single individual, group, or institution within western Christianity to operate through divine grace to effectuate good, while simultaneously perpetuating unspeakable acts of death, destruction, and genocide—all condoned and justified by scripture, creeds, confessions, and theological tradition. The possessed state is ego-syntonic in nature such that interior reflexivity is rendered obsolete: it is unable to reflect upon the death-dealing paradoxes and conflicts it has created. The split spiritual personality lacks the coherence and integrity to be touched with the feelings and infirmities of those it oppresses and terrorized. Consequently, the question of how the Christian world can utilize its texts, symbols, and traditions in a manner that facilitates centuries of evil and destruction is necessarily a pastoral theological question: how leads to such individual and collective corruption of the soul?

   Tillich is compelling in his observation that, "the demonic ecstasy brings about weakening of being, disintegration and decay...it reveals the divine, but as a reality which it fears, which it cannot love, with which it cannot unite...this relationship of divine and demonic ecstasy is the explanation of why in religious history the state of grace could so often change into a possessed state and why the moralistic attitude in religion denies both alike" (p. 88). To be sure, there is nothing redemptive about the cleaved consciousness—the demonic state. Even in its recognition of grace and the Divine (*i.e. what have you to do with us...I know who you are...the Holy One of God*), the telos of the demonic is death and destruction (*i.e. send us to the pigs...let us enter them...the unclean spirits came out and entered the pigs... and the herd, numbering about two thousand, rushed down the steep bank into the sea and drowned in the sea*). It is interesting to note in the latter parenthetical reference that the townspeople were more afraid of the healed and redeemed state of the formerly demon-possessed man such that they begged Jesus (the one with compassion and courage to confront the demonic) to leave their town (evidence of the consensus trance of evil). This is consistent with Tillich's observation that the demonic "reveals the divine, but as a reality which it fears, which it cannot love."

9. 2 Corinthians 4:16–18 ESV.

BIBLIOGRAPHY

Andrews, D. P. (2002). *Practical theology for black churches: Bridging black theology and African American folk religion.* Louisville: John Knox Press.

Baker-Fletcher, K. (1997). The strength of my life. In E. M. Townes (Ed.), *Embracing the spirit* (pp. 122–139). Maryknoll: Orbis Books.

Baker-Fletcher, K. (2006). *Dancing with God: The trinity from a womanist perspective.* St. Louis: Chalice Press.

Baker-Fletcher, K., & Baker-Fletcher, G. K. (2002). *My sister, my brother: Womanist and xodus God talk.* Eugene: Wipf and Stock Publishers.

Cone, J. H. (2012). Silence in the face of white supremacy. In D. N. Hopkins & E. P. Antonio (Eds.), *The Cambridge companion to black theology* (pp. 143–155). Cambridge: Cambridge University Press.

Cooper-White, P. (2003). "I do not do the good I want, but the evil I do not want is what I do": The concept of the vertical split in self psychology in relation to Christian concepts of good and evil. *The Journal of Pastoral Theology, 13*(1), 63–84.

Copeland, M. S. (2010). *Enfleshing freedom: Body, race, and being.* Minneapolis: Fortress Press.

Copeland, M. S. (2011). "Wading through many sorrows": Toward a theology of suffering in a womanist perspective. In K. G. Cannon, E. M. Townes, & A. D. Sims (Eds.), *Womanist theological ethics* (pp. 135–154). Louisville: Westminister John Knox Press.

Douglass, F. (1845). *Narrative of the life of Frederick Douglass, an American slave: Written by himself.* Boston: Published at the Anti-Slavery Office.

Douglass, F. (1855). *My bondage and my freedom.* New York: Miller, Orton & Mulligan.

Douglass, F. (1881). *Life and times of Frederick Douglass: His early life as a slave, his escape from bondage, and his complete history to the present time.* Hartford: Park Publishing Company.

Douglass, K. B. (2005). *What's faith got to do with it? Black bodies/Christian souls.* Maryknoll: Orbis Books.

Fluker, W. E. (1990). They looked for a city: A comparison of the idea of community in Howard Thurman and Martin Luther King, Jr. *Journal of Religious Ethics, 18*(2), 33–55.

Hopkins, D. N. (2005). *Being human: Race, culture, and religion.* Minneapolis: Fortress Press.

How, S. B. (1856). *Slaveholding not sinful: Slavery, the punishment of man's sin, its remedy, the Gospel of Christ.* New Brunswick: J. Terhune's Press.

Ray, S. G. (2009). Not as far off as once thought: Black theology and pentecostalism. In *American Academy of Religion Annual Conference*, Chicago.

Tillich, P. (1936). *The interpretation of history.* New York: Charles Scribner's Sons.

Townes, E. M. (1995). *In a blaze of glory: Womanist spirituality as social witness.* Nashville: Abingdon Press.

Woodson, C. G. (1933). *The mis-education of the Negro.* Washington, DC: The Associated Publishers.

CHAPTER 7

Remembering, Lament, and Public Ritual: Redeeming the Democratic Experiment

This chapter imagines the possibilities of redeeming the democratic experiment from the ongoing legacy of the slavocracy through the practices of remembering and lament using communal and public ritual. The legacy of the slavocracy remains entrenched in the emotional, spiritual, and psychic space of the democracy if we are not intentional about addressing it with countermeasures. Remembering, lament, and ritual are three such countermeasures. The Eucharist event offers a particularly compelling model for such public rituals of remembering and lament. Frederick Douglass understood well that how the story of the Civil War was told and remembered would have profound implications on the spiritual and emotional welfare of the nation—especially for black Americans.

The psychosocial urge to forget the tragic history of slavery in America, to deny how it was foundational to the national identity, and to ignore the present-day effects of this forgetting are all symptoms of defenses employed to maintain illusions of safety and innocence and to alleviate guilt and shame that stems from a painful history. Across many institutions within the democracy, whether it be the church, theological education, or the sociopolitical sphere, overcoming the entrenched practice of "not talking about" or "denying that oppression exists" is indeed a formidable practice that has deleterious effects if left unchallenged. Compelling individuals and communities to remember, mourn, and lament human tragedy is a practice consistent with pastoral sensibilities and pastoral ethics, as it promotes spiritual and psychological health, and emotional well-being. Master narratives

© The Author(s) 2018
D. G. Gibson, *Frederick Douglass, a Psychobiography*,
Black Religion/Womanist Thought/Social Justice,
https://doi.org/10.1007/978-3-319-75229-7_7

within the intersubjective matrix that forget the past, or remember in a disingenuous way, only perpetuate the legacy of the slavocracy in our collective psychic space. The communal effects of not remembering to mourn human tragedy are far from innocuous and have a profound impact on the clinical and spiritual state of individuals and groups. For black America and others at the margin, it reinforces a kind of cultural trauma. For white America (and others laboring to exist at the center), there is damage as well: the internalization of a caricature of American history and an illusion of an American dream—the illusion of whiteness—that all but ossifies the individual and collective soul in its capacity to recognize and dismantle structures of oppression, effectuate justice, and to care for the least of these among us.

The American democratic experiment has been crafted and fashioned by the unmourned legacy of slavery. The intersubjective matrix that embodies the democracy does not only consist of interpersonal relationships but also of historical and master narratives that form political, social, religious, class, and gender discourses. These unspoken meta-narratives inform how a person or group experiences herself as either spiritually and emotionally cohesive and compensated or fragmented and decompensated. Having examined how Frederick Douglass came to experience his selfhood in a way that propelled him to become one of the greatest thinkers of the nineteenth century, I now propose a pastorally—and psychoanalytically—informed public theology whose goal is the formation of an intersubjective milieu that no longer denies a tragic national history and its effect on individual subjectivity and psychic space. In addition to a pastoral theology of deliverance, I employ a model of the Eucharist that invites us to partake as often as we can as an intersubjective exercise that remembers and mourns the human tragedy imposed upon the subaltern by the dictates of empire. Publicly sharing in each other's suffering, especially the suffering of the marginalized, instead of ignoring that suffering, can begin to redeem the soul of the democratic experiment. Furthermore, a pastoral theology for the internal force of being better positions us to recognize how the psychosocial defenses of large groups (such as repression, moralization, and rationalization) have hijacked the western intersubjective milieu in favor of normalizing whiteness. Indeed, history is active (and can even repeat itself) in the present-day transference and counter-transference that plays out between individuals and groups when we ignore or repress the painful elements of the past. To this end, my proposed pastoral theology calls us to remember and lament the history and legacy of slavery for the sake of healing and reclaiming black subjectivity, and for the sake of redeeming the democratic experiment.

This is a monumental and contentious task, as history reminds us. Noted historian James Horton (1999) recalls Virginian Governor James Gilmore's declaration in 1998 that April be Confederate History Month. In comments at the time, Gilmore recognized the inhumanity of slavery and, as such, publically condemned the institution. The public backlash over the Governor's comment about slavery was immense. Horton observes:

> R. Wayne Byrd, president of Virginia's Heritage Preservation Association, labeled Governor Gilmore's reference to slavery an insult to the state and as bowing to what Byrd termed the political pressure of "racist hate groups such as the NAACP." He took issue with Gilmore's negative description of slavery, painting instead a picture of the plantation worthy of mid-nineteenth century proslavery apologists. It is alarming that at the end of the twentieth century, in a public statement, Byrd could call the slave plantation of the old South a place "where master and slave loved and cared for each other and had genuine family concern." (p. 25)

Horton goes on to note many such attempts to romanticize the interpretation of historical events. One is left to imagine why such an outrage manifested around this event. This is why I argue that historical and contemporary meta-narratives that prop up the illusion of a pure western democracy also underwrite the individual selfhood and subjectivity of those who stand to benefit the most from the democracy. Consequently I suggest that the outrage did not come from a place of historical accuracy but from an experience of threatened self-annihilation when a high-ranking figure (the governor) proposed change in the meta-narrative. In another place, Horton observes a woman who was in support of using Confederate flags as symbols of the county high school. Horton states she "claimed that they were neither racist nor a defense of slavery. Besides, she argued, 'Slavery was not all that bad. A lot of people were quite happy to be living on large plantations.' Then, in what seems a contradiction, she added, 'Blacks just need to get over slavery. You can't live in the past'" (p. 27).

It would be naïve to believe that such sentiments do not presently exist in the church and in Christian tradition. Even in today's sociopolitical environment, there remain few boundaries of shame when public officials claim that the last time America was great was during slavery. Group dynamics suggest that individuals who make such public claims reflect the sentiments of a much larger group.

Herein lays the danger of the intersubjective milieu that has not mourned or lamented the history and legacy of slavery: the heritage of the architects and perpetrators of the slavocracy permeates our intersubjective spaces in a way that undermines the health and well-being of individual and collective subjectivity—for both black and white people. Indeed, in my experience as a psychotherapist I have observed on many occasions a white client's extreme anxiety or chronic depression related to his or her self-perceived failure to attain middle-class conceptions of economic and social success, their assumption being that they are entitled to such success. Altman (2010) validates what I have observed in the therapist room when he posits that "whiteness is thus an omnipotent fantasy, a fantasy of mastery and fullness" (p. 103). I see the same effects of denying the heritage of the democratic experiment in the classroom when white students openly challenge the appropriateness of my syllabus or class lectures presenting black authors or what they perceive to be topics for black people. Sometimes this challenge is quite blatant, with a student asking, "What does this have to do with me?" Such students experience white authors as "standard" or "normal," rather than "white." Topics related to structural evil, systemic oppression, or theologies written by women and people of color they experience as off-topic, as they do not believe I can present such themes in a disinterested way (as if my white male counterparts teach in a disinterested way!).

Thus the unmourned legacy of the slavocracy precipitates a spiritual and clinical picture of neurosis and pathology in white subjectivity just as it does in black subjectivity. It does not follow that because an individual or group is in a position of power that their spiritual or clinical picture is normative and should be used as a baseline upon which to judge the psycho-spiritual health of all other people. To speak of a culturally traumatized black subjectivity in the intersubjective milieu necessarily means to speak of the pathology of whiteness and its related subjectivity in the same intersubjective space. Pastoral theology often overlooks this important dynamic. Altman captures this succinctly when he notes:

> What makes the fantasy of whiteness a pathological defense is the way it is paired with blackness as its disavowed double. The search for mastery becomes problematic when it becomes so desperate that it must entail the construction of a subjected group of people and the disavowal of one's own helplessness, that is, when the experience of helplessness is warded off, rather than integrated with the experience of mastery…most fundamentally, racism is a symptom, a manifestation, of an underlying disease that might be defined as an organization of experience around power, or a dominant-submissive structure that affects all of us, black and white alike. (p. 103)

This harm is perpetuated in the church, seminaries, and even in the room of the pastoral psychotherapist. For theologians often overlook and fail to acknowledge the legacy of the slavocracy and racism as a psychosocial and spiritual sickness. It is sin, and it is evil.

In another place, Altman (2004) argues persuasively that macro-level US history is both reflected and reenacted at the individual, small group, and dyadic levels. Altman concludes that as psychoanalysis was transplanted to the United States and as it evolved in a racist and capitalist society, the same dynamics and ideologies that have underwritten ideologies of American superiority became reflected in psychoanalytic discourse and enacted in the therapeutic space. History itself is reenacted in the therapeutic room. Taking a cue from one of his clients, Altman asserts that psychoanalysis in the United States has become a "white thing." In the final analysis, Altman posits:

> Our field thus became largely indifferent to poverty, oppression, discrimination, and the endless practical and psychological problems in living of persons who suffer these conditions...a blind spot was built into our field. Not wanting to see how we had disavowed part of our own backgrounds, our own selves, we took for granted the avoidance of the exploration of race, class, and culture in our clinical work, especially when it entailed the interaction of our own racial, class, and cultural backgrounds with those of our patients. (p. 811)

A black woman that I saw as a psychotherapy client for approximately one year always complained about how various social, economic, and political inequities depressed her when she reflected upon them. Without fail, her conversation during therapy would uncover new stories of injustices, both present and past. At first, I interpreted this as resistance to the therapeutic process and thought it was probably indicative of how she dealt with intimacy and closeness in other relationships. Whatever the reality, I realized that psychodynamic theory and training did not account for or give time and space to how history and narratives can conspire to denigrate individual selfhood, even in the therapy room. History was being reenacted in the therapeutic dyad, as I struggled to attend to the client's internal force of being that sought to reinscribe a counter-narrative in the intersubjective space.

The implications of the unmourned, unlamented intersubjective milieu that is laden with the legacy of slavery are great. In what follows, I unpack some of those implications as they pertain to the seminary, practical theology, and the church community—one small segment of our world. Ray (2008) observes this dilemma in theological education when the pedagogical process runs roughshod over African American religious tradition. The unspoken permeates the intersubjective milieu. The unconscious, high-stakes contest of undergirding selfhood within the pedagogical space of the institution is in play. For Ray, the educational process is undermined for everyone, not just black students, when the religious experiences of non-racialized bodies are rendered as normative. The messaging is that the religious experiences of racialized bodies are rendered as specialized interpretations of Christian tradition. Having attended both a conservative and liberal seminary, I can attest to this phenomenon personally. In each instance, I have struggled significantly not to experience my own religious tradition as negative because it does not align with what others have constructed as normal Christian tradition, whether among the most conservative or the most liberal. Ray observes that:

> Frequently our Black students come away from engagements with church history and various theological traditions with a feeling that their experience is neither present nor relevant, or our white students come away with an ambiguously diachronic sense of ownership and alienation that leads to the experience of their learning of Christian history as being contrived. This situation arises, of course, from one of the great tragedies of American church history, which has been the appropriation of the entire Christian tradition by the regime of white supremacy. By this I mean that it is too often the case that the "mainstream" Christian tradition is rendered as an ethic and racial legacy claimable only by those who share a particular identity. "Others," and their ecclesial traditions, are often treated as quaint interpretations of the tradition but rarely the embodiment of it. (p. 40)

Frederick Douglass understood the power of counter-narrative and remembering history in the intersubjective milieu. The selfhood of African Americans was at stake. This is still relevant today. Students of color, if not careful, can unconsciously learn either to despise or to underappreciate their indigenous faith traditions or mistakenly to interpret Christian tradition as the property of white heritage that must be internalized or sought. It is the perfect example of disciplinary power. Conversely, the unlamented intersubjective milieu harms white students as well, as they are left with an erroneous monolithic perception of the faith, as opposed to a Christian heritage that is ripe with a multiplicity of tradition, experience, and theological content. I recall taking a course during my graduate studies, a course whose title and objective focused on practical theology and African American experience during the Civil Rights era. In short, students were fully aware of what they were signing up for. About midway through the semester, several white students became uncomfortable and disengaged in the course, continuously making the point throughout the semester that white people have also suffered. One white male student even protested, "It's hard being a white male at this school." I recall thinking to myself, "Does he not understand how hard it is every moment of every day to be a black male in this country?"

What was occurring in this classroom was another example of a psychical contest within the intersubjective milieu. To center black history and experience into the pedagogical space white students experienced as a violation of the normal experience of selfhood and was thus rejected as nonnormative. When the "other," through the multiplicity of discourses (like black or womanist theology), pursue the same sense of selfhood, wellbeing, and justice that the majority has grown to experience as normative within the construct of whiteness, white people tend to experience people of color's pursuits or focus as irrelevant to mainstream Christian education and experience. Psychodynamically, we might call this annihilation anxiety. In observing this point in conservative circles, Bakke (1997) argues "there has been some hypocrisy in the evangelical community on these issues. I've watched Christians flock to the suburbs over the years so they could access the best our society could offer for their families, while raising suspicions about those of us who sought transformed communities of justice, peace, health and economic opportunity for those left behind. If we are brothers and sisters in Christ, how can we tolerate such disparities?" (p. 33).

Johnson's (2005) work offers a glimpse into the theological and religious potential of an intersubjective milieu that remembers and embraces the tragedy of slavery and the black experience. In his article "The Middle Passage, Trauma and the Tragic Re-Imagination of African American Theology," Johnson reflects on how African American subjectivity traumatized by the Middle Passage has shaped black theological consciousness. While his ultimate focus is the impact of such subjectivity on African American theological reflection, Johnson's work is useful here for exposing the lingering effects of western intersubjective milieu shaped by the unmourned legacy of slavery. For Johnson, the Middle Passage represents a keystone of western colonialism. It dominated the bodies and suppressed the selfhood and subjectivity of tens of thousands of slaves. The Middle

Passage attempted to erase the memory of a culture. Johnson further holds that the resulting psychological trauma imposed by this horrible historical event was replicated over generations and is still prevalent today. In an effort to justify the oppression of the other, Johnson observes the common portrayal of blacks in the eighteenth and nineteenth centuries as simple and without identity. He notes that while the literature of the time is filled with such notions, "these assumptions, while not explicitly held, are still the operative assumptions of many Europeans as well as African Americans when approaching the historical condition of African America and its historic struggle against the consequences of deeply embedded, culturally ubiquitous racism" (p. 543). However, because colonialism and oppression are commonly viewed and assessed only in political and physical terms, Johnson notes that the real impact and depravity of the Middle Passage is relegated to a "consistent underestimation of the significance of the initial conditions for what we are experiencing today…these initial conditions have determined the evolutionary course of African American cultural consciousness, race relations, as well as, the fragmented, refractory American identity, more broadly conceived" (p. 544). For Johnson, the historicity of the Middle Passage provides explanatory power in uncovering a rich theology and religious experience many would negatively categorize as the "otherworldliness" focus inherent in much of African American religious tradition. His observation is useful in understanding the intergenerational nature of the *harmful* intersubjective milieu created by the slavocracy. The passage of time does little to nothing to correct evil and oppression. He concludes that "it is especially difficult for white Americans to recognize the depth, damage, and violence of the cataclysm because they have had little in their experience to provide for the facilitation of the understanding of the experience at an empathic level… the trauma sustained and perpetuated through institutionalized violence—systemic and systematic, chronic marginalization developed early into a traumatic field that exists with unbroken continuity into the present" (pp. 544–545). This observation by Johnson then begs the question of how we might attend to the traumatic field in question—the ongoing legacy of the slavocracy.

> As Jesus went, the people pressed around him. And there was a woman who had had a discharge of blood for twelve years, and though she had spent all her living on physicians, she could not be healed by anyone. She came up behind him and touched the fringe of his garment, and immediately her discharge of blood ceased. And Jesus said, "Who was it that touched me?"

When all denied it, Peter said, "Master, the crowds surround you and are pressing in on you!" But Jesus said, "Someone touched me, for I perceive that power has gone out from me."[1]

In the above passage, Jesus allowed himself to be "pressed" by those who were rendered abject and marginalized in society. He allowed himself to be consumed in the intersubjective milieu of the subaltern subject. This experience put him in the unintended position of experiencing at close hand a woman who had suffered from a grievous ailment for 12 years, effectively bankrupting her due to ineffective medical treatment. Jesus' close proximity to her rendered this experience transformational, as he experienced a depletion of his own power or virtue that had sustained his selfhood up to that point. Similarly, we must allow our narcissistic virtue to be depleted in such a way that we are able to experience, even in some small way, the sufferings of those forced to exist on the underbelly of the democratic experiment. A pastoral theology of deliverance is Eucharistic in that it demands that we partake in the sufferings of the oppressed, that we witness in solidarity the suffering of the subaltern and how their bodies have been broken by the western democratic experiment. Eucharistic sensibilities posit that communal ritual and lament, commemoration of those lost to systemic oppression and evil, and granting voice to those whose bodies have been broken by the slavocracy and radical evil are all necessary elements of healing, sanctification, and well-being.

This project calls for a pastoral theology and praxis that allows itself to be subsumed in the intersubjective milieu that embraces the fullness of the story of the African American experience and the historic legacy of existence in the slavocracy. This calls for a pastoral theology and praxis that no longer considers the historicity of the African American experience as an outdated topic that is only relevant for black people. A pastoral theology for the interior force of being is necessarily subsumed by proximity in the history and legacy of slavery in the intersubjective milieu. A pastoral theology for the internal force of being recognizes and then mourns how a revisionist history that minimizes, represses, and ignores the culpability of western colonialism and the victimization of generations of African Americans has influenced the collective and individual psyche. A radical historicity then necessarily becomes a part of the theological. Here, W.E.B. DuBois' (1956) call for a hermeneutical ethic in history is relevant:

If history is going to be scientific, if the record of human action is going to be set down with that accuracy and faithfulness of detail which will allow its use as a measuring rod and guidepost for the future of nations, there must be set some standards of ethics in research and interpretation ... *If, on the other hand, we are going to use history for ... inflating our national ego, and giving us a false but pleasurable sense of accomplishment, then we must ... admit frankly that we are using a version of historic fact in order to influence and educate the new generation along the way we wish ... It is propaganda like this that has led men in the past to insist that history is "lies agreed upon";* and to point out the danger in such misinformation. It is indeed extremely doubtful if any permanent benefit comes to the world through such action. Nations reel and stagger on their way; they make hideous mistakes; they commit frightful wrongs; they do great and beautiful things. And shall we not best guide humanity by telling the truth about all this, so far as the truth is ascertainable? Here in the United States we have a clear example ... Our histories tend to discuss American slavery so impartially, that in the end nobody seems to have done wrong and everybody was right. Slavery appears to have been thrust upon unwilling helpless America, while the South was blameless in becoming its center.[2] (p. 714)

Constituents who inhabit the intersubjective spaces of the American democratic experiment must find the courage to experience the counter-narrative that calls attention to the perpetrators and victims of human tragedy. To encounter the other is not simply about taking classes or seminars on black history. The constituents of the espoused democracy must allow themselves to be subsumed into the community and intersubjective space of the other. To experience the other is formative and transformative. Until the power brokers of the experiment in question allows the hem of its ideological garments to be touched by the subaltern subject, they will never be exorcized of the inherited demonic tendencies that oppress and destroy the other or the corresponding propensity to deny and repress the tragic history of slavery and its continuing legacy within the intersubjective milieu.

Towards Redeeming the Democracy Experiment: A Eucharistic Model

The Eucharist event is a useful paradigm to this end, as it offers compelling imagery and insight into how we can envision redemptive possibilities. A pastoral theology for the internal *force of being* must allow for the counter-narrative in the intersubjective milieu. Contrary to the common practice of encouraging victims and survivors of atrocities to forget the past, overlook the culpability of perpetrators of evil, and "move on," a Eucharistic model embraces and recognizes the immediacy of the past on the individual psyche and its impact on the intersubjective community. To speak of pain, anguish, disgust, and anger in certain mainstream faith communities is to risk being pathologized, categorized as a troublemaker, or weak in the Christian faith. As observed by Oliver (2004), one must be silent and forgetful about their victimization in order to formulate an ego-identity that is consistent with an Eriksonian conception of human development and psychic maturity. At what cost does one gain such a colonized identity? Can black subjectivity only be recognized at the expense of losing its soul? The interrogative posed by the gospel writer still stands: "What does it profit a man to gain the whole world and forfeit his life? For what can a man give in return for his life?"[3] We must reassess the cost of admittance into the experiment—forfeiting identity, heritage, and agency—all for a synthetic ego-identity. Identity politics within the democratic experiment is dangerous and can extract life from both individual and community. James Baldwin's (1998) observation in his essay "The Price of the Ticket" sums up this point succinctly: "the price of the black ticket is involved—fatally—with the dream of becoming white...this is not possible, partly because white people are not white: part of the price of the white ticket is to delude themselves into believing that they are" (p. 835).

In order to be redeemed from the heritage of the slavocracy, the American democratic experiment must become a repository for vocalizing and dramatizing the experiences of all people in the service of healing and identity formation—especially those upon whose backs the experiment has been performed. Christian complicity must be named and owned in this as well. A life-giving Eucharistic model compels us to create intentional spaces where the subaltern can remember their history and heritage, in conjunction with the suffering and losses that constitute individual and collective identity. Faith communities, seminaries, academic guilds, public and private institutions, and public spaces of community must be reimagined as safe, accepting environments where the subaltern subject has agency to assert both counter-narratives that subvert the illusion of life, liberty, and the pursuit of happiness. A Eucharistic hermeneutic that stresses sharing in each other's sufferings demands a solidarity that will not passively tolerate the evils of the slavocracy, the very toleration that has defined the democratic experiment. Copeland (2010) proposes a vision of

Eucharistic solidarity designed to undermine disembodied theoethical frameworks that provide ideological currency to perpetuate the legacy of the slavocracy and white supremacy. For her, "Eucharistic solidarity contests any performance of community as 'an atomized aggregate of mutually suspicious individuals' or as self-righteously self-sustaining or as historically innocent or as morally superior or as monopoly on truth" (p. 127). Emilie Townes (2006) expresses the potential in such practices as countermemory, which to her "is not a rejection of history, but its emendation" (p. 52). Active practices of countermemory are accretive to both selfhood and the interior force of being, for both individuals and the larger black community. Countermemory reflects appropriate countermeasures that are able to expose and deconstruct ideologies or white supremacy underwritten by disciplinary and productive power. Highlighting the possibilities of countermemory, Townes posits that "countermemory can open up subversive spaces within dominant discourses that expand our sense of who we are and, possibly, create a more whole and just society in defiance of structural evil" (p. 23).

In the Eucharist event, Jesus is clear that those who are in relationship with him are not to forget the terror, subjugation, torture, and execution he experienced at the hands of empire. The Eucharist does not allow us to "move on" or "forget about the past," as western ideology prefers. In the intersubjective space created by the Eucharist, we must recount the past in order to garner hope for healing in the future. *We must be willing to engage the historical reality of the grotesque by placing our hand in the wounds of those who have existed on the underside of modernity.* It is in this model of the Eucharist that we must attempt to refashion the intersubjective milieu that still supports and perpetuates the heritage of the unmourned history and reality of slavery. In his conception of the Eucharist, Rogers (2001) envisions a space where both victims and perpetrators can meet. This in no way implies cheap forgiveness but a movement toward an eschatological event of redemption and reconciliation. For Rogers then:

> The Eucharist ... enables Jesus to meet his victimizers face to face. The one they had betrayed, denied, abandoned, condemned, and crucified, is back again, walking the streets, before their faces ... The story of the victim's terror becomes the story of the victimizer's terror. The unnamed woman, the holocaust victim, meets and judges the executioners. Jesus meets and judges them with—forgiveness. They must live differently—and they may, because the resurrection restores their victim as the one in whom alone there is judgment, and therefore hope. (p. 277)

Yet, this project compels us to extend our understanding of the Eucharist event beyond the meal that Jesus shared with his disciples before he suffered, to the meal that Jesus shared with his disciples after he suffered. While the theological resources to underwrite this suggested endeavor fully are not yet available, the proposed attempt at this juncture does not render undue violence to Eucharistic theology. I cannot overstate the importance of this reimagining of the Eucharist. The gospel writers[4] compel us to imagine a post-resurrection theoethical praxis that includes Jesus communing with his disciples in a body that still bore the marks of its brokenness. This image presents us with a complex paradigm of community and communion in which trauma, healing, and resurrection are all embodied in the broken body of an outcast Jewish male from Palestine. Similarly, in an effort to redeem a western democratic experiment shaped in iniquity and forged on the backs of generations of black people victimized in the slavocracy, we must embrace a robust Eucharistic ethic that no longer compels a "forgetting" of the past for the sake of peace and tranquility in the intersubjective milieu but welcomes a full recognition of the broken bodies and silenced voices that represent the casualties of modernity's colonial project. In this way, we can begin to reimagine subjectivity and the American democratic experiment.

NOTES

1. (Luke 8:42–47 ESV).
2. My emphasis.
3. (Mark 8:36–38 ESV).
4. Luke 24 and John 20.

BIBLIOGRAPHY

Altman, N. (2004). History repeat itself in transference: Countertransference. *Psychoanalytic Dialogues, 14*(6), 807–815.

Altman, N. (2010). *The analyst in the inner city: Race, class, and culture through a psychoanalytic lens* (2nd ed.). New York: Routledge.

Bakke, R. (1997). *A theology as big as the city*. Downers Grove: InterVarsity Press.

Baldwin, J. (1998). The price of the ticket. In J. Baldwin & T. Morrison (Eds.), *James Baldwin: Collected essays* (pp. 830–842). New York: Literary Classics of the United States.

Copeland, M. S. (2010). *Enfleshing freedom: Body, race, and being*. Minneapolis: Fortress Press.

Du Bois, W. (1956). *Black reconstruction in America: An essay toward a history of the part which black folk played in the attempt to reconstruct democracy in America, 1860–1880.* New York: Russel & Russel.

Horton, J. O. (1999). Presenting slavery: The perils of telling America's racial story. *The Public Historian, 21*(4), 19–38.

Johnson, S. M. (2005). The middle passage, trauma and the tragic re-imagination of African American theology. *Pastoral Psychology, 53*(6), 541–561.

Oliver, K. (2004). *The colonization of psychic space.* Minneapolis: University of Minnesota Press.

Ray, S. G. (2008). E-racing while black. In N. L. Westfield (Ed.), *Being black teaching black: Politics and pedagogy in religious studies* (pp. 39–59). Nashville: Abingdon Press.

Rogers, E. F., Jr. (2001). The stranger. In J. J. Buckley & D. S. Yeago (Eds.), *Knowing the Triune God: The work of the spirit in the practices of the church* (pp. 265–283). Grand Rapids: William B. Eerdmans Publishing Company.

Townes, E. M. (2006). *Womanist ethics and the cutlural production of evil.* New York: Palgrave Macmillan.

Index[1]

[1] Note: Page numbers followed by 'n' refer to notes.

© The Author(s) 2018
D. G. Gibson, *Frederick Douglass, a Psychobiography*,
Black Religion/Womanist Thought/Social Justice,
https://doi.org/10.1007/978-3-319-75229-7

Made in the USA
Middletown, DE
29 December 2020